States of
RAGE

States of
RAGE

Emotional Eruption, Violence, and Social Change

EDITED BY

Renée R. Curry AND Terry L. Allison

NEW YORK UNIVERSITY PRESS
New York and London

NEW YORK UNIVERSITY PRESS
New York and London

© 1996 by New York University

Library of Congress Cataloging-in-Publication Data
States of rage : emotional eruption, violence, and social change/
edited by Renée R. Curry and Terry L. Allison,
p. cm.
Includes bibliographical references and index.
ISBN 0-8147-1525-7 (alk. paper). —ISBN 0-8147-1530-3 (pbk—
alk. paper)
1. Violence—United States.   2. Anger—United States.   3. Social
change—United States.   4. Mass media—Social aspects—United
States.   I. Curry, Renée R., 1955-   .   II. Allison, Terry L.
HN90.V5S83   1996
306'.0973—dc20   95-41244
                                                     CIP

New York University Press books are printed on acid-free paper,
and their binding materials are chosen for strength and durability.

Manufactured in the United States of America

10 9 8 7 6 5 4 3 2 1

CONTENTS

v

ACKNOWLEDGMENTS

We would like to acknowledge receipt of a California State University San Marcos Affirmative Action Grant and a California State University San Marcos Multicultural Center Grant, both of which enabled us to conduct the RAGE! Across the Disciplines Conference, July, 1993. We want to thank Provost Rich Millman for his last minute additional support of the conference as well as volunteer extraordinaire, Sherri Williams, faithful participants, Diane Martin, and Don and Carolyn Funes, our student presenters, and the wonderful performers whose work we could not include in this format. We would also like to thank California State University San Marcos for encouragement and support of the project. More personally, we thank Judy Stagg and Norma Long for hours of typing. Further thanks to student assistants: Karen Huck, Garrett Collins, and Dominique Rousseau.

We sincerely appreciate the years of commitment to this project demonstrated by the contributors, Dianne Layden, Vanessa Friedman, Ian Barnard, William Brigham, Susan Stryker, Sharon O'Dair, Sheng-mei Ma, and Don Keefer. Further appreciation goes to Niko Pfund and Jennifer Hammer at New York University Press, who believed in this project and who persisted in editing the manuscript into fruition. A general thanks to colleagues who have kept discussion of rage alive. A special thanks to Patty Seleski for all the listening.

Terry would like to acknowledge in particular the encouragement of Dean of Library Services, Marion T. Reid, and co-workers Susan Baksh,

Cathie Dorsett, Dannis Mitchell, Suzanne Rios, and Marge Hohen-berger. He also thanks Roddey Reid for valuable ideas and Winnie Woodhull for encouragement to carry on intellectual pursuits. Terry also wants to acknowledge a number of long-time friends without whose support he could not have continued this project: Larry Heiman, Stacy Nelson, Gary Kukus, Anne Terrell, Janet Volkmann, and Karen Kinney. And thank you, Renée Curry.

Debra Curry and Cathy Bradeen Knox always must be acknowledged as Renée's consistent source of encouragement and comfort throughout writing projects and throughout life. And thanks, of course, to Terry.

CONTRIBUTORS

TERRY L. ALLISON is a graduate of the University of California, Berkeley and has Master's degrees from that campus and from UC San Diego. He is currently the Collections Librarian at CSU San Marcos and is also completing his doctorate in Comparative Literature at UCSD. Mr. Allison is the author of several papers in librarianship, gender studies, and popular culture.

IAN BARNARD teaches in the Department of English and Comparative Literature, and the Department of Rhetoric and Writing Studies at San Diego State University. His book *Queer Race* is forthcoming from New York University Press.

JULIE BRICKMAN writes in Toronto, Ontario.

WILLIAM BRIGHAM holds graduate degrees in social work and sociology, and is currently a lecturer in the Sociology program at California State University, San Marcos. His primary area of interest is mass media, with particular focus on the news media and film. Professor Brigham's analysis of filmic depictions of homelessness and poverty will be published in an anthology on ideologies in popular film. He is currently studying various connections between the tobacco industry and mass media, including advertising and product placement in films. Professor Brigham thanks Roberta and Caitlin for their patience.

RENÉE R. CURRY is Associate Professor of Literature and Writing at California State University, San Marcos, where she teaches American literature and film studies. Dr. Curry edited *Perspectives on Woody Allen*, and has also authored several articles on American women's poetry and on film.

MOSHE DAVIDOWITZ writes on the Jewish historic experience.

VANESSA FRIEDMAN is a Ph.D. candidate at the University of Maryland at College Park, where she has taught "Political Theory" and "The Politics of the Family." She is completing her dissertation, *Over His Dead Body: Women, Violence, and Murder As Metaphor,* after which she intends to pursue research on the politics of the body.

CLAIRE KAHANE teaches at SUNY-Buffalo and writes on modern British and American fiction, psychoanalysis, and feminist theory. Her new book, *Passions of the Voice,* explores the intersection of hysteria and narrative voice in late nineteenth-century fiction. She is currently at work on a collection of essays on mourning and representation.

DON KEEFER is Assistant Professor of Philosophy at Rhode Island School of Design. He has written on the philosophy of music, cultural criticism, art, and interdisciplinary studies. He is currently engaged in a "Dewey-eyed" exploration of the connections and disconnections between aesthetics and the practices of art, past and present, from both psychological and sociological points of view.

D. S. LAWSON is Assistant Professor of English at Lander College, Greenwood, South Carolina.

DIANNE R. LAYDEN teaches human resource management and labor relations at the University of Redlands in Redlands, California. Her field is American Studies. Research interests include employee discipline, women and the workplace, working conditions of immigrant workers, labor culture, and hate crime in America.

SHENG-MEI MA received a Ph.D. from Indiana University and is currently Assistant Professor of American Thought and Language at Michigan

State University. He is the author of *Immigrant Subjectivity in Asian American and Asian Diaspora Literatures.* His articles have appeared in such journals as *Journal of American Culture, Modern Language Studies,* and *Holocaust and Genocide Studies,* as well as in such collections as *English Studies/Culture Studies: Institutional Dissent* and *Literature of Asian Immigration/Emigration.*

SHARON O'DAIR teaches Shakespeare at the University of Alabama. She is the author of essays on Shakespeare, literary theory, and social science, and the issue of class in the profession. A co-editor of *The Production of English Renaissance Culture* (1994), she is completing a manuscript entitled "Bottom Lines: Class, Critics, and Shakespeare."

ALAN CLARKE SHEPARD teaches English at Texas Christian University in Fort Worth, Texas. His work on theatrical masculinity has appeared in *Theatre Journal* and *Renaissance Quarterly,* and he is finishing a book on Christopher Marlowe's plays, English military handbooks, and the Spanish Armada.

SUSAN STRYKER is an independent scholar, writer, and activist living in the San Francisco Bay area. Her book on transgender theory is forthcoming (1997).

Invitation to Rage

TERRY L. ALLISON and RENÉE R. CURRY

Being a black woman means frequent spells of impotent, self-consuming rage. —*The Black Woman's Gumbo Ya-Ya*

WHY TALK ABOUT RAGE?

In our daily consumption of media, "rage," "outrage," "enraged" increasingly appear in print or are splashed at us from our televisions and radios. Rage appears to define the daily existence of some groups in the United States;[1] further, our own experience suggests that few individuals in our media-dominated culture fail to encounter en-, out-, or just plain rage each day. Contemporary society appears suddenly willing to employ the term more often to describe our own or others' mental states or actions. Rage seems to have gained a currency in the past decade which it previously did not possess.

The rise of rage in discourse begs many questions. Has the experience of individuals in our society shifted so significantly that vastly more people experience rage? Or, have we simply hyperbolized such a term as "anger" in an ever more sensationalized multimedia market? Could the rising discourse about rage reflect an ever less reticent public, now willing to discuss their rage along with the whole range of their other previously private and family emotions? Or, are we suddenly hearing the expressions of rage that have been speaking to us all along? In some respects these questions also ask whether or not we believe in rage as a present and/or ongoing cultural phenomenon or whether we consider rage primarily a catchword, manufactured or inflated for our consumption, even for our entertainment. Will the term, au courant, fade into obscurity, or will rage continue to describe in some more profound sense our daily experience in contemporary society?

In preparing this collection of essays, we claim that rage as a personal and social construct deserves more than our passing interest. The term *rage* succinctly describes an ongoing emotional state for many residents and citizens of the United States and elsewhere, not only for those whom we usually name as outrageous or outraged. While we do not wish to claim that everyone continuously stalks our landscape in rage, this anthology aims to suggest why this emotional state has increasingly intruded into our social, artistic, and academic existences.

WHY DEVELOP AN ANTHOLOGY ABOUT RAGE?

States of Rage seeks to gather for the first time a critical mass of writing about rage in various disciplines. In first planning a national conference, "Rage! Across the Disciplines," we began with the assumption, stated above, that we could no longer avoid rage, that it has intruded, welcome or unwelcome, into our emotional, social, cultural, and academic lives. Rage has become both an increasingly legitimated method of expression and a feared outcome of interchange in several areas of our lives. The expression of rage at the very least has challenged an agreeable, centrist consensus that we must remain polite when discussing our differing views. At its greatest force, the unleashing of rage has translated into dead bodies on our campus and city streets, in our public buildings and our homes.

Some of the essays collected here and on our list of readings at the end of this introduction illustrate that our social interactions have long manufactured rage and our cultural productions historically have both reflected and produced their own degrees of rage. Until only quite recently, however, does it appear that our safer realms of academia have fully experienced both the social and cultural arenas of rage. Certainly rage appeared in academic settings in the 1960s with the outburst of civil rights and anti-war protests. However, now we legitimate rage when discussing previously "non-political" arenas such as what gets taught and by whom.

At base, rage is an emotion that, when expressed, either individually or collectively, manifests itself in multiple and unforeseen ways usually perceived to be violent. Manifestations of rage come in many forms including volatile and violent actions, artistic productions, discourse and political activism. This collection addresses a range of such manifestations: killings by postal workers; killings of feminists; killings of husbands, wives, and lovers; arguments regarding political correctness; depictions of deaths by AIDS; filmic and fictional representations of racism; riots against injustice; queer militant acts; and representative sites of rage.

Yet, few writers have asked the basic questions about rage: Who defines rage? How do they define it? Does rage merit serious analysis? What sorts of analyses of rage would prove most fruitful? What can we learn by looking at rage across disciplines rather than strictly within disciplinary boundaries?

This anthology, a first interdisciplinary gathering of writing about rage, does not seek definitive answers to these questions, but does seek to begin a structured conversation about them. By gathering these essays, we seek to enable readers to discern rage in terms of its psychological and social origins, its relationship to the self, its connection to culture, and its possible predictors. The essays do not, however, announce with any surety the exact people(s) among whom, the exact moments at which, nor the exact forms in which rage will occur.

In compiling this collection, we sought out connections from a wide variety of contemporary writing, looking for patterns of rage to emerge. An initial chord was struck when we realized that for some people *mere discussion of rage* produced rage. For some of the critics of our conference, for example, to discuss various people's rage immediately qualified one for Allan Bloom's "culture of complaint" or Harold Bloom's "school of resentment." To some cultural critics, rage implies invasion by an intruder, a loss of self, thus a lack of responsibility that threatens the concept of a powerful, moral, autonomous self. The fear of bringing rage into more conscious discourse preserves the illusion either that rage does not exist or that to address rage necessarily incites further rage. In editing this anthology we wanted, among other purposes, to legitimize the discussion of rage, to propose rage not as unadulterated complaint or resentment, but as a constant, perhaps increasing, provocation in our daily lives.

We seek first to focus attention on recent work about rage, work that considers basic questions:

How do various theorists multiply define rage, and do their definitions work across disciplines?

How have writers constructed rage in terms of its supposed opposites: Reason: sanity, stoicism, normality, order and politeness?

Can we ritualize rage, or is it always spontaneous?

What is the relationship between rage and power(lessness)?

Is rage a response to loss? Loss of what?

How does rage relate to personal or social injustice?

What provokes rage and what is provocative about it?

The essays in this anthology begin to provide definitions, context, and shape to the multiple meanings of rage.

A problem implicitly raised by defining rage, yet infrequently addressed by this collection, remains that of whether or how to curtail the often violent results of unleashed rage. This collection does not purport a prevention mode. The authors represented here provide insight and commentary into the operations of rage as they see it apparent primarily in contemporary U.S. culture. In some cases they make judgments; in other instances they analyze and interpret. Some of the authors infrequently mention the word, "rage," and yet the intense emotion they describe resonates with the more explicitly defined moments of rage that the authors here discuss.

SOCIAL, ARTISTIC, AND ACADEMIC ARENAS OF RAGE

We have gathered the essays here into broad categories of disciplines that employ similar methodologies, styles, and vocabularies to address rage. Naturally, some of the essays reach across the disciplinary boundaries that we have imposed on them. Nevertheless, within the broad groupings provided, the essays reflect on each other's vocabulary, thematics, production, and interpretation of the meaning of rage.

Social Constructions of Rage

Both Julie Brickman ("Female Lives, Feminist Deaths") and Dianne R. Layden ("Violence, the Emotionally Enraged Employee, and the Workplace") focus on men's rage that explodes into violence. Brickman draws more of a continuum between outbreaks of killing rage and what she perceives as more "normal" or common male behaviors of rape and incest, while Layden describes rage as a manifestation of various levels of pathology. Still, for Layden as well as for Brickman, men's murderous rage can reveal itself among those who display a whole range of mental illness to those who are "generally not deranged." Layden reports that these outbreaks of rage into murder at the workplace are small in number, but growing. Brickman's focus on the continuum of male violent behaviors means that she is not so concerned with charting the growth of the outbreaks of murderous rage, but with tackling the whole range of men's socialization into violent, outrageous behaviors.

Though both Brickman and Layden describe similar outbursts of male rage, Layden sees more practical steps to counter rage that eventually may break out into violence. However, reading Layden's essay closely will reveal that she, like Brickman, believes that only broad social changes will diminish the production of male rage. For both Brickman and Layden, rage is a likely outcome of social pressures. There may be warning signs, but responding to these signals from isolated individuals alone will not stem all of male rage.

Vanessa Friedman examines the rarer case of female murderous rage. Women's rage, for Friedman, is a reaction to patriarchal abuse and a means of stating a woman's very existence. Yet, Friedman shares with both Brickman and Layden the reaction that our social structure itself unfailingly will produce rage. Friedman asks: "What happens when the [social] structure which serves to contain anxieties becomes the source of anxiety itself?" For Friedman, female rage counters the essential denial of female language and voice within the patriarchy. Murderous rage becomes one of the few means that women possess to turn themselves into speaking subjects. While acknowledging the damage of rage, "the ultimate unacceptability" of murderous rage, Friedman still finds it "honest and genuine."

By directly confronting his own rage, Ian Barnard speaks in a different voice than the three previous authors. Barnard takes the highly threatening and damaging act of "gay bashing" and turns the phrase into a figurative bashing of those gays and lesbians who "collude" with the same power structures that Brickman, Layden, and Friedman criticize to varying degrees. Barnard, who aligns his rage with that of the fag bashing queer 'zines, specifically names the social structures that would need to change to alleviate his rage: "reductively binary models of identity, oppositionality, and political activism." Barnard's work suggests the complicated nature of undoing social structures that manufacture rage. Beyond simple homo/hetero issues lie a whole matrix of class, race, and gender issues that will likely produce and reproduce rage.

Artistic and Cultural Representations of Rage

In his essay "Whatup in the 'Hood," William Brigham discusses the artistic practice of black filmmakers as one that closely reflects their social experience of rage, thus providing an effective transition between considering rage in its social and its artistic manifestations. Brigham demonstrates that when African-Americans depict themselves independently of the white-owned and dominated film industry, the portraits of African-Americans shift from accommodating and assimilationist to enraged. However, Brigham argues, African-American directors also in part have used their recent films to demonstrate the misdirection of this rage towards other blacks. Several of the recent films produced by African-Americans suggest that turning this rage towards white institutions would provide the most effective means of resolving the characters' rage.

D. S. Lawson ("Rage and Remembrance") also sees rage as a central, structuring emotion for a group of texts, plays about AIDS, that spring directly from a known social condition. Similar to Brigham's argument, Lawson's analysis finds that the dominant society's dismissal of the crisis (black poverty or AIDS, respectively) produces as much rage as the crisis itself. Lawson agrees with Brigham as well that artists from minority or oppressed groups may often direct their rage at the "inner group"; the seeming hopelessness of the group working together to accomplish change may unleash the artist's rage against the insiders as well as the outsiders.

Claire Kahane ("The Aesthetic Politics of Rage") defines varying types of rage produced in nineteenth-century, upper-middle-class women: repressed rage, displaced rage, and outrage. As opposed to the earlier essays collected here, Kahane finds that "the experience of rage is powerful, but not political." Kahane separately defines "outrage" as a political act. Thus, while both Brigham and Lawson see filmmakers and playwrights expressing rage directly in artistic form, Kahane sees this direct expression of rage as outrage, manifested in essay writing and feminist action. Kahane defines rage in literary expression as an act of displacement, describing this displacement in more explicitly Freudian, psychological terminology than the previous authors in this section.

Our essay ("All Anger and Understanding") finds rage more literally expressed in film and literature than Kahane suggests. The essay describes how narrative in the cinema and in fiction represents what we describe as an ultimately uncontainable concept, rage. We argue, as does Lawson, that complex, experimental narrative structures more effectively allow for rage to emerge from the text. Through examining the work of several writers and filmmakers, notably Hanif Kureishi, we interrogate rage in fictional texts for its content, its structural challenges, and its cultural significance.

The next two essays in the collection discuss how artistic works can work to conceal or to deflect (abort) rage. Moshe Davidowitz's essay ("The Psychohistory of Jewish Rage and Redemption") defines rage as a probable psychological reaction to persecution and hatred. Davidowitz alone among the authors here discusses pictorial art as a symbolic means of expressing a rage that could not be expressed directly in words or action, nor even figuratively through drama; if medieval European Jews expressed their rage, they could be killed. Using psychological theory similar to Kahane, Davidowitz describes rage as an emotion that must be directed *somewhere*. Pictorial art, then, can serve as a safe, symbolic outlet of rage for a particular group that dares not express it directly.

Alan Clarke Shepard also discusses repressed rage, but in this case, the artistic work both expresses and deflects the rage. In our contemporary society, certainly, expressions of rage by oppressed groups are more tolerated than in the society that Davidowitz discusses. Still, female playwright Beth Henley, Shepard argues, nearly always hesitates to express or aborts the rage so evidently mounting within her work. Shepard's essay echoes both Friedman's analysis of female reluctance to assume the male prerogative of rageful revenge and Kahane's demonstration that female rage often turns inward onto the female self. Even in our so-called age of feminism, female rage may never develop into the acts of violence it threatens. Though Henley's heroines "relish murderous and suicidal fantasies, they repudiate them."

As in the first section, "Social Constructions of Rage," we end our group of essays on artistic and cultural representations of rage with a work that mixes a personal experience of rage with a broader theoretical engagement with it. Susan Stryker ("My Words to Victor Frankenstein above the Village of Chamounix") furthers some of Barnard's ideas regarding the unfixed self as a particularly productive site of rage. Stryker offers the transsexual body as a metaphoric site of cultural rage. Transsexuality and the rage it screams "represents the prospect of destabilizing the foundational presuppositions of fixed genders upon which a politics of personal identity depends." Stryker radicalizes the idea of an artistically constructed self transformed into a symbol of rage.

Rage in the Academy

Our last section of essays demonstrates how the previously polite discourse common to higher education in the United States increasingly breaks down in the face of rage. As we began the anthology with the bloody, murderous intrusion into a Canadian university of a male outraged against feminism, so we end by showing how feminist, working-class, and multicultural intrusions into academia have outraged all parties on any side of the debates. Each of the essays in this grouping reflects the personal focus of Barnard or Stryker while raising larger issues about rage in the academy as an institution.

Sharon O'Dair discusses her outrage as a university professor, forced to separate herself from her working class roots, but constantly humiliated by middle- or upper-class professors who recognize her performance, both in trying to retain working-class roots and in trying to pass as an intellectual, therefore, not a person of the working class. Academics who claim working-class solidarity while denying their privilege as elites fuel O'Dair's outrage. O'Dair does not finally propose a means to resolve the rage that a professor of working-class origins faces. However, she states that the academy has only begun to acknowledge this issue and must continue to confront it.

In the essay, "Second-Rate or Second Rank: The Human Pyramid of Academe," Sheng-mei Ma provides a connection between ethnicity and rage in the academy. Ma writes to unveil the outrageous attempt on the part of U.S. academic institutions to keep hidden the facts of hierarchy prevalent throughout. Ma argues that "by retrieving into scholarly debates such terms as second-rate, as harsh as they may sound, we import to our profession some degree of honesty" and make possible "the revolution of turning the communication channel upside down." He suggests a revolution of honesty that would afford academic institutions opportunities for change.

In "The Rage of Innocents: On Casting the First Stone in a Sea of Cultural Pain," Don Keefer also asserts that a "cold civil war" exists in academia and that it has everything to do with the political correctness movement. He cautions against the execution of a politically correct agenda: "A consequence of the politically correct depth-psychological search and destroy mission to eradicate prejudice is a style of intolerance not tolerable within the academic community." Here too issues of academic freedom and justice infiltrate the rage debate.

The essays we collect here do not represent all theoretical stances on rage, nor do they attempt to survey rage to a great extent beyond the borders of the United States (with one significant extension into Canada and a foray into nineteenth- and twentieth-century England.) This anthology serves to expand and to complicate an understanding of rage, its relationship to social, artistic, and academic life. It provides an introduction, a beginning, an invitation to rage.

Further Reading

During the course of our research, we found rage a surprisingly undertheorized term. Though we read and heard the word often in our daily experience, rage had received few significant theoretical analyses. We recommend the following works for their analysis of rage, for their central representation of it, or for the fears they express about rage. This list by no means represents a definitive bibliography of rage, but it should provide some key directions for those readers who want to pursue the topic further:

Alan-Williams, Gregory. *A Gathering of Heroes: Reflections on Rage and Responsibility: A Memoir of the Los Angeles Riots.* Chicago: Academy Chicago Publishers, 1994.
Brooks, Gwendolyn. *Maud Martha.* New York: Harper & Row, 1953.
Burack, Cynthia. *The Problem of the Passions: Feminism, Psychoanalysis, and Social Theory.* New York: New York University Press, 1994.

Cleage, Pearl. *Deals with the Devil: And Other Reasons to Riot.* New York: Ballantine, 1993.

Cocks, Jay. "A Nasty Jolt for the Top Pops." *Time,* 1 July 1991, 78–79.

Cose, Ellis. *The Rage of a Privileged Class.* New York: Harper Collins, 1953.

Friedman, Murray. *Overcoming Middle Class Rage.* Philadelphia: Westminster Press, 1971.

Gaylin, Willard. *The Rage Within: Anger in Modern Life.* New York: Simon and Schuster, 1984.

Glick, Robert A., and Steven P. Roose. *Rage, Power, and Aggression.* New Haven: Yale University Press, 1993.

Grier, William H., and Price M. Cobbs. *Black Rage.* New York: Harper Collins, 1992.

Handling, Piers, ed. *The Shape of Rage: The Films of David Cronenberg.* New York: New York Zoetrope, 1983.

Jewell, Terri L., ed. *The Black Woman's Gumbo Ya-Ya: Quotations by Black Women.* Freedom, Calif.: Crossing Press, 1993.

Johnstone, Peggy Fitzhugh. *The Transformation of Rage: Mourning and Creativity in George Eliot's Fiction.* New York: New York University Press, 1994.

Jordan, June. *Naming Our Destiny.* New York: Thunder's Mouth Press, 1989.

Leo, John. "City Rage and Revival." *U.S. News and World Report,* 1 Nov. 1993, 21.

Lewis, Michael. "The Development of Anger and Rage." In Glick and Roose. 148–68.

Lockridge, Kenneth A. *On the Sources of Patriarchal Rage: The Commonplace Books of William Byrd and Thomas Jefferson and the Gendering of Power in the Eighteenth Century.* New York: New York University Press, 1992.

Lorde, Audre. *Zami, A New Spelling of My Name.* Trumansburg, N.Y.: Crossing Press, 1982.

Moraga, Cherríe and Gloria Anzaldúa, eds. *This Bridge Called My Back.* New York: Kitchen Table, Women of Color Press, 1983.

Morrison, Toni. *Beloved.* New York: Knopf: Distributed by Random House, 1987.

Parmar, Pratibha. *A Place of Rage.* New York: Women Make Movies, 1991.

Person, Ethel Spector. Introduction. *Rage, Power and Aggression.* Eds. Robert A. Glick and Steven P. Roose. New Haven: Yale University Press, 1993. 1–9.

Scheff, Thomas J. and Suzanne M. Retzinger. *Emotions and Violence.* Lexington, Mass.: Lexington Books, 1991.

Thomas, Sandra P. Introduction. *Women and Anger.* New York: Springer, 1993. 1–19.

———. *Women and Anger.* New York: Springer, 1993.
Valentis, Mary, and Anne Devane. *Female Rage: Unlocking Its Secrets, Claiming Its Power.* New York: Carol Southern Books, 1994.
Wright, Richard. *Black Boy.* New York: Harper & Brothers, 1945.
Wright, Robin B. *Sacred Rage: The Wrath of Militant Islam.* New York: Simon & Schuster, 1986.

NOTES

1. This collection of essays contains only one essay about Canada, another which divides its attentions between England and the United States. All the other essays focus on rage as it develops and manifests itself within the United States. We intended all along to center our attention on U.S. experience, but added the other two essays which closely parallel situations in the United States as they have occurred in other Western societies. In no way do we want to claim that people across different cultures experience, feel, or manifest their rage in similar ways.

PART I

Social Constructions
of Rage

CHAPTER 1

Female Lives, Feminist Deaths

The Relationship of the Montreal Massacre to Dissociation, Incest, and Violence against Women

JULIE BRICKMAN

On Wednesday, December 6, 1989 a young man, 25 years old, product of a violent home, failed military candidate and lover of war films, entered the University of Montreal's School of Engineering building. He was not a student, although he had once studied for admission to the school. He was carrying a .223 calibre semi-automatic rifle.[1] It was a little after 5:00 p.m.

Walking into a classroom, he shouted "I want the women" (Kuiten-brouwer, Scott, Lamey & Heinrich, 1989). He separated the men from the women, ordered the men to leave the classroom, and lined the women up along one wall. "You are all feminists!" he yelled and began shooting to kill (Kuitenbrouwer et al., 1989). According to the professor, all nine women in his class were either killed or wounded (Shepherd, 1989). There were approximately 48 men in the classroom (Came, Burke, Ferzoco, O'Farrell & Wallace, 1989; "The gunman's trail," 1989).

The young man continued his hunt, stalking his victims without obstruction. He had already murdered one woman near the copying room prior to entering that first classroom. He killed six more in the classroom, left, walked through the corridors firing randomly, entered the cafeteria, killed three more women, then went into a second classroom, where he murdered four more women and killed himself. By the end of

Reprinted by permission of the Canadian Psychological Association, copyright © 1992 by the Canadian Psychological Association.

his spree, he had murdered fourteen women and injured thirteen others: nine women and four men.

According to Elliott Leyton, anthropologist and author of *Hunting Humans: The Rise of the Modern Multiple Murderer* (1986), this pattern is characteristic of multiple killers. Their murders are their social statements, and their social statements embody central themes and tensions of the civilization in which they live. Typically, they are men who view themselves as failures and blame their lack of success and status on a target group.

Marc Lépine targeted women: successful women and feminist women. For him, the two categories were the same. His explanatory letter contained a tirade against women as well as a list of nineteen prominent women, whom he particularly despised.

What, then, was Lépine's social statement? How does it embody tensions central to our age? There seemed to be at least three implied statements concerning women:

1. Women are responsible for the failures of men;
2. Any woman who stands in the way of a man's success deserves to be punished;
3. Successful women have abdicated their right to protection by individual men (through heroic actions) or collective mankind (through theory, social policy and law).

Feminism, a label earned by scholarship, political action and/or particular theoretical understandings of the world, should not be denigrated by allowing it to be applied willy-nilly by those with the least comprehension of what it signifies. To examine these murders as actions against successful (and therefore feminist) women would be to define women from the stand-point of Marc Lépine and to endorse traditional sexist theories about women, which collapse unrelated characteristics of women such as successful, feminist and anti-male into a single dimension or constellation. During their lives most, if not all, of the murdered women did not define themselves as feminist, and one of the basic tenets of most feminist thought is the right of women, individually and collectively, to define themselves.

If they did not live as feminists, they certainly died as them. The nature and circumstances of their deaths has reshaped the meaning of their individual lives, transforming these fourteen women into symbols, tragic representatives of the injustice against women that has been built into the fabric of the society in which we live. This is violation of the highest order.

To understand this injustice, to prevent similar crimes in the future, we need to look towards those fields that would predict, even expect, the occurrence of unprovoked outbreaks of rage against women. These areas are encompassed by the label violence against women and include the related fields of sexual violence (incest, sexual assault, sexual abuse), physical violence (battering, child abuse), sexual harassment, and pornography. Using my experience of 14 years of working with victim/survivors of incest, I shall focus primarily on sexual violence as one path to clarifying the occurrence, purpose and effects of violence against women.

SENSITIZATION TO VIOLATIONS

According to a study by Linda MacLeod (1989) 56% of urban Canadian women are afraid to walk alone in their own neighbourhoods after dark. It would be interesting to know what these figures would have been right after the massacre. If the media reaction is any index, for a few days, perhaps a few weeks, after the massacre everyone's awareness of the fear and lack of personal safety that are part of the daily context of women's lives was heightened. During that brief time, background became foreground and dialogue increased.

An editorial, "We Mourn All Our Daughters," by James Quig of the (Montreal) *Gazette* reflected this awareness. Quig (1989) wrote:

> But he was sick, good men will say.
> Of course he was sick. Of course all men don't think like that.
> But let good men not hide. Let us not look the other way.
> There were no men on Marc Lépine's hit list and good men must look harder to find the reason why.
> Men abuse women. Men throw the punches.
> Men pull the trigger. Men build the walls.
> And only men can end it.
> Why is violence against women the domain of women?
> How did a man's fist in the woman's face ever get to be a women's issue? (p. A-1)

Within two weeks or less this heightened awareness had disappeared both from the media and from daily social discourse. The social forms of defenses typically used to avoid either the existence, uniqueness, seriousness or consequences of violence against women reappeared: "It's the random act of a madman" (not part of the spectrum of violence against women); "How could they ban men from their mourning" (not an issue unique to women); "Why is everyone jumping on the bandwagon, diminishing the tragedy with women's issues?" (which are neither serious nor tragic); "How angry those women are" (denial that the consequences of violence against women include rage against men and social institutions that perpetuate violence).

Women who have been violated physically or sexually or both (and those of us who work with them) cannot afford the luxury of these denials. We all live in a state of heightened awareness and reactivity to undercurrents and threats of violence between genders that are invisible to most others. Originally, the survival of violated women depended on this sensitization. I have come to believe from my work with them that this sensitization is essential to the containment of such violence, that just as each act of individual violence remains forever in a relationship, forming its unwritten rules, so each act of social violence remains forever in the collective unconscious of a culture, and that how it gets written depends on the response of the onlookers.

The Statistics on Sexual Violations

Incidence and prevalence statistics on rape and sexual abuse have now been available for a long time. A representative survey of 551 women drawn from both the English and French communities in Winnipeg in 1978–9 found that 6% reported having been raped and 21% having been sexually assaulted at some point in their lives, 50% before they were 17 (Brickman, Briere, Ward, Kalef & Lungen, 1979; Brickman & Briere, 1984). In a random sample of 930 adult women in San Francisco 16% reported at least one incident of intrafamilial and 31% of extrafamilial sexual abuse (Russell, 1983). Herman (1981), reviewing five surveys of sexual abuse, concludes that the results were "remarkably consistent" (p. 12), that one-fifth to one-third of all women reported that as children they had had some kind of sexual encounter with an adult male. The Badgely Commission (1984), from a national population survey in

Canada, reported that one in two females and one in three males had been victims of "unwanted sexual acts" (p. 175). Citing these statistics in *Reaching for Solutions*, the report of the Special Advisor to the Minister of National Health and Welfare on Child Sexual Abuse in Canada (1990), Rix Rogers broke down the unwanted sexual acts category into attempted and actual penetration (16.3%), unwanted sexual fondling (18.1%), threats of sexual acts (7.8%) and exposure (14.8%); of the total assaults, 71.8% were against females and 28.2% against males (Badgely, 1984).

The statistics are likely to underestimate the rates of the most severe abuse, since complete amnesia in the forms of atypical dissociative disorder and multiple personality disorder (MPD) seems to correlate with early onset and severity of trauma (Herman & Schatzow, 1987; Briere & Conte, 1989). In the most severe cases, those who are diagnostically MPD, over 90% of the victims are female (Putnam, Guroff, Silberman, Barber & Post, 1986; Coons, Bowman, & Milstein, 1988; Ross & Norton, 1989).

These statistics mean that a large number of females and a smaller number of males experience sexual violation at the hands of an adult male; more than 90% of the offenders are male—98.8% according to Badgely (1984). Thus, a large segment of the adult female population exists, at least partly, in a perpetual state of heightened awareness to gender violations. The experience and perceptions of these women may help the rest of us understand the nature and purpose of these violations, and how they illuminate a central theme of our society.

The Stages of Sexual Abuse

In the study of sexual abuse, three stages may be examined (see table 1). The first stage describes the actual abusive events that occur between offender and victim and provides a foundation and a context for understanding what follows. The second stage focuses on the harm experienced from the abuse by moving into a closeup of the experience of the victim and how she copes.

The third stage, the stage of illness and dysfunction, encompasses the long-term consequences from abuse and harm. In this stage, the victim has usually become a patient, coping strategies have become defenses, harm has become illnesses and syndromes, and the offender and the

TABLE 1 States of Sexual Abuse

States	1 Abuse	2 Harm & Damage	3 Illness & Dysfunction
	Victim and Perpetrator	Victim only	Patient
	Description of typical progression of incestuous assaults (who does what to whom, when and how)	Description of experience of trauma and coping (victim still defined as normal)	Clinical description of long-term effects of trauma and defensive structures (victim defined as sick)

abusive events have disappeared into the vaguaries of clinical language, re-emerging as the blur of perceptions, attributions, memories and fantasies which is antecedent to the clear, clinically observable malfunctions.[2] In the next sections of this paper, I shall discuss each of these stages.

The Victim Experience

The pattern of severe incestuous abuse appears remarkably constant across victims.[3] The abuse starts early, occurs frequently, continues over a long period of time and becomes increasingly brutal until the victim is sufficiently subdued to behave as if she were a willing partner. The abuser (father, stepfather, mother's boyfriend) assaults his victim in secret, cornering her when no one else is around: pulling off the street during a car ride, taking her into a clearing during a hike or a picnic, sneaking into her bedroom late at night.

The sexual acts are usually whatever the victims' body can be made to accommodate. With an infant, the offender may poke a finger into her anus or vagina, stroke and tickle her in a sexual manner, masturbate over her or against her skin, or insert his penis as far into her mouth as he can. With a toddler, digital penetration has the goal of stretching the orifice enough to accommodate an erect penis and oral rape and thigh rape become increasingly common. Objects may also be inserted either to continue to stretch the orifice or as a type of coercive manoeuvre to get her to choose or appear to want penetration by his penis. The onset of penile penetration into her vagina and anus seems to occur as soon as possible; in my own clinical practice, this has varied between the ages of 4 and 12.

Threats and other forms of intimidation occur simultaneously (Summit, 1983). These include slapping, punching, smothering, choking, and verbal threats of abandonment or of additional violence, e.g. "I'll kill you if you tell; your mother will never believe you; you'll break up the family and end up in a foster home." These tactics are not only to prevent the child from telling, but to stop her from making audible noise while the rapes are taking place. Most incest victims cry, scream, kick, punch and push until these self-protective actions are beaten and smothered out of them. Their silence builds gradually until their screams, cries, and tantrums are internal only. The classical "passive" victim is usually the end result of a long, abusive process which teaches that active protests only make the abuse worse: longer, more violent, and harder to endure.

A second, subtler agenda is often present; incestuous fathers seem to want their daughters to behave like cooperative, sometimes loving, and certainly willing, partners. They want their victims not only to do it, but to like it: to smile, initiate, relax, kiss, hear confidences, become passionate and orgasmic, and in general simulate the ideal (adult) consenting partner. Once the context of force and violence has been established, they teach their child-victims the full repertoire of sexual behaviour, including fellatio, cunnilingus, anilingus, vaginal and anal intercourse.

At the same time, the father-offender is often contemptuous of his daughter's sexuality and uses her responsiveness to prove that she is the vixen, the seductress, the one to blame. If she lubricates, he may smear it under her nose or in her mouth to demonstrate that she is enjoying it. Often, there is a battle of wills over orgasm; in a typical scenario the daughter holds out as long as possible against having an orgasm while her father stimulates her relentlessly until she does, then uses that fact to demonstrate that she liked it and wanted it, that she is the little slut-whore who made him do it. Eventually she starts, at least partially, to believe this agenda or at least to believe that everyone else will think as he does. She begins to lose her own thoughts, her own version of experience. Now he controls not only the responses of her body, but her mind. This control is essential to prolonged victimization. The undermining of her self-confidence is deliberate, a way to bind her more completely to him (Stone, 1989). As her personal experience increasingly eludes her, the rage and deep shame at what the offender is doing turn inward; one of my patients remembered throwing herself down the stairs when she was a toddler, thinking it was her only way out.

The second agenda is, in fact, the traditional rape fantasy or rape myth: Just lie back and eventually you'll enjoy it (Malamuth, Heim & Fesbach, 1980; Malamuth & Check, 1980; Burt & Albin, 1981; Broth & Hobson, 1983; Marshall & Barrett, 1990). Father-offenders may actually believe this or convince themselves via their own tactics that it is the case. For their victims, the reverse is true. Rape does not become sex; instead, sex becomes rape. Severely abused women often have a difficult time distinguishing between sex with someone they choose and sexual victimization (e.g. Kluft, 1990). Because sexuality has been linked to pain, nausea, fear, rage, helplessness and overwhelming trauma, sex with a loved partner may be experienced as traumatic. They may also develop the "compulsion to inflict new suffering" on themselves in order "to keep former suffering repressed," which superficially resembles "masochism" (Miller, 1990, p. 73), and which can lead them to become targets for revictimizations (van der Kolk, 1989; Kluft, 1990).

Coping with Trauma: Victim Defenses

Three fundamental problems exist for incest victims: how to tolerate the overwhelming trauma at the time it occurs; how to deal with irreconcilable extremes in a single parent; how to define a place in a familial and social context that does not recognize the existence of the trauma.

If the abuse starts early and is chronic, like the pattern outlined earlier, then the victim will generally adopt the more extreme dissociative defenses and show greater amnesia (Horevitz & Braun, 1984; Kluft, 1985a; Herman & Schatzow, 1987; Herman, Perry & van der Kolk, 1989; Briere & Conte, 1989). She has to find a way to manage sitting at the breakfast table with the same man whose penis descended over her face the night before. The most effective way to do this is to split them: good daddy and the monster; daddy who loves me and abusive daddy. Confronting this division can be startling: "But how come they wear the same clothes?" one of my patients asked while in a dissociated child state.

To keep the two daddies separate, the self divides forming a nontraumatized part who lives in the house, goes to school, maintains a relationship with good daddy, and knows nothing about the abuse (but shows symptoms) and a traumatized part or parts, who carry the memories and feelings associated with the abuse and have the relationship with bad daddy or the monster.

The traumatic experiences are stored behind a barrier of denial, which originates by the repetition of statements like "This can't be. This isn't true. This isn't happening to me. Oh no!" statements which are common to anyone confronted with an event too shocking to absorb. A repressive barrier augments the denial and helps to push events and feelings farther from consciousness. With the addition of dissociative defenses, the traumatic events themselves are splintered, shattered like a puzzle into manageable chunks (Braun, 1989; Putnam, 1989). Unlike the retrieval of a repressed memory, which usually reappears in a relatively complete form, a dissociated memory comes up fragmented and splintered with barriers that can be as thick as repression between each piece. In his BASK model of dissociation, Braun (1989) describes the divisions within each traumatic experience as occurring between behaviour, affect, sensation and knowledge (BASK) in various ways. Moving from one piece to the next is like changing channels; two cannot be on at the same time without fuzziness and static. Summit (1989) believes that this process is so active that he calls it "remembering it away" (p. 421).

The fragmentation of severe trauma has been extensively described by Kluft (1985a & b), Braun (1986, 1989) and Putnam (1986, 1989)—all experts on the dissociative disorders. Basically, the dissociated, traumatized parts may become separate enough to form distinct personalities that alternatively emerge and take control as in classical MPD or may remain separate at a more underlying level as in atypical dissociative disorder.

The boundaries between the parts or personalities are thick; those between self and other are thin. While some personalities emerge with names and quite separate histories, personalities or parts are often organized by: (1) emotion: the sad one, the violent one, the angry one, the scared one, the sexy one; (2) age: the little one(s), the seven-year old, the adolescent; (3) function: personalities who keep the barriers in place (the persecutor, the one like father, the censor), personalities who help (internal self-helper, the explainer, the one who figures it out, the nurturer, the soother), personalities who know (the librarian, the file clerk, the objective one); (4) place or venue: the one on the bed, the one in the garage; (5) job: the one who swallowed the sperm, the one who was choked; (6) and many more. Each contains different knowledge or different aspects of the same knowledge. The person in therapy (who represents only one personality, often called the host) usually knows nothing of this for she is the nontraumatized part, who has the relationship with the good daddy. She will typically struggle with a strong desire to disbelieve or doubt these memories as they emerge, so that only a therapist comfortable with the dynamics of dissociation and familiar with the patterns of abuse will be able to resist colluding with her against the enormity of the pain, rage and trauma.

As the memories coalesce and the amnestic and dissociative barriers begin to yield, post-traumatic stress disorder (PTDS) symptoms may emerge or worsen (Herman & Schatzow, 1987; Goodwin, 1988; Coons, Bowman, Pellow & Schneider, 1989; Braun, 1989; Kluft, 1990) and it becomes obvious that the person is traumatized. At this point, some combination of the symptoms seen in rape victims or late onset, less dissociated incest victims emerge: flashbacks, sleep disturbances, eating problems, irritability, difficulty concentrating, somatic complaints, anxiety, self-destructiveness, suicidality, fear of being alone, low self-esteem.

The central issues, the ones that the person is defending against, are contained in the physical and psychological experience of trauma. These include the overwhelming feelings of pain, rage, helplessness, despair and loss of authentic self (Spiegel, 1986) as physical, sexual and emotional injuries are being concurrently inflicted by *someone who is loved and trusted*. The experience that she is trying to avoid retrieving is the shattering of her spirit, which has been called soul murder (Shengold, 1979).

Consequences of Trauma: Victim Losses

The consequences of prolonged abuse are severe. Pieces of the self, too overwhelmed to function, slowly split away from the central personality. These self-parts, frozen at the time of trauma, each representing an aspect of functioning, are unable to mature or develop and remain inaccessible. Often only a tiny part of the self stays conscious and untraumatized; that part is all that truly grows up. The complex web of internal resources that compose an integrated individual's personality fails to develop. Consequently, many incest survivors function well in only one dimension of adult life: their professional work (Herman & Schatzow, 1987), if that.

Each lost self-part or ego-state (Watkins & Watkins, 1982), which initially separated for a reason related to managing repeated abuse (Braun, 1989) usually represents a major aspect of functioning. The ability to take initiative disappears (Goodwin, 1988), not only in the sexual sphere, but in every sphere. Initiative is related to the ability to desire, to want, to get a grip on, to be passionate about, to abandon oneself to a goal or an experience. Desire makes incest victims anxious and frightened; they fight it as they once fought orgasm, as if to experience it compromises their very being. Without initiative, life slips into a kind of passivity and, ultimately, drifts by.

A second major loss is in cognitive functioning (Horevitz & Braun, 1984; Ross & Gahan, 1988; Fine, 1990). The ability to self-monitor or self-examine disappears (Kluft, 1984). In other words, the objective, inner, personal voice fails to develop and victim/survivors become dependent on the opinions of others to make decisions. The evaluation of the personal—relationships, friendships, life—requires clear knowledge of what is happening. Not knowing, once crucial to survival, has become a way of life, perpetuated by remaining too close to experience to sort it out, experiencing life without perspective.

Self-caring functions are also lost (Herman & Schatzow, 1987). As children, victim/survivors have gone through over-whelming disasters, variously described as "electrical shock all over my body," having "seizures," being penetrated "by a train," with no one to comfort, soothe or calm them. A second stage of trauma is the response of others (Kluft, 1984).The combination of shock and the absence of comfort from others leaves part of the person in constant panic; physiologically, they are frequently in a state of hyperarousal (van der Kolk, 1989). They are hypervigilant and externally focused. One of my patients described how only parts of her sleep; others remain alert and watchful. A second dissociated in my office and described the tonsillectomy she had had at age four while under general anaesthetic. Instead of internalizing self-soothing and self-care (Schultz, 1990), which was never received, they internalize what the abuse felt like: hatred, loathing, turmoil, chaos, an internal uproar from which there was no escape or relief. When this becomes self-loathing, which it invariably does, the strategies for relief include a spectrum of self-punitive acts rather than self-caring ones. Hence, incest victims are frequently found to constitute a large segment of severely disrupted groups such as prostitutes (James & Meyerding, 1977a, b; Silbert & Pines, 1981), alcohol and drug addicts (Yeary, 1982; Cohen & Densen-Gerber, 1982; Coleman, 1982), self-injurious and suicidal patients (De Young, 1982; Briere & Runtz, 1986), delinquent and acting-out patients (Briere & Runtz, 1987). To counteract this fundamental sense of worthless self, incest victim/survivors often look to others to provide care, soothing, approval. Actually, of course, only a disappeared part of the self can adequately fulfill this function.

Other profound losses include the ability to trust and remain intimate with self and others, the ability to experience spontaneity and genuine pleasure (Spiegel, 1986), the ability to handle power and influence (Brickman, 1984), and, to some extent, the ability to concentrate, learn and achieve (Schetky, 1990).

RELATIONSHIP TO THE MONTREAL MASSACRE

The fundamental mechanisms employed to cope with the ongoing trauma—denial, dissociation, minimization, false normality—are but extreme versions of the ones we all use to distance ourselves from public traumas: the Massacre, the Gulf War, the homeless. Without these mechanisms, raw human misery might permeate our consciousness to an unbearable extent and the boundary between ourselves and the suffering of others might diminish. A firm boundary between self and others is considered a major criterion for individual psychological health, yet a striking characteristic of most incest victims with whom I have worked is a strong identification with the "wretched of the earth," (Fanon, 1963), an identification which seems attributable to boundary permeability.

In the health fields we maintain a boundary firmness between ourselves and traumatized others by ignoring a problem until it can be clinically pathologized, then pathologizing it on an individual basis, treating the pathology out of context (e.g. talking about powerlessness—in this case women's—as if it occurs as a symptom in a vacuum while keeping the powerful others—men—invisible in clinical language), and

consequently addressing neither the causative social, political and economic aspects of the problems, nor the individuals and groups who
systematically gain from them and how their pathologies operate (Stark,
Flitcraft & Frazier, 1979; Brickman, 1984; Mitchell, 1990).

Focusing on the final stage of illness and dysfunction (table 1) removes
abuse from its cultural context and creates a clinical and social category
called "victims," who are usually women; this allows large portions of
the female population to be classified individually as dysfunctional and
to be marginalized as a group. When the focus moves back a stage to
the consequences of abuse, harm and damage, the division between
healthy, normal individuals and maladjusted, unhealthy ones begins to
break down. Because these harmful consequences can (and do) happen
to anybody who is traumatized, it becomes evident that childhood injury
is as random an event as Lépine's rampage. Since injurious circumstances
probably hold for a large percentage of children, especially female ones,
in the world than noninjurious ones, what we have termed "normal"
development might best be conceptualized as childhood under ideal or,
following Winnicott (12960), "good-enough" conditions, which form
an emotionally privileged developmental stream, and that another normative development sequence is from an injurious childhood to a marginalized, damaged adulthood.

Then, if stage one of abuse is also included and the typical phenomenology of assault described, the commonalities between assaults that
seem as superficially different as incestuous abuse and Lépine's murderous rampage begin to emerge, showing all assaults against women to be
part of a prevailing social tendency of misogynist[4] men to frighten,
harm, marginalize and control women as a shortcut in the path to
establishing themselves.

The Montreal Massacre left us face to face with a trauma perpetuated
by misogynist rage without time to pathologize the victims. It was
absolutely clear that fourteen women, who were innocently going about
their daily lives, were suddenly murdered, finished. There was no way to
pathologize them—to say they shouldn't have been there, that they
cooperated in some way, or at least failed to resist. They didn't live long
enough to develop post-traumatic symptoms, become permanent victims
or even show evidence of the Stockholm syndrome. There was no way
to ask stage three questions: why didn't she leave? Why didn't she say
no? Why is she so depressed and anxious? What is wrong with her

character? Ultimately, the meaning of their short lives was altered; they went from being women in charge of their own destinies to (massacre) victims, a transformation which may be the social effect of all victimization; to create a servile class.

From the perspective of violated women, the Montreal Massacre was neither a surprising nor an isolated event. Many, if not most, abuse victims expected to be killed if they did not conform to the demands, expectations and fantasies, explicit and implied, of their abuser. The massacre, in a sense, represented a public version of their private lives. When this parallel is understood, the massacre of fourteen women by a misogynist male can be placed in a context and viewed as an illustration of various types of violence committed by (some) men against women, one part of a broad spectrum of misogynist male rage and violence that can erupt any time against randomly selected women in any one of its multiple forms of rape, incest, battering, harassment, vilification and abuse. It can be understood statistically as a common event in the lives of some women and psychologically as a feared event in the lives of all women.

This raises the crucial question implicit in the initial stage of the problem when the (usually male) perpetrator is violating the (usually female) victim, the stage which is rarely formulated into a general description in the literature but included usually in fragmentary forms as part of individual case vignettes. This question is *why women?* Why did Marc Lépine kill the women and spare the men? Why do so many men select female victims? What advantage accrues to men from keeping women at least partially debilitated by fear?

From my work with violated women I have learned that particular women are targeted for no other reason than that they are women and, like the fourteen women at the Polytechnique, they are accessible. Nevertheless, they are carriers of a social message that disperses to all women:

1. Women are responsible for failures in the lives of men;
2. Any woman who stands in the way of a man deserves to be punished;
3. Independent women have abdicated their right to protection by individual men (through heroic actions) or collective mankind (through theory, social policy and law).

Fundamentally, women are targeted because men, individually and collectively, stand to gain. Men who harm women gain by doing so— otherwise they wouldn't do it. They gain sexual pleasure, reduction of tension, anger, and other unpleasant emotions. They gain interpersonal control: they get their way, impose their will, have their whims catered to. They coerce women into staying with them who do not wish to. They get sexual partners who do anything they want, whenever they want. Because the violence of their methods has been private and socially invisible, they get all this without a taint on their sexuality and reputation. By keeping individual male sexuality free of such taints, there is no spillover to taint men in general, no equivalent of being a little rape-ish like being a little sluttish, no warnings in the general code of sexual ethics to aid women in avoiding the repugnant forms of male sexuality.

Men may also gain status. We all know and remember the name Marc Lépine. We know his life story, how he thought, what he believed. He has gained a permanent place in Canadian social history; soon someone will write a book about him. The spillover to men in general is to augment the male reputation as aggressive, powerful, forceful, dangerous figures. The spillover for women is quite different; in death the victims have lost their individuality. How many of us know anything about the lives of even one of the fourteen women Lépine murdered? How many of us know what they cherished, believed, stood for? How many of us even remember their names?

Geneviève Bergeron, 21
Hélène Colgan, 23
Nathalie Croteau, 23
Barbara Daigneault, 22
Anne-Marie Edward, 21
Maud Haviernick, 29
Barbara Maria Klueznick, 31
Maryse Laganière, 25
Maryse Leclair, 23
Anne-Marie Lemay, 27
Sonia Pelletier, 23
Michèle Richard, 21
Annie St-Arneault, 23
Annie Turcotte, 21

NOTES

The author would like to thank Paula Pasquali, Pam Gahan and Judith Golden for their thoughtful comments on this manuscript.

1. The sale of these rifles increased in the days following the massacre (Kaihla & Burke, 1989).

2. The first attempt to differentiate abuse from its medical construction appeared in a classic paper by Stark, Flitcraft and Frazier (1979) in which they documented how the physical injuries of battered women were ignored until they could be defined as psychiatric. They describe the stages of medical treatment as (1) the appearance of the injury in the emergency room, (2) the transition from injury to self-abuse, that is abuse that is caused by the patient's own problems, and (3) the transition from self-abuse to a medical definition of battering.

3. Much of the detail in this section is gathered from the author's clinical experience working with incest victims, from talking to other therapists in the field and from details embedded in case studies reported in the literature.

4. Because misogynist and misogyny are respectively defined as "a woman hater" and "women hating" *(The Compact Edition of the Oxford English Dictionary)* without respect to the gender of the person who hates women, I have chosen to use the term here as a way to distinguish misogynist men from all men.

REFERENCES

Badgely, R. (1984). *Sexual offences against children, vol. II.* Report of the committee on sexual offences against children and youths appointed by the Minister of Justice & Attorney General of Canada & the Minister of National Health & Welfare, Ottawa, Canada: Canadian Government Publishing Centre.

Braun, B. G. (Ed). (1986). *Treatment of multiple personality disorder.* Washington, D.C.: American Psychiatric Press.

Braun, B. (1989). Psychotherapy of the survivor of incest with a dissociative disorder. In R. P. Kluft (Ed.), Treatment of victims of sexual abuse (Special issue). *Psychiatric Clinics of North America, 12,* 306–323.

Brickman, J., Briere, J., Ward, M., Kalef, M. & Lungen, A. (1979, June). Preliminary report of the Winnipeg Rape Incidence Project. Paper presented at the annual meeting of the Canadian Psychological Association, Quebec City, Quebec.

Brickman, J. & Briere, J. (1984). Incidence of rape and sexual assault in an urban Canadian population. *International Journal of Women's Studies, 7,* 195–206.

Brickman, J. (1984). Feminist, nonsexist and traditional models of therapy: Implications for working with incest. *Women and Therapy, 3,* 49–67.

Briere, J. & Runtz, M. (1986). Suicidal thoughts and behaviours in former sexual abuse victims. *Canadian Journal of Behavioural Science, 18,* 413–423.

Briere, J. & Runtz, M. (1987). Post sexual abuse trauma: Data and implications for clinical practice. *Journal of Interpersonal Violence, 2,* 367–379.

Briere, J. & Conte, J. (1989, August). Amnesia in adults molested as children: Testing theories of repression. Paper presented at the annual meeting of the American Psychological Association, New Orleans, L.A.

Burt, M. R. & Albin, R. S. (1981). Rape myths, rape definitions and probability of conviction. *Journal of Applied Social Psychology, 11,* 212–230.

Came, B., Burke, D., Ferzoco, G., O'Farrell, B. & Wallace, B. (1989, December 18). Montreal massacre. *Maclean's,* pp. 14–17.

Cohen, F. S. & Densen-Gerber, J. (1982). A study of the relationship between child abuse and drug addiction in 178 patients: Preliminary results. *Child Abuse and Neglect, 6,* 383–387.

Coleman, E. (1982). Family intimacy and chemical abuse: The connection. *Journal of Psychoactive Drugs,* 153–158.

Coons, P. M., Bowman, E. S. & Milstein, V. (1988). MPD: A clinical investigation of 50 cases. *The Journal of Nervous & Mental Disease, 176,* 519–527.

Coons, P. M., Bowman, E. S., Pellow, T. A. & Schneider, P. (1989). Post-traumatic aspects of the treatment of victims of sexual abuse and incest. In R. P. Kluft (Ed.), Treatment of victims of sexual abuse (Special issue). *Psychiatric Clinics of North America, 22,* 325–335.

De Young, M. (1982). Self-injurious behaviour in incest victims. *Child Welfare, 61,* 577–584.

Fine, C. (1990). The cognitive sequelae of incest. In R. P. Kluft (Ed.), *Incest-related syndrome of adult psychopathology* (pp. 161–182), Washington, D.C.: American Psychiatric Press.

Fanon, F. (1963). *The wretched of the earth.* N.Y.: Grove Press.

Goodwin, J. (1988). Post-traumatic symptoms in abused children. *Journal of Traumatic Stress,* 475–488.

Groth, A. N. & Hobson, W. F. (1983). The dynamics of sexual assault. In L. B. Schlesinger & E. Revith (Eds.), *Sexual Dynamics of Anti-Social Behavior* (pp. 159–172), Springfield, Ill.: Charles C. Thomas.

Gunman's trail of death (1989, December 8). *The Gazette,* p. A-5.

Herman, J. L. (1981). *Father-daughter incest,* Cambridge, Mass.: Harvard University Press.

Herman, J. L., Perry, C. & van der Kolk, B. (1989). Childhood trauma in borderline subjects. *American Journal of Psychiatry, 146,* 490–495.

Herman, J. L. & Schatzow, E. (1987). Recovery and verification of memories of childhood sexual trauma. *Psychoanalytic Psychology, 4,* 1–14.

Horevitz, R. P. & Braun, B. G. (1984). Are multiple personalities borderline? *Psychiatric Clinics of North America, 7,* 69–87.

James, J. & Meyerding, J. (1977a). Early sexual experience as a factor in prostitution. *Archives of Sexual Behavior, 7,* 31–41.

James, J. & Meyerding, J. (1977b). Early sexual experience and prostitution. *American Journal of Psychiatry, 134,* 1381–1385.

Kaihla, P. & Burke, D. (1989, December 18). A lethal choice for a murderer. *Maclean's,* p. 16.

Kluft, R. P. (1984). Treatment of multiple personality disorder. *Psychiatric Clinics of North America, 7,* 9–29.

Kluft, R. P. (Ed.) (1985a). *Childhood antecedents of multiple personality disorder.* Washington, D.C.: American Psychiatric Press.

Kluft, R. P. (1985b). Hypnotherapy of childhood multiple personality disorder. *American Journal of Clinical Hypnosis, 27,* 201–210.

Kluft, R. P. (Ed.) (1990). *Incest related syndromes of adult psychopathology.* Washington, D.C.: American Psychiatric Press.

Kuitenbrouwer, P., Scott, M., Lamey, M. & Heinrich, J. (1989, December 7). Campus massacre, *The Gazette,* pp. A1–A2.

Leyton, E. (1996). *Hunting humans: The rise of the modern multiple murderer.* Toronto: McLelland and Stewart.

MacLeod, L. (1989). *The city for women: No safe place.* Secretary of State, Canada.

Malamuth, N. M. & Check, J. V. P. (1980). Sexual arousal to rape and consenting depictions: The importance of the woman's arousal. *Journal of Abnormal Psychology, 89,* 763–766.

Malamuth, N., Heim, M. & Fesbach, S. (1980). Sexual responsiveness of college students to rape depictions: Inhibitory and disinhibitory effects. *Journal of Personality & Social Psychology, 38,* 399–408.

Marshall, W.C. & Barrett, S. (1990). *Criminal neglect: Why sex offenders go free.* Toronto: Doubleday.

Miller, A. (1990). *Banished knowledge.* New York, Doubleday.

Mitchell, T. (1990). *Male violence: Language, lying and lechery.* Unpublished paper.

Putnam, F., Guroff, J. J., Silberman, E. K., Barber, L. & Post, R. M. (1986). The clinical phenomenology of MPD: Review of 100 cases. *Journal of Clinical Psychiatry, 47,* 285–293.

Putnam, F.W. (1989). *Diagnosis and treatment of multiple personality disorder.* Washington, D.C.: American Psychiatric Press.

Quig, J. (1989, December 10). We mourn all our daughters. *The Gazette*, p. A-1.

Rogers, R. (1990). *Reaching for solutions: The report of the special advisor to the Minister of National Health and Welfare on child sexual abuse in Canada.* Ottawa: Ministry of Supply and Services, Canada.

Ross, C. & Gahan, P. (1988). Cognitive analysis of multiple personality disorder. *American Journal of Psychotherapy, 42,* 229–239.

Ross, C. & Norton, G. R. (1989). MPD: An analysis of 236 cases. *American Journal of Psychiatry.*

Russell, D.E.H. (1983). The incidence and prevalence of intrafamilial and extrafamilial sexual abuse of female children. *Child Abuse and Neglect, 7,* 133–146.

Schetky, D. H. (1990). A review of the literature on the long-term effects of childhood sexual abuse. In R. P. Kluft (Ed.), *Incest-related syndromes of adult psychopathology* (pp. 35–54). Washington, DC: American Psychiatric Press.

Schultz, R. (1990). Secrets of adolescence: Incest and developmental fixations. In R. P. Kluft (Ed.), *Incest-related syndromes of adult psychopathology* (pp. 133–159). Washington, DC: American Psychiatric Press.

Shengold, L. (1979). Child abuse and deprivation: Soul murder. *Journal of the American Psychoanalytic Association, 27,* 533–559.

Shepherd, H. (1989, December 8). Gunman 'had cool eyes' professor remembers. *The Gazette*, p. A5.

Silbert, M. H. & Pines, A. M. (1981). Sexual child abuse as an antecedent to prostitution. *Child Abuse & Neglect, 5,* 407–411.

Spiegel, D. (1986). Dissociating damage. *American Journal of Clinical Hypnosis, 29,* 123–131.

Stark, E., Flitcraft, A. & Frazier, W. (1979). Medicine and patriarchal violence: The social construction of a "private" event. *International Journal of Health Services, 3,* 461–493.

Stone, M. H. (1989). Individual psychotherapy with victims of incest. In R. P. Kluft (Ed.), Treatment of victims of sexual abuse (Special issue). *Psychiatric Clinics of North America, 12,* 237–255.

Summit, R. (1983). The child sexual abuse accommodation syndrome. *Child Abuse & Neglect, 7,* 177–193.

Summit, R. (1989). The centrality of victimization. In R .P. Kluft (Ed.), Treatment of victims of sexual abuse (Special issue). *Psychiatric Clinics of North America, 12,* 413–430.

van der Kolk, B. (1989). The compulsion to repeat the trauma. In R. P. Kluft (Ed.), Treatment of victims of sexual abuse (Special issue). *Psychiatric Clinics of North America, 12,* 389–411.

Watkins, J. H. & Watkins, H. H. (1982). In L. E. Abt and I. R. Stuart (Eds.). *The newer therapies: A source book.* N.Y.: Van Nostrand Reinhold.

Winnicot, D. W. (1960). The theory of the parent-infant relationship. *International Journal of Psychoanalysis, 41,* 585–595.

Yeary, J. (1982). Incest and chemical dependency. *Journal of Psychoactive Drugs, 14,* 133–135.

CHAPTER 2

Violence, the Emotionally Enraged Employee, and the Workplace

Managerial Considerations

DIANNE R. LAYDEN

In 1986 in Edmond, Oklahoma, postal worker Patrick Henry Sherrill fatally shot fourteen persons, wounded six others, and committed suicide at the U.S. Post Office, after being reprimanded by his supervisor and told that he would receive a poor performance report.[1] Sherrill's crime marks the first landmark case of violence in the workplace. "While there had been a small number of limited cases, workers basically vented their anger and frustration in non-violent ways and workplaces were generally free from the threats of intruders. Now, and perhaps permanently, violence has become commonplace."[2]

The treatment below attempts to shed light on possible social causes of workplace violence, behavior by the "emotionally enraged" employee, managerial practices possibly associated with violence, and managerial practices that may reduce the risk of its occurrence. Readers may consult the source materials for details of the cases. It should be noted at the outset that profiles of potentially violent employees are of limited use in preventing workplace violence, and managerial plans that address workplace violence should balance the needs of employee privacy, employee safety, and employee dignity.

The study of the rise in workplace violence since the 1980s would strongly benefit from an interdisciplinary approach. Fields that may contribute to the discourse are psychology, sociology, criminology, occupational safety and health, human resources management, labor relations, security management, and business law. By sharing perspectives and information regarding the phenomenon of workplace violence, academicians and practitioners of these disciplines may begin to depend more upon scholarship than news coverage for information.

OVERVIEW

The recent rise in violence in the workplace—a threefold increase over the past five years[3]—is cause for alarm. In 1992, one in four workers reported harassment, threats, or assaults in a survey by Northwestern National Life Insurance Company (tables 1 and 2).[4] Thirty percent of the attackers were co-workers, bosses, or former employees (table 3). After traffic accidents, homicides were the second leading cause of workplace deaths, although the vast majority occurred during robberies.[5] Of 1,004 workplace homicides in 1992, 87 resulted from business-related confrontations, or 9 percent (table 4). Of these, 45, or 4 percent, involved co-workers or former co-workers. In their analysis of Federal Bureau of Investigation (FBI) data in 1976–1991, Fox and Levin concluded that employer-directed homicides have doubled in the last decade.[6] Currently, about two such cases occur each month in the United States. Workplace violence has wide-ranging ramifications for organizations, according to Thomas Harpley of National Trauma Services in San Diego: " 'The company never will get back to business as usual. Everyone has been changed forever. ... You have to try to find a new normal.' " [7]

In their book on workplace violence, Kinney and Johnson estimated

TABLE 1 Incidence of Workplace Harassment, Threats, and Attacks, July 1992–July 1993 [1]

On-the-job Incident Experienced	Percentage of Workers	Rate per 100,000 Workers	Number of Workers (Millions)
Harassment	19	18,667	16.1
Threat of physical harm	7	7,333	6.3
Physical attack	3	2,500	2.2

NOTE: Sample Size: 600 full-time American workers.
[1]Based on 1991 Census Bureau estimates of 96,575 million full-time workers less 10,341 million self-employed workers, or a total of 86,234 million workers.
SOURCE: *Fear and Violence in the Workplace* (Minneapolis, MN: Northwestern National Life Insurance Company, 1993).

TABLE 2 Extent of Workplace Harassment and Violence

Violence, Threat, Harassment, or Fear	Percentage of Workers
Worker was harassed, threatened, or attacked on the job in the past 12 months	25
Someone was threatened with physical harm in employee's workplace in the past 12 months	22
Worker was threatened with physical harm on the job during lifetime	21
Worker was harassed on the job in the past 12 months	19
Worker was physically attacked on the job during lifetime	15
Someone was physically attacked in employee's workplace in the past 12 months	14
Worker considered carrying teargas or mace for protection on the job	11
Worker is often worried about being a victim of violence on the job	10
Worker considered bringing a gun or other deadly weapon to work for protection	4

NOTE: Sample size: 600 full-time American workers.
SOURCE: *Fear and Violence in the Workplace* (Minneapolis, MN: Northwestern National Life Insurance Company, 1993).

the average cost of a serious incident at $250,000.[8] Expenses included: medical and post-trauma stress treatment; lost productivity; lost wages to workers; training costs for replacement workers; property damage and theft; increased security investigations by outside consultants; enhanced managerial training; legal advice and litigation; diversion of attention of senior management to react to the incident, respond to the crisis, and plan for the future; and diminished image in the minds of stockholders and customers, which results in reduced sales potential and lower stock value.

The rise in workplace violence has led to interest in its social causes, profiles of homicidal people, and managerial practices associated with violence. Social causes include the existence of a violent culture in America, where handguns were involved in 12,489 homicides in 1992.[9] In comparison, in 1990, Switzerland and Japan reported 91 and 87 handgun homicides, respectively.[10] A recessionary economy is a factor,

TABLE 3   Harassers and Attackers at the Workplace
(Percentage of Workers)

Perpetrator	Workplace Attack Victims [1] (N = 89)	Workplace Threat Victims [1] (N = 127)	Workplace Harassment Victims [2] (N = 112)
Customer or client [3]	44	36	15
Stranger	24	16	2
Co-worker other than boss	20	32	74
Boss	7	5	39
Former employee	3	6	2
Someone else	3	7	2
Total	101	102	107

NOTE: Sample size: 600 full-time American workers. Columns total more than 100 percent if more than one person attacked, threatened, or harassed the worker.
[1] Most recent event in lifetime.
[2] Most recent event in past year.
[3] Includes students, patients, and inmates.
SOURCE: *Fear and Violence in the Workplace* (Minneapolis, MN: Northwestern National Life Insurance Company, 1993).

as rising unemployment is associated with increases in violence, crime, and disease.[11] Domestic violence also spills over into the workplace, as does violence resulting from client dissatisfaction with provision or denial of goods and services.

Kinney and Johnson identified three control processes that may provide conditions known to discourage violent behavior: an efficient economic system that creates full or nearly full employment; an effective legal system that prevents crime and protects citizens against crime; and a cultural system that maintains a norm of good behavior.[12] Unfortunately, the United States may be characterized as having high rates of unemployment, a relatively inefficient criminal justice system and liberal gun laws, and a popular culture that glamorizes violence.

Homicidal people at the workplace generally are depicted as white males in their thirties and forties with migratory job histories; they tend to be loners, strongly interested in weapons, and alcohol or drug abusers.[13] They have poor self-esteem, coping skills, and interpersonal relations. Many come from dysfunctional families and have experienced

TABLE 4   Circumstances of Workplace Homicides, 1992

	Homicides	
Type of Circumstance[1]	Number	Percent
Total	1,004	100
Business disputes	87	9
Co-worker, former co-worker	45	4
Customer and client	35	3
Other	7	1
Personal disputes	39	4
Relative of victim (primarily husband, ex-husband)	24	2
Boyfriend, ex-boyfriend	7	1
Other	8	1
Police in the line of duty	56	6
Robberies and miscellaneous crimes	822	82

[1]Some cases listed under business disputes, personal disputes, and police in the line of duty may also qualify as robberies or other crimes.
NOTE: Percentages may not add to totals because of rounding.
SOURCE: Janice Windau and Guy Toscano, "Workplace Homicides in 1992," *Compensation and Working Conditions* (Washington, DC: U.S. Department of Labor, Bureau of Labor Statistics, February, 1994), citing *Census of Fatal Occupational Injuries,* Bureau of Labor Statistics, in cooperation with Federal and State agencies, 1992.

child abuse. Religious or political proselytizing is a common behavior. At the time of the violent act, multiple life stressors may have been occurring, particularly the threat of job loss. Harpley averred, "Often-times, their life is their job. When their job is in jeopardy, their life is in jeopardy." [14]

Kinney and Johnson contended that workplace violence results from "career dissonance" among men. "Only somewhat over-simplified, the critical anchor for women is the *relationship;* for men, their *chosen job* or *profession.* Both overt and covert life-stress effects are made more manageable while these anchors are in place, because they afford a sense of control that permits us to tolerate less critically-perceived pressures. When lost or jeopardized, however, these essential life components increase vulnerability to stress more than additively."[15] Notably, there are gender differences in behavioral consequences when these anchors fail; women seek counseling, while men display aggression—and may kill. Layoffs in recent years have threatened the most critical anchor for men.

In addition, "as women have gained ground in their struggle for equality in the workplace, often to the perceived disadvantage of men, there has been a marked increase in assaultive crime by males on females, reflecting the destruction of a secondary anchor that men see as a challenge to their authority and potency."[16] At the workplace, women are at risk from both violence and sexual harassment, itself often a precursor to battery, rape, or murder.[17]

> The essence of career dissonance is that the very "branch we clung to" in order to cope with moderate life stressors turns into the "straw that breaks the camel's back" when it is lost as an anchor. The incongruity is enhanced by the realization that the long-held, generalized expectation that loyalty, diligence and hard work would be rewarded with job stability and security is a relationship which no longer holds.[18]

Kinney and Johnson predicted an increase in assaultive crime by males against females and figures perceived as having authority over jobs as the number of jobs continue to diminish.

Indeed, of 6,956 workplace homicides in 1980–1988, 972 victims (14 percent) were managers, the third largest category.[19] "Most employees who kill managers or colleagues have been fired or feel mistreated."[20] Managerial practices possibly associated with violence include those described as negligent, unjust, and abusive, but that may go unchecked until violence results. Following a violent incident, managerial practices will be assessed as a possible causal factor in news coverage by the communications media, medical inquiries, and court testimony by employees, union officials, family members and friends of the perpetrator and victims, health care professionals, and other observers involved in lawsuits filed against the organization.[21] News coverage of the organization may continue for years.

The "Emotionally Enraged" Employee: Reviews of the Cases

Reviews of workplace violence cases by Baron, Kinney and Johnson, and Fox and Levin are discussed below. Although their profiles of violent employees developed from the cases are remarkably similar, each is presented separately in the interest of clarity.

S. Anthony Baron, in his book on workplace violence, used the term "emotionally enraged" employee to describe the perpetrator of workplace violence.[22] In this context, rage is defined as "an employee's attempt to regain control by verbally abusing or physically attacking the source of their frustration."[23] His review of the cases found that the emotionally enraged employee almost always fell within one or more of these categories: history of violence, psychosis, romance obsession, chemical dependence, depression, pathological blamer, impaired neurological functioning, elevated frustration with the environment, interest in weapons, and personality disorders, such as the antisocial and borderline personality disorders.[24]

The cases also revealed that warning signs existed, although they often went undetected.[25] Baron outlined three levels in the forms that violence may take:

Level One: Refuses to cooperate with immediate supervisor; spreads rumors and gossip to harm others; consistently argues with co-workers; belligerent toward customers/clients; constantly swears at others; makes unwanted sexual comments.

Level Two: Argues increasingly with customers, vendors, co-workers and management; refuses to obey company policies and procedures; sabotages equipment and steals property for revenge; verbalizes wishes to hurt co-workers and/or management; sends sexual or violent notes to co-workers and/or management; sees self as victimized by management (me against them).

Level Three: Frequent displays of intense anger resulting in recurrent suicidal threats, recurrent physical fights, destruction of property, utilization of weapons to harm others, commission of murder, rape, and/or arson.[26]

Kinney and Johnson developed the following baseline profile of a perpetrator of workplace violence: male; white; 35 + years old; history of violence toward women, children, or animals; weapon owner; self-esteem heavily dependent on job; few interests outside of work; withdrawn or a "loner"; often externalizes blame for disappointments; military service; alcohol or drug abuse; history of mental health issues; fascination with violence or weapons; proselytizes for cause(s); perceives that he will be laid off or terminated; and interpersonal conflict.[27] They noted that "Seger adds the tendency to function at menial job levels, or if professionals, persons who had experienced great personal frustration characterized by 'enormous pent-up rage'; and includes as an important component, 'people who are depressed or even suicidal and who see no way out of their troubles.' "[28]

They found that a secondary but crucial set of risk factors included actual or perceived impending dismissal or layoff; argumentative or uncooperative behavior towards co-workers and perhaps customers; extremist opinions and attitudes; unwelcome sexual comments or threats of physical assault; preoccupation with weapons; violation of company policies and procedures; expressed desire to harm co-workers or management; difficulty accepting authority; history of interpersonal conflict with co-workers, supervisors, or both; and sabotage of equipment and/or property.

Kinney and Johnson identified 125 cases of workplace violence with sufficient data to permit analysis; all but a few were preceded by warnings. Some specific findings are summarized below:

Of 121 perpetrators for whom gender was specified, 118 were male, or 97.5 percent.

Ages ranged from 17 to 66 years; in cases in which ages were stated, the average was 36.1 years.

In 122 cases, or 98 percent, the perpetrator acted alone.

Of the total number of 607 victims, 393 were killed, or 65 percent.

Firearms were used in 90 of 111 assaults for which weapons were specified, or 81 percent, mostly handguns.

Suicide by 3 1 of 1 3 0 perpetrators, or 2 4 percent, followed their assault.

California was over represented as a locale with 3 7 cases, or 3 0 percent; New York had 1 0 (8 percent), Florida and Texas had nine each (7 percent), and Illinois had seven (6 percent). No other state had more than five cases, or 4 percent.[29]

Fox and Levin presented a similar picture of the perpetrator of workplace violence, drawn from FBI data compiled on 2 4 1 murders in 1 9 7 6– 1 9 9 1. The "vengeful worker" typically a middle-aged, white male who faces job loss, sees little opportunity for finding another job, and blames others for his plight. He tends to be a loner for whom work provides the only meaningful part of his life. "Here too we see a trend in society which places more and more middle-aged men at risk. An increased rate of divorce, greater residential mobility, and a general lack of neighborliness mean that, for many Americans, work is their only source of stability and companionship."[30]

Citing considerable evidence that frustration tends to increase aggressive motivation, Fox and Levin identified two kinds of job frustration which engender enough resentment to be translated into extreme violence:

[S]ome vengeful workers have suffered long-term, cumulative frustration—repeated failures in their careers, resulting in a diminished ability to cope with life's disappointments. From their point of view, they never get the right job, the deserved promotion, or a decent raise. Their firing at a crucial time in their lives becomes the final straw. . . . [O]ther vengeful employees come to feel invulnerable to job loss because of their long-term employment with the same company. They feel a strong sense of entitlement, as though they have tenure. From their perspective, they have given their best years to the boss, have unselfishly dedicated their careers to the firm, have helped build the business . . . and what do they get in return? Fired![31]

The vengeful worker treats the gun as the "Great Equalizer" in his quest for justice. "Not only does the gun correct the power imbalance between the employee and his superior, but it is simply far more lethal, particularly if he wants to go after multiple victims. Although full of rage, he might be deterred were it necessary to kill with hands. By contrast, a gun makes it very easy." [32]

Fox and Levin also found most vengeful, violent workers do not act spontaneously and "just explode," but deliberate and engage in well-planned ambushes to gain revenge. "Workplace killers may be despondent, disillusioned, disappointed and even clinically depressed—but generally [are] not deranged." [33]

Kinney and Johnson found that workplace violence, unlike robbery and commercial crime, belongs to a "genre" that almost always follows the same sequence:

> The sequence begins with a traumatic experience that creates the perception of an unsolvable psychic state, which in turn produces extreme and chronic emotional tension or anxiety. The traumatic experience may be caused by a single major event, such as job termination, or it may be more cumulative in nature, preceded by a series of seemingly minor events, such as several reprimands, one or two negative performance reviews, etc.

> Once traumatized, the individual projects all responsibility for his or her internal tension or anxiety onto the situation, in effect externalizing blame for the unsolvable psychic state.

> At this point, the individual's thinking turns inward, and becomes increasingly egocentric, progressing to self-protection and self-preservation as objectives, to the exclusion of all other concerns.

> Within this frame of reference, the idea is conceived that a violent act is the only way out; and following a period of internal conflict, which may be prolonged, the violent act is attempted or committed. [34]

According to John Monahan, author of works on predicting violent behavior, research studies "demonstrate how difficult it is to predict violence in general, much less violence specific to the workplace." [35] He observed that given a labor force of more than 125 million people, and a small number of workplace homicides annually, it is impossible to predict accurately an event with such a low base rate except in extreme circumstances. Monahan suggested the following indicators of the propensity of an individual toward violence: history of violence, sex, race, age, intelligence scores, educational attainment, employment stability, base rate of violent behavior among people of same background, sources of stress, predisposition to cope with stress in a violent or non-violent manner, similarity of the contexts in which violent coping mechanisms have been used in the past to those in which the person likely will function in the future, who the likely victims are and how available they are, and what means are available to commit violence.[36]

Perpetrators of workplace violence generally do not fit Monahan's profile. For example, Frank Kuzmits applied the model to the case of Joseph Wesbecker, an emotionally disturbed employee on long-term disability leave from the Standard Gravure Company in Louisville, Kentucky, who killed eight co-workers and injured twelve others with an assault rifle before committing suicide.[37] Wesbecker did not fit the demographic profile of a violent person, had not previously engaged in violent behavior at work, and had no police record of violence; two harassment suits filed by his first wife resulted in not-guilty verdicts. Considerable sources of stress existed in his work environment, however; and he was predisposed to respond to stress in either a non-violent or violent manner.

Fox and Levin noted that profiles designed to predict rare events tend to produce a large percentage of false positives: "Regardless of the specific profile characteristics, many more employees will likely fit the profile than will in fact seek revenge at work. Moreover, an effort to identify the problem worker may actually create a self-fulfilling prophesy whereby combative employees become enraged when singled out in a negative way."[38]

Several observers have warned against reliance on profiles as a means of preventing workplace violence.[39] For example, at the U.S. Postal Service, where 33 postal workers died and 20 were wounded in 1983–1993, a study conducted of a sample of "assaults" in 1989–1992, ranging from verbal threats to armed attacks, hoped to yield a profile of potentially violent employees for use in the hiring process.[40] Some workplace violence experts responded by calling attention to the high-pressured, authoritarian, and frequently hostile work environment at post offices, which fosters emotional and psychological instability among employees, while postal workers expressed fear the results would be used to make "scapegoats" of broad groups of employees and applicants, particularly military veterans, two of whom were responsible for the 1993 shootings at post offices in Dana Point, California, and Dearborn, Michigan. Indeed, following the shootings, former Postmaster General Anthony Frank called for reexamination of the hiring preference in federal employment given to military veterans.[41]

MANAGERIAL CONSIDERATIONS

While it may be impossible to predict workplace violence, its prospect compels managers to examine their practices from the standpoint of preventing or discouraging its occurrence. Kinney and Johnson depicted the high-risk work environment as having the following characteristics: chronic labor-management disputes; frequent employee grievances; an extraordinary number of injury claims (especially psychological claims); understaffing or excessive demands for overtime; a high number of psychologically stressed personnel; and an authoritarian management approach.[42] In the Northwestern Life survey, employees who said their employers have effective grievance, harassment, and security programs reported lower rates of workplace violence and lower levels of job dissatisfaction, job "burn-out," and stress-related illnesses (table 5).

Four steps an employer may take to reduce the risk of workplace violence are to identify managerial practices possibly associated with violence, to identify its legal obligations with respect to workplace violence, to establish and maintain sound human resources management (HRM) practices, and to develop comprehensive plans that address workplace violence, which include plans for coping with a violent incident should one occur.

The first step is to identify managerial practice that may be characterized as negligent, unjust, and abusive. Negligent practices include failure to maintain communication with employees on all work-related matters, particularly regarding HRM decisions such as performance ratings, promotions, layoffs, and dismissals. Unjust practices include absence of a grievance procedure, or presence of a one-sided procedure, which in effect precludes amending or rescinding a managerial decision. The import of communication programs and complaint procedures is widely observed throughout the HRM literature.[43]

TABLE 5   Impact of Improved Interpersonal Relations and Effective
Preventive Programs on Workplace Violence (Percentage of Workers)

Employees Report They:	Employer Has Grievance, Harassment, and Security Programs	Employer Does Not Have All Three Programs
Will burn out in the next year or two	28	44
Experience a lot of job stress	22	32
Have been attacked, threatened or harassed in past 12 months	18	31
Worry about being laid off or fired in the next year	14	21
Experience high levels of stress-related illness	13	29
Have no harmony in their work group	13	27
Have been harassed on the job in the past 12 months	13	23
Cannot rely on supervisor for support	11	30
Were attacked or threatened on the job in the past 5 years	11	21
Are dissatisfied with their job	5	21

NOTE: Sample size: 600 full-time American workers.
SOURCE: *Fear and Violence in the Workplace* (Minneapolis, MN: Northwestern National Life Insurance Company), 1993.

The post office supervisor killed in 1991 in Royal Oak, Michigan, was known for such abusive practices as requiring a custodian to scrub urinals with a toothbrush as punishment for allegedly not properly cleaning the restrooms.[44] Complaints against the supervisor led only to transfers, not his removal. Post office managerial practices are described as paramilitary. Time clocks calibrated on military time measure attendance in hundredths of a second and dock employees for seconds of tardiness. Sometimes, employees have to ask permission to use the bathroom.

Employee surveys have found a high incidence of abuse at work.[45]

According to Anderson and Militello, about 25 percent of managers are abusing their employees because they in turn were abused when they were young.[46] The personalities of most managers feature one or more of the following characteristics—aggression, control, paranoia, and narcissism—which managers often display when under pressure. These leadership styles and their roots in childhood are defined as follows:

Aggressive managers assume that the world is a hostile place and leaders should develop self-protective behavior that includes striking first. Supervisors in this category generally are abrasive and contemptuous of authority. Such behavior usually can be traced to parental hostility or rejection.

Controlling managers show common characteristics that include orderliness, parsimoniousness, obstinacy, rigidity, and perseverance. These managers are concerned with organization and efficiency and the pecking order. They do not question their bosses. These managers often are indecisive because their parents did not tolerate mistakes.

Narcissistic managers are concerned primarily with self-preservation. They often are perceived as having strong personalities, and as being aggressive, independent, and action-oriented. Many employers think these traits and the need to validate self-esteem make these people ideal managers. Such managers are playing a role in which they idealize parents they are or were never able to please.

Paranoid managers are acutely aware of the dynamics of power. They value status and position highly and they envy people in higher-ranking jobs. Most such managers had extremely intrusive parents.[47]

Anderson and Militello found that "[r]ather than discharge abusive managers, many corporations reward them for their behavior because it may have increased productivity in the short run, as employees scramble to avoid antagonizing their bosses."[48]

In their book on fear at the workplace, Ryan and Oestreich presented a scale of aggressive managerial interpersonal behavior and a continuum of intensity (figure 1).[49] Intimidating actions range from glaring at some-

FIGURE I. What Managers and Supervisors Do to Threaten Their
Employees

Light	1	Silence
gray	2	Glaring eye contact: "the look"
	3	Brevity or abruptness
	4	Snubbing or ignoring people
	5	Insults and put-downs
	6	Blaming, discrediting, or discounting
	7	An agressive, controlling manner
	8	Threats about the job
	9	Yelling and shouting
Dark	10	Angry outbursts or loss of control
gray	11	Physical threats

A	B	C	D	E

Lower Intensity				Higher Intensity
Subtle				Obvious
General				Personal
Rare				Frequent
Private				Exposed

SOURCE: Kathleen D. Ryan and Daniel K. Oestreich, *Driving Fear out of the Workplace* (San Francisco: Jossey-Bass Publishers, 1991). The "gray scale" arranges various types of behavior in order of increasing impact. The authors describe behaviors near the light gray end as *abrasive* and behaviors near the dark gray end as *abusive*. Letters A to E represent the intensity dimension.

one across the desk to losing control of one's emotions, with the intensity ranging from subtle, general, rare, and private actions to those obvious, personal, frequent, and exposed actions. Intentionally or unintentionally, such actions demean, humiliate, isolate, insult, and threaten people.

The Northwestern Life survey found that workplace violence and harassment affected the health and productivity of victims (table 6). An additional finding was that workplace stress was both a cause and effect of workplace violence, in that highly stressed workers experienced twice the rate of violence and harassment as less-stressed employees, and threats of workplace violence were linked with higher burn-out rates.

In 1993, U.S. Postmaster General Marvin Runyon informed Congress of the following initiatives by the U.S. Postal Service to improve its

TABLE 6   Effect of Workplace Violence and Harassment on Health and Productivity of Victims (Percentage of Workers)

Effect on Worker	Workplace Attack Victims (N = 89)	Workplace Threat Victims (N = 127)	Workplace Harassment Victims (N = 112)
Affected psychologically [1]	79	77	88
Disrupted work life [2]	40	36	62
Physically injured or sick	28	13	23
No negative effect	15	19	7

NOTE: Sample size: 600 full-time American workers.
[1] Victim was angry, fearful, stressed, intimidated, or depressed.
[2] Victim reported at least one of the following effects: interpersonal problems, quit or changed jobs, wanted to quit, lowered productivity, or adjusted work schedule or routine.
SOURCE: *Fear and Violence in the Workplace* (Minneapolis, MN: Northwestern National Life Insurance Company, 1993).

work environment: including representatives of unions and management associations in weekly senior leadership meetings at headquarters and major facilities across the country; conducting employee opinion surveys to measure factors related to employee commitment; holding managers and supervisors accountable for improving employee commitment; measuring executive performance through the process called "360 degree feedback," which utilizes assessments by supervisors, peers, and subordinates; and attempting to award advancement only to executives with "people skills." [50]

The second step in reducing the risk of workplace violence requires identifying the employer's legal obligations. The social responsibility of employers has long been a matter of public concern. Employment law regulates practices in such areas as discrimination, compensation, pensions, safety and health, collective bargaining, polygraph use, notice of layoffs, employee privacy, and personnel records. Wrongful dismissals are subject to judicial review under principles of tort and contract law. [51]

Although no regulations exist under the Occupation Safety and Health Act (OSHA) of 1970 for preventing workplace violence, Section 5(a), the general duty clause, requires employers covered by the Act to provide a safe working environment. In 1992, OSHA inspectors were told to cite workplaces where criminal activity endangers workers. [52] In 1992, Cal/OSHA, California's workplace safety and health program, released guidelines on improving the safety of health care and community service workers, and Governor Pete Wilson signed a law requiring hospitals to have plans to assess violence in their facilities. Legal issues that may be raised under common law in suits for damages filed against the organization following a violent incident include negligent hiring, negligent retention, the "duty to warn," and the post-discharge duty to provide security.[53]

Employers find particular difficulty with the issue of negligent hiring. There is a general duty to refrain from hiring an applicant the employer knew or should have known was unfit for the job so as to create a danger of harm to others, and a heightened duty of inquiry into an applicant's background when the job involves weapons, substantial public contact, and supervision of children. However, prior employers generally are unwilling to furnish information about former employees other than employment dates, position titles, and salaries earned, to avoid risk of defamation suits. Criminal records also prove difficult to assess because past violent behavior may not be predictive, and their use in hiring decisions must meet the test of business necessity if the applicant is a member of a group protected by Title VII of the Civil Rights Act (CRA) of 1964, as amended, which forbids discrimination on the basis of race, color, religion, sex, or national origin.

All tests for employment must be job-related and valid under U.S. Equal Employment Opportunity Commission guidelines. Psychological tests may not be intrusive without a compelling reason, such as involving a life-endangering occupation or a high-stress position. According to Kinney and Johnson, questionable scores should be followed by clinical interviews, not outright rejection of the applicant. The Americans with Disabilities Act (ADA) of 1990 forbids discrimination in hiring against persons with mental disabilities, unless a person poses a "direct threat" established by objective evidence to the health and safety of self or others.[54]

The employer has a duty to take notice of threats and harassment within the workplace, and to respond to employee complaints and warnings about potentially dangerous employees. Sexual harassment is illegal under Title VII of the CRA. The ADA may require provision of mental health counseling to employees with violent propensities related to mental impairment and may preclude suspending or discharging an employee suspected as posing a danger.

Although individuals have no general duty to act affirmatively to protect another from harm, some states impose a duty to warn potential victims of threats under three conditions: if a "special relationship" exists between the one who has knowledge of potential harm and either the dangerous person or potential victim, such as the employer-employee relationship; the risk of harm is foreseeable; and the potential victim is readily identifiable.[55] The duty covers employee assistance programs at the workplace that provide counseling on work-related and personal problems, independent psychiatrists and psychologists, and mental health clinics. Following a discharge, the employer has a duty to protect its employees' safety by taking keys and passcards, changing locks and codes, transferring a threatened employee, or increasing the security at a work location.

To avoid liability for workplace violence, employers are advised to conduct background investigations of job applicants with reference to employment history, criminal record, references, and prior employers, and maintain records of the results; investigate all complaints of harassment and take disciplinary action when necessary; provide honest, accurate, bias-free evaluations of employee performance; to be alert to and prepared to act on dramatic changes in attendance, attitude, performance, and behavior; and, apply disciplinary procedures in a consistent and equitable manner. In addition, employers should maintain a continuing review of applicable federal and state statutes and case law on pre-employment inquiries, discrimination under the CRA and ADA, employee privacy, and employee threats.

The third step in preventing or discouraging workplace violence is to establish and maintain HRM practices that promote trustful relationships in the drive for organizational productivity. The following HRM practices constitute managerial practices in their own right. Key elements include careful selection of managers, continuous management development, and refusal to tolerate abusive behavior. "Simply firing abusive managers without changing the corporate culture does little to prevent their successors from also being abusive."[56] Ryan and Oestreich recommended adoption of a program of developing positive group norms for relationships with employees by increasing awareness of threatening behaviors, collaboratively developing codes of conduct in each work group, coaching supervisors in how to reinforce positive communication when others exhibit either threatening or supportive behaviors, working with resistant supervisors, and fostering organizational commitment to positive interpersonal behavior.[57]

Other desirable HRM practices include open communication, absence of discrimination and favoritism, adequate compensation, training and promotional opportunities, employee participation in decision-making, feedback on performance, employee assistance programs, stress-reduction programs, just cause and due process in discipline, impartial grievance procedures, out placement services for terminated employees, exit interviews, and attitude surveys on managerial performance and satisfaction with the HRM program.

A display of sensitivity in disciplinary and downsizing matters is essential. Baron noted the importance of understanding the psychology of job loss, noticing what has value to employees, and recognizing that what is valued differs from employee to employee. He argued that *any* "take-aways" at the workplace, material or intangible, "should be orchestrated and planned with the same forethought and care as a major relocation, merger, or product launch. . . . [W]hen the environment is uncertain and resources are diminished, people will hang on that much tighter to what they have, and will be that much more threatened by the potential loss of that which they value."[58]

Finally, employers are urged to develop comprehensive plans for preventing as well as coping with violent incidents. Such plans must balance the interests of employee safety, employee privacy, and employee dignity in all dealings with the organization. These plans should address the following actions: (1) provision of security measures to limit exposure of employees; (2) promotion of an organizational climate free of stress and abuse; (3) maintenance of sound HRM practices, with attention to selection, appraisal, disciplinary, and layoff procedures; (4) management training on communication, the psychology of job loss, workplace violence, and the potentially violent employee; (5) adoption and communication of a policy statement that declares violence of any sort is contrary to business purposes and designates personnel to receive and act on reports of employee threats; (6) adoption of procedures for the confidential handling of reports and investigations of threats, followed by intervention through counseling, when appropriate; (7) appointment of a broad-based, crisis-management team, which includes a mental health professional, to respond to warning signs and violent incidents; and (8) post-incident implementation of trauma response procedures for dealings with police, medical personnel, communications media, clients, and particularly employees and their families, who may require treatment for post-traumatic stress disorder.[59]

The handling of threats is a sensitive matter. Experts on workplace violence propose the use of telephone hotlines for reporting threats and triggering investigations of any employees who inspire fear. Such programs may generate other forms of conflict. For example, postal workers reportedly file reports against each other alleging threats at the slightest hint of trouble rather than attempting to resolve the problem, which has created an atmosphere of paranoia.[60] New legal issues are likely to arise if investigations are conducted without cause, or employees are defamed or adversely affected in their employment opportunities by allegation of having made threats.

James S. Cawood recommended the following process for the analysis of threats: a background investigation of the employee alleged to have made a threat; interviews by a psychologist with the person who reported the threat, persons knowledgeable about the employee's state of mind, and the employee who is the subject of the investigation; and a determination as to the proper disposition of the threat by a crisis-management team that includes a psychologist and members of the human resources, legal, and security professional staff.[61] Alternatives for managerial action include no action, voluntary or mandatory counseling, a disability leave of absence, an offer of the opportunity to resign, dismissal, obtaining a temporary or permanent restraining order, notifying law enforcement agencies or filing civil or criminal charges, notifying persons who are the targets of threats so that they may protect themselves, and providing additional security at the worksite.

According to Baron, insensitivity to employees following a violent incident can further victimize and traumatize people:

If management responds slowly or with disinterest or blame, employees may experience feelings of betrayal. Individuals are at risk of ongoing stress reactions, and even rage, if management is perceived as resistant to providing information or taking corrective action. . . . Most people report losing a sense of safety and well-being. This can affect a person's entire life, including relationships with family as well as the ability to work and carry out everyday activities.[62]

In conclusion, the rise in violence at the workplace since the 1980s is a social development of significance to employers. One possible cause is "career dissonance" experienced by men in the wake of economic and social changes affecting job availability and perceptions of male authority. Profiles of the "emotionally enraged" employee provide an aid to understanding the psychology of violence and patterns of occurrence, but may be of limited usefulness in predicting violent behavior.

The prospect of workplace violence compels employers to examine their managerial practices and legal obligations in the hope of reducing the risk of occurrence of a violent incident. Negligent, unjust, and abusive practices should be eliminated or discouraged. Sound human resources management practices, desirable in their own right, should be established and maintained. Such practices should be supplemented by comprehensive plans that provide employee security, management training on workplace violence, policies and procedures for handling threats, and trauma-response procedures should a violent incident occur. Cooperation among the human resources, legal, and security professional staff is essential, and management must forge relationships with mental health professionals in responding to workplace violence issues. Finally, managerial plans must balance the needs of employee privacy, employee safety, and employee dignity.

NOTES

1. See, generally, S. Anthony Baron, *Violence in the Workplace: A Prevention and Management Guide for Businesses* (Ventura, CA: Pathfinder Publishing of California, 1993), 55–69.

2. Joseph A. Kinney and Dennis L. Johnson, *Breaking Point: The Workplace Violence Epidemic and What to Do about It* (Chicago: National Safe Workplace Institute, September 1993), 15.

3. Edward Iwata, "Violence in the Workplace," *Albuquerque Journal, Business Outlook*, May 31, 1993, 14.

4. See, generally, *Fear and Violence in the Workplace* (Minneapolis, MN: Northwestern National Life Insurance Company, 1993). See also Frank Swoboda, "Growing Violence Clouds Nation's Workplaces," *Albuquerque Journal, Business Outlook*, January 10, 1994, 3, citing the results of a December, 1993, survey of workplace violence by the Society for Human Resource Management in Alexandria, Virginia. The survey of 479 randomly selected personnel officers found one-third of the respondents reported incidents of workplace violence,

half of which were committed by employees toward fellow workers. The types of incidents were as follows: fist fights, 74.8 percent; shootings (not necessarily homicides), 17 percent; stabbings, 7.5 percent; rape and sexual assault, 6.3 percent; use of explosives, .6 percent; other, 26.4 percent. (The figures total more than 100 percent because of multiple incidents.)

5. See, generally, Janice Windau and Guy Toscano, "Workplace Homicides in 1992," *Compensation and Working Conditions* (Washington, DC: U.S. Department of Labor, Bureau of Labor Statistics, February 1994). Of 6,083 fatal work injuries in 1992, traffic accidents accounted for 1,121, or 18 percent, and homicides for 1,004, or 17 percent. See also *NIOSH Alert: Request for Assistance in Preventing Homicide in the Workplace,* DHHS (NIOSH) Publication No. 93–109 (Cincinnati, OH: National Institute for Occupational Safety and Health, September 1993). In 1980–1989, workplace homicides accounted for some 7,600 deaths—12 percent of the total. Homicides were the third leading cause of death from injury in the workplace, and the leading cause of occupational death among women. Minorities and workers aged 65 and older incurred a disproportionate share of workplace homicides. Industries with high incidence rates were the retail trades, public administration, and transportation/communications/public utilities. High-risk occupations were taxicab driver, law enforcement officer, hotel clerk, gas station worker, security guard, stock handler/bagger, store owner/manager, and bartender. For a detailed analysis of differential rates among industries, see Dawn N. Castillo and E. Lynn Jenkins, "Industries and Occupations at High Risk for Work-Related Homicide," *Journal of Occupational Medicine* 38, no. 2 (February 1994): 125–32.

6. James Alan Fox and Jack Levin, "Firing Back: The Growing Threat of Workplace Homicide," manuscript for forthcoming publication in The Annals of the American Academy of Political and Social Science, November 28, 1993, 2–3, citing Supplementary Homicide Reports compiled by the FBI as part of the Uniform Crime Reporting Program, which "surely underestimate the prevalence of workplace murder in the United States," (2). Fox and Levin also comment on the inadequacy of NIOSH data in revealing the extent of workplace homicide. News coverage represents one source of data on workplace homicides. See "War in the Workplace," *Early Warnings* 2, no. 2 (February 1994): 1, 4, published by the Institute for Crisis Management (ICM) in Louisville, Kentucky. According to the ICM database, the number of business-crime news stories increased 39 percent between 1989 and 1993, and jumped 23 percent in 1993.

7. Peggy Stuart, "Murder on the Job," *Personnel Journal,* February 1992, 84. See, generally, 27, 72–84.

8. Kinney and Johnson, op. cit., 26–27. For 1992, Kinney and Johnson estimated a total cost of 4.2 billion for 111,000 incidents of all phenomena associated with workplace violence—homicide, injury from battery, psychologi-

cal trauma, stress-related mental disorders stemming from violence, assault, verbal abuse, sexual assaults, property damage, sabotage, and theft and other property crimes.

9. Robert Davis, "Gun Foes Sense a Time to Seize the Moment," *USA Today,* October 19, 1993, 9A.

10. "Stop Handguns before They Stop You," poster by Handgun Control, Inc., Washington, DC. In 1990, handguns killed 10,567 people in America, 91 in Switzerland, 87 in Japan, 68 in Canada, 22 in Great Britain, 13 in Sweden, and 10 in Australia.

11. Richard L. Vernaci, "Crime, Disease Linked to Economy," *Riverside Press-Enterprise,* October 16, 1992, A1, A10. Merva and Fowles found a 1 percent rise in unemployment resulted in 17,654 deaths annually from heart disease, 1,386 deaths from stroke, 730 homicides, 31,305 violent crimes, and 111,775 property crimes. See Kinney and Johnson, op. cit., 77. In the first half of the 1980s, about 4.3 million workers were reported as displaced, and in 1987–1992, 5.6 million were displaced; the term "displaced" applies only to those who lost jobs held three years or more. "Those who lost jobs of less tenure would swell the 1987–1992 number by an additional 9.7 million," (77).

12. Kinney and Johnson, op. cit., 32–33. See *Fear and Violence in the Workplace,* op. cit., 9: "Most workers blamed alcohol or drug abuse, layoffs or firings, and poverty in society as major causes of on-the-job violence. To a lesser but important degree, the availability of guns, violence on TV or in the movies, job stress and job-related conflicts were identified as major causes," (9).

13. Iwata, loc. cit., and National Trauma Services, *Defusing Workplace Violence: How to Avoid Violence in the Workplace,* a Seminar on Responding to Workplace Violence, San Diego, CA, October 7, 1993, 9.

14. Thomas F. O'Boyle, "Disgruntled Workers Intent on Revenge Increasingly Harm Colleagues and Bosses," *Wall Street Journal,* September 15, 1992, B7. See also Bob Filipczak, "Armed and Dangerous at Work" *Training,* July 1992, 43, citing San Diego psychologist Michael Mantell, co-author of a forthcoming book on workplace violence, who attributed its surge to worker powerlessness: "After a decade of instability and the death of job security, many employees feel they have no control over their jobs or their futures. He [Mantell] describes the corporate environment as 'a beaker of frustration that continues to stir and stir, and frustration leads to aggression.' "

15. Kinney and Johnson, op. cit., 37. See also Curt Suplee, "Berserk! Violent Employees Obsessed with Revenge Are Turning the Workplace into a Killing Zone," *Washington Post,* October 1, 1989, D1, citing sociologist David Phillips: " 'The late 20th-century male particularly defines himself as a worker, much more than as a family man or member of a religious community. . . . So when he strikes out, he strikes out at the most significant part of his world.' "

16. Kinney and Johnson, op. cit., 37.

17. Ibid., 72. See, generally, chapter 5, 69–73.

18. Ibid., 37.

19. O'Boyle, op. cit., B1. Most victims were in sales (1,529, or 22 percent) or service (1,268, or 18 percent). By geographic region, the incidence of workplace homicides was as follows: South, 49 percent; West, 24 percent; North Central, 19 percent; Northeast, 8 percent.

20. "Waging War in the Workplace," *Newsweek,* July 19, 1993, 30.

21. Summary of media coverage of shooting by Joseph Wesbecker at Standard Gravure Corporation, Louisville, Kentucky, in 1989, furnished by Institute for Crisis Management, Louisville, KY, 1991. See, for example, John Filiatreau, "A Life in Pieces," *Louisville Magazine* 41, no. 1 (January 1990): 26–41, which examines Wesbecker's life prior to the shooting.

22. See, generally, Baron, op. cit.

23. Telephone interview with S. Anthony Baron, Scripps Center for Quality Management, Inc., San Diego, California, April 1, 1994.

24. Baron, op. cit., 23–31.

25. Ibid., 50–52. Warning signs include attendance problems, extensive counseling of the employee required of the supervisor, decreased productivity, inconsistent work patterns, poor working relationships, concentration problems, safety problems, poor health and hygiene, unusual or changed behavior, fascination with guns or other weapons, evidence of possible drug or alcohol abuse, evidence of serious stress in the employee's personal life, continual excuses or blaming, and unshakable depression.

26. Ibid., 31.

27. Kinney and Johnson, op. cit., 40. See, generally, 39–67.

28. Idem., citing Karl A. Seger, "Violence in the Workplace: An Assessment of the Problem Based on Responses from 32 Large Corporations," *Security Journal* 4, no. 3 (1993): 139–49.

29. Ibid., 40–42. The data were insufficient to support conclusions regarding the presence of substance abuse or mental health issues.

30. Fox and Levin, op. cit., 10. The FBI data show that "when younger workers kill, they typically are perpetrating a robbery or some other felony, whereas older workers who kill do so as a result of an argument or dispute with the boss" (6). See, generally, 5–11.

31. Ibid., 7, 9. See also the discussion of "murder by proxy," in which victims are chosen because they are identified with a primary target against whom revenge is sought, such as the supervisor or employer (5).

32. Ibid., 11. Fox and Levin also cited gender differences with respect to violence, in that "men regard violence as a means for establishing or maintaining control, whereas women see it as a breakdown of control. Thus, men who suffer

psychologically because of the loss of a job are more likely to respond violently in order to 'show who's boss' " (7). See, generally, Anne Campbell, *Men, Women, and Aggression* (New York: Basic Books, 1993).

33. Ibid., 3.

34. Kinney and Johnson, op. cit., 30.

35. John Monahan, "Editorial: Violence in the Workplace," *Journal of Occupational Medicine* 32, no. 10 (October 1990): 1021.

36. See, generally, John Monahan, *Predicting Violent Behavior: An Assessment of Clinical Techniques*, Sage Library of Social Research 114 (Beverly Hills, CA: Sage Publications, Inc., 1981).

37. Frank E. Kuzmits, "When Employees Kill Other Employees: The Case of Joseph T. Wesbecker," *Journal of Occupation Medicine* 32, no. 10 (October 1990): 1014–20. See also Suplee, loc. cit. Perpetrators of workplace violence are said to fit the Monahan profile only in two respects: "They are almost invariably mean and they tend to have migratory job histories."

38. Fox and Levin, op. cit., 14.

39. See Bob Filipczak, op. cit., 40–41. For example, Thomas Harpley of National Trauma Services in San Diego distinguished lethal violence, an attempt to kill a co-worker, from non-lethal violence, such as threats or physical assaults not intended to kill. "Non-lethally violent employees tend to be under 30, have a history of violence, and may have trouble with drugs and alcohol. Lethally violent employees, on the other hand, are usually older, have no history of violence, and very often have no substance-abuse problem" (40).

40. "Postal Study Aims to Spot Violence-Prone Workers," *New York Times,* July 2, 1992, A7, which referred to 34 persons killed at post offices since 1983. The figure of 33 postal workers killed, which includes four suicides by the shooters, was furnished by Roy Betts, Corporate Relations, U.S. Postal Service, Washington, DC, telephone interview, April 6, 1994.

41. Martin J. Smith, "Postal Killing: Postwar Stress?" *Orange County Register,* May 19, 1993, 1. See 1–2.

42. Kinney and Johnson, op. cit., 44.

43. See, for example Arthur W. Sherman, Jr., and George W. Bohlander, *Managing Human Resources,* 9th ed. (Cincinnati, OH: South-Western Publishing Co., 1992), chapters 14, 15, and 16 on employee motivation, communications, and discipline; William P. Anthony, Pamela L. Perrewe, and K. Michele Kacmar, *Strategic Human Resources Management* (Fort Worth, TX: The Dryden Press, 1993), chapter 11 on total quality management, and chapter 16 on ethics, employee rights, and employer responsibilities; and Cynthia D. Fisher, Lyle F. Schoenfeldt, and James B. Shaw, *Human Resource Management,* 2nd ed. (Boston: Houghton Mifflin Company, 1993), chapter 16 on organizational exit.

44. David Moberg, "The Michigan Post Office Killings Were a Tragedy

Waiting to Happen," *In These Times*, November 27–December 10, 1991, 9. See also "Postal Study Aims to Spot Violence-Prone Workers," loc. cit.

45. Teri Randall, "Abuse at Work Drains People, Money, and Medical Workplace Not Immune," *JAMA, Journal of the American Medical Association* 267, no. 11 (March 18, 1992): 1439–40.

46. Violence and Stress: The Work/Family Connection, BNA Special Report Series on Work & Family, Special Report #32 (Washington, DC: The Bureau of National Affairs, Inc., August, 1990), 1, 2, 7. The 25 percent figure is based on estimates of the population that was abused while growing up. The problem is said to be declining among younger managers, who have different views than their elders of how to motivate employees, are aware of the effects of their actions, and are more willing to examine their behavior.

47. Ibid, 8.

48. Ibid, 9.

49. Kathleen D. Ryan and Daniel K. Oestreich, *Driving Fear out of the Workplace* (San Francisco: Jossey-Bass Publishers, 1991), 74, 133.

50. "Statement by Marvin Runyon, Chief Executive Officer and Postmaster General of the United States before the Joint Hearing of the Subcommittee on Census, Statistics, and Postal Personnel and the Subcommittee on Postal Operations and Services, Committee on Post Office and Civil Service, U.S. House of Representatives, Washington, DC," August 5, 1993, 6–7.

51. See, generally, James Ledvinka and Vida Gulbinas Scarpello, *Federal Regulation of Personnel and Human Resource Management*, 2nd ed. (Boston: PWS-Kent Publishing Company, 1991), which also covers regulation under state labor laws and judicial developments in the employment-at-will doctrine.

52. "Workplace Violence: Dear Outlines Strategy to Address Issue; Special Assistant Named to Spearhead Effort," *Occupational Safety & Health Reporter* (Washington, DC: The Bureau of National Affairs, Inc., January 19, 1994), 980–81. See also "Workplace Violence: Data Lacking on Non-Fatal Violent Injuries; Speakers Question Inclusion of Verbal Attacks," 981–82.

53. See, generally, Kinney and Johnson, op. cit., 103–13; Stephen P. Pepe, O'Melveny & Myers, "Violence in the Workplace," Legal Update '94, PIRA Association of Human Resource Management Professionals, Los Angeles, California, January 26, 1994; and William W. Floyd, Best, Best & Krieger, "A Seminar on Workplace Violence for the Inland Area Personnel Management Association," Riverside, California, November 4, 1993.

54. "Tip of the Month," *Tennessee Employment Law Update* 8, no. 12 (December 1993): 2–3. The "direct threat" must constitute a "high probability of substantial harm," and be established by objective evidence as opposed to "mere speculation." Such evidence may be obtained in a pre-employment physical examination, during which the physician may inquire into a history of mental

illness and violence-related problems. Regarding current employees, factual evidence of psychological behavior that suggests a threat to safety may constitute evidence of "direct threat," such as an employee's violent, aggressive, destructive, or threatening behavior (3).

55. Pepe, op. cit., 4–6. Other examples of special relationships are bank-depositor, carrier-passenger, and psychotherapist-patient. Regarding forseeability, factors may include whether the employer had notice of the potential risk of harm, and whether the perpetrator made any threats or had a criminal or violent background. An identifiable victim probably would include a victim who had complained to the employer regarding violent acts or harassment by the perpetrator.

56. *Violence and Stress: The Work/Family Connection,* op. cit., 6.

57. See, generally, Ryan and Oestreich, op. cit., 139–51.

58. Baron, op. cit., 82. See also Kinney and Johnson, op. cit., chapter 6, 75–85.

59. See, for example, Baron, op. cit., 93–124, Kinney and Johnson, op. cit., 87–94, and National Trauma Services, op. cit., 46–58, for plans for responding to workplace violence. See "Statement by Marvin Runyon, Chief Executive Officer and Postmaster General of the United States," op. cit., 3–6. Since the shooting at the Royal Oak, Michigan, post office in 1991, the U.S. Postal Service has doubled the amount of time devoted to threats and assaults. Its efforts include enhancement of management training; consultation with behavioral scientists; attendance at academies on workplace violence prevention; maintenance of a national hotline for reporting threats and employee concerns about safety; conduct of a study of threats and assaults to identify common factors; formation of a national task force on workplace violence, which includes union representatives; conduct of meetings with employee focus groups to discuss workplace violence concerns; provision of progress reports on the recent restructuring, which involved no layoffs; development of new pre-employment screening techniques; and expansion of the employee assistance program to include broader issues than substance abuse, provide more and better-qualified counselors, and improve the referral process.

60. Stuart Silverstein, "The War on Workplace Violence," *Los Angeles Times,* March 18, 1994, A1, A20, citing Omar Gonzales, American Postal Workers Union, Los Angeles area.

61. See, generally, James S. Cawood, "On the Edge: Assessing the Violent Employee," *Security Management,* September 1991, 131–36. See also Baron, op. cit., 127–38, and Kinney and Johnson, op. cit., 95–101.

62. Baron, op. cit., 114–15.

CHAPTER 3

Over His Dead Body

Female Murderers, Female Rage, and Western Culture

VANESSA FRIEDMAN

I stand now where I struck him down. The thing is done. Thus have I wrought and I will not deny it now. That he might not escape nor beat aside his death, as fishermen cast their huge circling nets, I spread deadly abundance of rich robes, and caught him fast. I struck him twice. In two great cries of agony he buckled at the knees and fell. When he was down I struck him the third blow, in thanks and reverence to Zeus the lord of dead men underneath the ground.   —*Aeschylus*, Agamemnon

Unspeakable female rage, when enacted, expresses the darkest, deepest secrets of Western patriarchal order. The first thought that probably comes to mind when people hear about a woman who has committed murder is that a crime against nature has occurred. That is, primarily a crime against *her* culturally prescribed nature. Somehow, almost nothing would seem as horrible or perverse as a woman who can kill. Women, after all, give life—they are not supposed to take it away. Men kill frequently in many deliberate ways (i.e. as soldiers in war) and our sensitivities do not seem nearly as offended when we encounter men who have murdered, unless they have done so in a particularly gruesome way. However, when confronted by a murder of the so-called fairer sex we somehow feel repelled at a much deeper level, as if what has occurred is not only a crime against society, but a perversion of nature, a perversion of her nature as woman.

Western culture fears the woman who kills and her rage in a way quite unlike the fear held towards the more common male murderer. A woman who murders, like any woman who steps outside her socially sanctioned role, tests society, pushes against not only its social and political boundaries, but its ideological underpinnings and substructure. An inquiry into *why* a woman would murder (and, indeed, why more do not), along with *whom* they murder (the vast majority murder mates, and occasionally, their own children), and *how* they commit their acts, offers at root an exploration into the political and philosophical relationship between the woman, her act, and the culture/society in which she lives. We can, of course, come up with a number of social theories concerning the nature of her oppression, abuse, economic status, etc. Often her murderous act can be seen as an understandable, although unacceptable, response to her situation, especially when confronted by an abusive partner. But these theories provide only the partial truth about her act, and one that I believe conceals a deeper meaning, the rage behind it.

The woman who murders the one she loves often expresses more than merely her acute distress with her particular personal situation. Although one should not generalize to all such cases, I do believe that frequently her crime is not only a self-preservative act, but also, in a political and philosophical way, the dramatic expression of her repulsion towards and violent rejection of the social order of patriarchal abuse, the phallocentric culture which has successfully muted her and made her an invisible human being. Her enactment of rage ruptures this success. Her act may be interpreted as a statement of deepest need, a declaration of Self ("I'm here—I matter!") in a social order where she perceives herself as unseen, or at most a reflection of her male partner. Her act expresses the otherwise inexpressible. Her crime provides an articulation in a social order where she perceives herself as misunderstood. She may feel unrepresented by a language in which she is not allowed her own voice or original words, except perhaps in certain forms of madness or as a somatic symptom such as hysteria.[1] This is not to say that men do not feel misunderstood or invisible at times. However, men are generally much better represented linguistically, with fewer narrowly defined categories and polarities than in language for women.

This silencing of women, according to Luce Irigaray, perpetuates the atrocious and primitive phantasies of woman as monster, demon, or lunatic, the "archaic projections" of the male imaginary—from which women as a group have suffered tremendously.[2] Irigaray presents us with a way to better understand these enduring and powerful images of enraged women as evil and terrifying. These phantasies are part of the dreadful images roused in us when confronted by a crime as hideous as a woman murdering within the family, and are so powerful in fact that whole mythologies have been created around them. In Western civilization, these images have their beginnings in ancient Greek mythology, in the stories, for example, of Clytemnestra and Medea, and the fearful tales of the Amazon women or the Furies, the avengers of (familial) injustice. These legends of mythical women who committed acts of such heinousness have persisted for over two thousand years. What could be the significance of such an enduring and intense preoccupation with "mad" women? Could it be that female rage, which most often goes unspoken and is, perhaps, "unspeakable," represents the darkest, deepest fears of the male order?

Myths, often interpreted as historical commentary on the social consciousness of their time, may also be viewed as windows into the unconscious. A re-examination of ancient Greek myth reveals the function of these phantasies, especially as, according to Irigaray, "our imaginary still functions in accordance with the schema established through Greek mythologies and tragedies."[3] Irigaray's reinterpretations of classical mythology stem from her belief that we can see a struggle taking place between the maternal and paternal genealogies in them, a struggle that eventually ends in the establishment of the patriarchy.[4] The phantasies may also be seen as the psychological defenses of the male social order, used to alleviate social anxieties and conceal the underlying nature of that order.[5] That which is concealed is, according to Irigaray, the original connection with Mother, and her consequent murder. The overwhelming anxiety brought on by the knowledge of this concealment would cause too much anxiety for the culture to cope with. Women who step outside the bounds of their socially sanctioned roles, as women who publicly express rage do, are represented in myth and symbolized in language as lunatics and monsters, all of which helps settle and manage these deep-seated anxieties. These women can be excused easily as "crazy" and therefore not threatening to the dominant order, but more than that, they help contain, physically and psychologically, the projected fears of that order. But at what cost, and whose cost, does this structure of anxiety containment operate?

My purpose is certainly not to excuse or make light of the actions of these women. (There can, it seems to me, ultimately be no justification for murdering your own children.) But beyond the obvious, the life stories of women's crimes have dramatic political and philosophical implications for the community around them. The internal life of an individual human being is not an insulated thing, but is deeply affected by and can have striking consequences for the public world, especially when that interior is fraught with fear, hate, and violence. Ordinarily, society and community offers a way for the individual to manage overpowering emotions and difficulties by providing appropriate psychological defenses, shared by the community, which bind the individual to social conventions. The structure of the patriarchy itself can be interpreted as a psychological defense which tries to contain anxieties about the underlying social order.[6] But what happens when these defenses, and targets of externalization, do not work or when they break down? What happens when the structure which serves to contain anxieties becomes the source of anxiety itself?

To be a member of any social structure creates special problems, both socially and politically, but also certain psychic difficulties which can manifest themselves in particular and peculiar ways.[7] In the masculine-based social order of Western civilization, women may not perceive their representation or symbolization adequately in language and may feel little recognition by the public space, where the predominant subject-position is the masculine one. Language contains within it the ability to affect identity by giving individuals within the community the necessary means by which to interact and to establish intersubjectivity, while at the same time also representing a particular symbolic system. Recognition by the community, as an empowered human being, as an individual capable of self-actualization, is necessary to attain a sense of identity. The community can not exist without language, as anything to do with "community" necessitates cooperation, and cooperation must include consensual use of language. The realm of community offers the individual the opportunity to see oneself as others do, with its shared symbolisms and structures of relations, recognition of reciprocal rights, acceptance of responsibility beyond the needs of the self, etc. The public space is where the individual discovers intersubjectivity. Yet this intersubjectivity is precisely what women lack in a male social order. In this community, the "individual" is generally taken to be masculine; the standard to which our social imaginary refers is generally a white male. The actual operation of this language can be observed, as summarized in Irigaray's 1990 *Sexes et genres à travers les langues: Éléments de communication sexuée* (Sex and genders across the languages: Elements of sexuate communication): (1) Men are more likely than women to take up the subject-position in language; (2) The use of "I" does not necessarily indicate a feminine identity even when used by a woman; (3) Woman's own self-representation is more or less absent in language; (4) Women privilege dialogue and interpersonal communication, while men privilege relations with the world and the object; (5) Woman's speech is likely to efface the expression of their subjectivity; and (6) Women are less abstract than men, more context oriented and collaborative.

Although several of these propositions may represent sexist stereotyping, the others I interpret as claiming that the feminine, for the most part, goes unrepresented in patriarchal language. What this means for women is that they do not have readily available to them a public language which may accurately and satisfactorily express their needs and desires, one that is accepted and understood by the masculine social order. In other words, the predominant mode of communication for woman, if she is to function understandably in patriarchal society, is only that available by bequeath from the patriarchy. In this "man"-made language, she may perceive herself as ignored. Her own voice may often go unspoken (except, perhaps, in her private conversations with her female friends), her own language unidentified or misunderstood, her desire unrepresented symbolically. Insofar as her desire exists at all in discourses, or the imaginary of Western culture, it has been as an "other," mirror, or "use value" for men, as with her orgasms which "are necessary as a demonstration of masculine power. . . . Women are there as witnesses."[8] Women have very few of their own symbolic forms represented in language or the public space, and those that do exist function to contain her in the categories most acceptable to the masculine order. That is, as mother, daughter, sister, wife, all of which are defined in relation to a male figure. Perhaps the only other public identity available to women in patriarchal culture, other than that which is in relation to the male and the maternal which itself is systematically constituted as a patriarchal institution, is as a defective or castrated male.

Implicit in the public discourse in general, including psychoanalytic theory and the biological sciences (of Aristotle), is woman defined as a disadvantaged man, an imperfect or flawed male with no inherent status of her own. As Adrienne Rich has said, "The power of the fathers has been difficult to grasp because it permeates everything, even the language in which we try to describe it."[9] Thus, with little or inadequate representation in language and in the shared symbolics of community, many women may feel a loss of recognition, misunderstood, or at worst, invisible, especially when confronted by a situation of abuse.

This invisibility may be what initiates and sustains her rage and what makes a woman destructive both to herself and to men. When a woman murders her mate, it may be the most extreme enactment of her rage, a rage felt by her to be the result of a community which ignores her, and a system which mutes her. Murder may be one of the only, albeit most extreme examples, of an abused woman's need to express her rage. Her act certainly articulates the rage she feels about her own situation, but can also be interpreted as an expression of her feelings about the patriarchy, as well as an effort at reconstituting her own identity and representation.

LANGUAGE AND DESIRE

This chapter is concerned, at its roots, with the identity, or lack thereof, of the woman-self in Western patriarchal society. Identity is enacted in large part through self-positioning in language, and as identity is formed in the unconscious, language helps to form the unconscious.[10] In a language system where the underlying structure is Oedipal, as Irigaray believes, the only possible subject-position is the masculine one. The only symbolization that occurs is masculine, and the only imaginary represented is male. Accordingly, women have no representation or possibility of self-positioning in language. Without that, the only available original identity for her, aside from her maternal one, is as an imperfect or castrated male. Without her own social symbolic forms or representation, with biased, phallocentric translation modes, she perceives herself as invisible, with no possibility of intersubjectivity which is needed to be a fully participating member of society and community. Even woman as "chaos," "disorder," or "nature," images which have predominated in Western myth, literature, and imagination, can be viewed as a projection by the male imaginary, fixed on her in order to disown his "bad" or irrational desires.[11] Her desires can not be fully expressed because she has no feminine symbology or language to express them with; her own death drives are deflected or mediated, as instead she is used by the male imaginary to mediate the masculine death drive by being immobile, the silent one (life = movement, death = stasis). Only her desires are interpreted as madness, whether she be in fact "mad" or not: "All desire is connected to madness. But apparently one desire [the masculine one] has chosen to see itself as wisdom, moderation, truth, and has left the other to bear the burden of the madness it did not want to attribute to itself, recognize in itself." [12]

Although I part here with Irigaray in reference to her belief in the total absence of representation, my fundamental position remains akin to hers. To desire, you must be able to take up the subject-position, but in a social order where you have little representation, this action proves difficult at best and at worst not possible. As Irigaray explains, "Food is a need. It can become desire, but it needs speech for that to happen. So long as women are imprisoned in the reality of need, where is desire?" [13] Where and how does women's desire become expressed? How does a woman who has deep rage at her perceived invisibility linguistically, politically, existentially, physically, express herself? How far will she go to express herself?

MYTHOLOGY AND THE PATRIARCHY

What could be as horrible as a woman who murders as Clytemnestra did? Or women like the Furies (Erinyes) who are the wild and animal-like punishers of injustice? Or the Bacchae and Amazons? These women and their acts provide immediate shocks but also serve as reminders of the supreme social order of the patriarchy. They must be loathed, feared, and demonized as opposing the natural order of things, or seen as forces to be overpowered and controlled for the patriarchy to continue unquestioned.

But these stories can be reinterpreted, as Irigaray has suggested. Clytemnestra's story can also be seen as an account of the founding of the patriarchy at the expense of the mother, where the husband-killer gets slain herself. Clytemnestra is, perhaps, the quintessential Furie or amazon warrior-woman, a woman, according to the patriarchy, to be hated and feared more than anything else. Therefore, she must be silenced. What is being concealed by the/her silence is a social order which has been established upon the murder of the mother/Clytemnestra. According to Irigaray, women as mothers provide the unacknowledged foundation of our social order. Western culture is founded *not* on patricide, as Freud says in *Totem and Taboo,* but on matricide. To interpret Aeschylus's *Oresteia* in this fashion, the phallic order was initiated not on the murder of the father, as Sophocles' Oedipus would have it, but on the murder of the mother (Clytemnestra) along with the sacrifice of the daughter (Iphegenia). Upon this the patriarchy, and Greek democracy, are erected by the matricidal son (Orestes).

In other words, the major taboo in Western culture is the acknowledgment of the original relationship with the mother, and the final severance of that relationship, symbolically through the murder of the mother (Clytemnestra). This murder embodies the effort by the masculine order to deny an "other" or different way of perceiving, or desiring in the world, a way that is now "submerged by the logic that has dominated the West since the time of the Greeks."[14] The phallic order conceals this original relationship through its fundamental emphasis on the Oedipus and castration complexes as the perceived foundations of Western civilization.[15] Accordingly, the sons must plot to commit the murder of the father in order to possess the mother, thereupon initiating the development of the superego, the conscience, a higher moral order, "civilization". The relationship with/between father, son, brother that remains seminal in the establishment of the social order of Western civilization, at the expense of women, who cannot participate in this conspiracy.[16]

Clytemnestra, the Furies, Amazon women, all women who murdered men, are demonized forever for it. The image that comes to mind when we hear about a woman who has murdered her mate is indelibly imprinted on our brains — she is the incarnation of enraged Clytemnestra — vengeful, venomous, and dreaded. But through a careful reinterpretation of these ancient Greek myths, where the roots of our own civilization began, we can perhaps come to understand these crimes in a different light. In many ways myths can be interpreted as both expressions of, and formative of, the social unconscious. They may not only express what organizes a society at any particular time, but also reinterpret the unresolved anxieties of a culture and its people. Interpreting ancient Greek myth in this light may bring us closer to understanding not only the social unconscious that has formed the moral, ethical, and intellectual bases of Western civilization, but additionally, the way the self envisions its own intersubjectivity and place in the community. By beginning with ancient Greek mythology, where the imaginary of the patriarchy first took hold, we can begin to understand some of our present-day Clytemnestras, our modern mad-women, their rage, and their sometimes seemingly incomprehensible acts. Their ancient dialogue, enacted publicly for all to see and participate in, operated as not only the ethical and moral training ground for the social public, but also as the container for social and individual psychic anxieties. Their discourses reveal more than just the common moral and social dilemmas of their time; they reveal deeply pervasive and disturbing anxiety about the place of women in an established patriarchy. Understanding these myths will help to uncover the foundation mythology of our own time, and to recognize the ways our mythology not only perpetuates the misunderstanding and underrepresentation of woman, but may, indeed, give her impetus to act in ways society considers abhorrent.

GETTING BACK TO THE BODY: THE BODY AS LIVING TEXT

The visceral body, with its *capacity* for language, is the foundation of all human institutions and culture. Speech is only a surplus of our existence over our material being; it is only one of the ways in which the human body achieves expression.[17] Language, discourse, can be interpreted, however, as an attempt to contain the body, to make its desire controllable, to dominate it, suppress it. But, as Jane Gallop wrote, "the body always exceeds the mind's order." The body is outside logic, outside language. It can not be rationalized and subordinated to discourse. The body can never be totally dominated by man-made meaning.[18] We are opened to the world through the body first, rather than the mind. As infants, our first contact with the world is through our physical senses, our skin. So, perhaps a return to the body, the most primal of all communicative spaces, would be appropriate when the ready-made, man-made institutions, especially that of language whose original expressivity is no longer available to women (except perhaps to artists and musicians, etc.) can not express their desire. Men too, of course, can return to the body, but because men gain in large part their masculine identity by being estranged from their bodies (the mind-body/public-private split) and dominating the bodies of others, a return to the body for a man may have a different meaning.

Although the abused woman may not have recourse to her own original words, although she may feel neglected, misunderstood, unrepresented, or invisible, she still has the desire to speak and to be acknowledged. So how does she do this, how does she express her rage about her perceived invisibility, in a culture which she experiences as abusive and devaluing?

She may speak her rage through her murderous act. She uses her body, and his body, as tools—his body, his blood fertilizes the (re)creation of her identity. The murder she commits is not only an act of rage in the face of an abusive situation, but a corporeal metaphor; the content of her act of murder is about using his body to speak, to make a final statement, to make herself understood and visible at last. She may even experience her rage as a transcendent thing, a sacred thing. Her rage, which is honest and genuine, as all rage is, purifies that which is ugly. Her act of murder releases blood which is sacred; his blood purifies that which is ugly.

Clytemnestra herself recognized this paradox when she uttered, after striking her fatal blows:

"as he died he spattered me with the dark red and violent driven rain of bitter savored blood to make me glad, as gardens stand among the showers of God in glory at the birth time of the buds." (Clytemnestra, standing over the dead body of her husband, Agamemnon, in Aeschylus's *Agamemnon*, lines 1389–91).

NOTES

1. Hysteria has traditionally been a women's disorder, and perhaps an attempt to communicate that which she is otherwise unable to articulate: "Yet there is a revolutionary potential in hysteria. Even in her paralysis, the hysteric exhibits a potential for gestures and desires." (*The Irigaray Reader*, "Women-Mothers, the Silent Substratum of the Social Order," 1991, 47.)

2. See Margaret Whitford's introduction to Irigaray's essay "The bodily encounter with the mother" in *The Irigaray Reader*. Also, "women as a group" is a flawed and inaccurate concept. Women of color have been silenced in ways that white women have not. There are different modes of invisibility attached to each "group" or class of women affected by differing structural positions in society. Yet, the patriarchy exists everywhere, albeit in different forms and strengths, and women "as a group" have suffered and been oppressed by it.

3. *Reader, 36.*

4. See *Philosophy in the Feminine* by Margaret Whitford, 102.

5. It seems probable to me that all complex cultures and societies conceal, at least to a certain extent, the real natures of their social orders by using foundation myths. Whether it is a culture based on gender hierarchy, race hierarchy, or class, the revealed true nature of a social order would be likely to cause too much social unrest and chaos, if it were ever to be revealed.

6. Any social structure could be interpreted this way, i.e. as a social device to contain and control anxieties that arise in individuals within groups.

7. See Sigmund Freud, *Civilization and Its Discontents.*

8. Irigiray, *This Sex Which is Not One,* 199.

9. See *Of Woman Born,* Adrienne Rich, 57–58. To imply that experience can be directly represented by language is false. I believe it probably has more to do with biased translation modes.

10. See Jacques Lacan, *Ecrits.*

11. See Melanie Klein, *Contributions to Psychoanalysis 1921–1945;* and M. Klein and D. Tribich, "Kerberg's Object Relations Theory."

12. Irigaray, *Reader,* 35.

13. *Reader,* 52.

14. *This Sex,* 25.

15. My point is not, of course, that Sigmund Freud and his psychoanalytic theories go unquestioned, or that we, as a culture, "believe" his theory of the Oedipus complex. Rather, my point is that the symbology, the collective imagination underlying Western culture, assumes this scenario to be correct, and organizes society accordingly.

16. Consequently, Freud, of course, believed that women were not capable of achieving as developed a superego as men, and in fact were inhibitors of the development of civilization.

17. John O'Neill, *The Communicative Body,* 3, 4, 9.

18. Jane Gallop, *Thinking about the Body,* 4, 1

Works Cited

Aeschylus. *Oresteia.* Eds. David Grene and Richard Lattimore. Trans. Richard Lattimore. Chicago: University of Chicago Press, 1953.

Freud, Sigmund. *Civilization and Its Discontents.* Trans. James Strachey. New York: W. W. Norton, 1961.

———. *The Standard Edition of the Complete Psychological Works of Sigmund Freud.* Ed. James Strachey. London: Hogarth Press, 1953–74.

Gallop, Jane. *Thinking Through the Body.* New York: Columbia University Press, 1988.

Irigaray, Luce. *Sexes et genres à travers les langues: Éléments de communication sexuée*. Paris: Grasset, 1990.

———. *This Sex Which Is Not One*. Trans. Catherine Porter. Ithaca, N.Y.: Cornell University Press, 1985. Originally published in French, 1977.

Klein, Melanie. *Contributions to Psychoanalysis 1921–1945*. New York: McGraw-Hill, 1964.

Klein, Melanie, and D. Tribich. "Kerberg's Object Relations Theory: A Critical Evaluation." *International Journal of Psychoanalysis* 62 (1981): 27–43.

Lacan, Jacques. *Ecrits*. Trans. Alan Sheridan. New York: Norton, 1977.

O'Neill, John. *The Communicative Body: Studies in Communicative Philosophy, Politics, and Sociology*. Evanston: Northwestern University Press, 1989.

Rich, Adrienne. *Of Woman Born: Motherhood As Experience and Institution*. London: Virago, 1977.

Whitford, Margaret, ed. *The Irigaray Reader*. Cambridge, London: Blackwell, 1991.

———. *Luce Irigaray: Philosophy in the Feminine*. New York: Routledge, 1991.

CHAPTER 4

Fuck Community, or Why I Support Gay-Bashing

IAN BARNARD

I am sick and tired of hearing these matter-of-fact references to "the gay community," as if everyone knows what this community is, as if everyone is included in it, as if everyone wants to be included—or should want to be. If I hear another reference to "the community" or "the gay community," I am going to scream. I direct my rage as much against racism as against the gay-bashers. I am sick and tired of guppies of all colors, self-centered white fags, and smug lifestyle lesbians telling me that I am divisive, too radical, too extreme. I am sick and tired of people rolling their eyes when I speak—here comes the party pooper again. I am sick and tired of being reprimanded for not "supporting my gay brothers"—I am sick and tired of people assuming that I have everything in common with someone else just because that person is gay. Am I supposed to "support" gay Nazis or gay KKK members or gay women-haters just because I, too, am gay?

> You are entering a gay and lesbian-free zone. . . . Effective immediately, [we are] at war against lesbians and gays. A way in which modern queer boys and queer girls are united against the prehistoric thinking and demented self-serving politics of the above-mentioned scum. . . . This is a civil war against the ultimate evil, and consequently we must identify us and them in no uncertain terms. . . . So, dear lesbian woman or gay man . . . prepare to pay dearly for the way you and your kind have fucked things up.[1]

Part of this chapter has appeared previously in *Harvard Gay & Lesbian Review* (Summer 1995). Reprinted by permission.

These words are not the scurrilous rantings of right-wing homophobes. On the contrary, they represent a reclamation of the radical roots of modern lesbian and gay activism in North America and elsewhere by guerrilla queer insurgents. Johnny Noxzema and Rex Boy's characterization of their queer fan magazine *BIMBOX*, enacts a renewed politicization and fragmentation of "sexual identity" in the nineties. Many queerzines articulate what is by now a familiar opposition in social and cultural realms between lesbian and gay activists and queer militants, and in academia, between lesbian and gay studies and queer theory.

The relationship of the 'zines towards the lesbian and gay establishment is oppositional—often enraged. A blurb for the 'zine *Scab* takes *BIMBOX*'s threat a step further: it describes the contents of *Scab* as "pro-gaybashing with map of gay areas" ("'Zine," n.p.). This violent stance towards the lesbian and gay establishment is a sign not of homophobia, but of disgust at this establishment's collusion with and reproduction of homophobic and other oppressive power relations. The 'zines reject a lesbian and gay politics of assimilation (we're just like everyone else, please give us our rights . . .), and instead construct a queer proliferation of difference. They despise the comfort of single issue identity politics, and instead multiply, connect, and undo their own identifications.

A striking characteristic of the 'zines is their difference from each other in their appeal to and identification with a specialized readership within "the lesbian and gay community"— indeed, their contestation of the idea itself that any unified unitary lesbian and gay community exists. Almost every 'zine has a very local constituency. The 'zine *Swish*, for instance, was primarily written by, for, and about white gay male skinheads, while *Thing* focused on aspects of black drag queen culture. There is no delusion that there is something for everyone here, no pretense at being for or about most people, claims made by mainstream publications despite the fact that they are just as exclusionary as the 'zines are. As each 'zine irreversibly invokes a queer specificity, so the 'zines' multiple voices illustrate that queer is not one thing. In their opposition to the lesbian and gay metropolis and their difference from each other, they smash the myth of the gay community.

This fantasized gay community is ritually invoked by the institutions of the state as they attempt to enforce the regimen of compulsory heterosexuality. And those assimilationist lesbians and gay men who seek access to these institutions invoke this fantasy gay community as insistently. I don't want to see any more wealthy queers on the cover of *Newsweek* or interviewed on TV and hear lesbians and gays celebrating this "positive" depiction of "our community"; I don't want to hear another lesbian or gay man who is criminally ignorant of homeless queers, poor queers, and jobless queers, telling me proudly about polls proving that queers are generally more prosperous than straight people. By exploding open the phantasmatic gay community, the 'zines undo comfortably but reductively binary models of identity, oppositionality, and political activism.

Those who think of their own identity as singular, those who remain unable to imagine multiple subjectivities in others, and those who experience only one site of oppression against themselves tend to universalize their limited understanding, colonizing other subjects. Since middle-class gay white men control and dominate most institutionalized lesbian and gay organizations in this country, these organizations inevitably have infused the category gay with a middle-class white male content. This isn't news. However, I want to insist that even non-assimilationist groups that organize around singular categories reproduce dominant structures. For instance, in the late eighties and early nineties conflicts within ACT UP and Queer Nation regularly centered around the opposing interests of white men, on the one hand, and people of color and white women, on the other. It's a struggle over whose experiences and agendas will define the group's identity and politics. Most of the white men usually wanted the group to devote itself exclusively to contesting homophobia and/or to AIDS activism, while many of the white women and people of color often felt that racism and sexism demand as urgent attention. The white men replied that these issues were irrelevant and divisive. The white women and people of color were unwilling to condone sexism and racism for the sake of so-called queer unity, and unable to divide up their identities in order to decide whether a particular act of discrimination was being committed against them because of their race, gender, HIV status, or sexual orientation. Identity was thus constructed so that one's concerns were only pertinent to the group if they resulted from one's gayness: if you were being attacked on the street because your sexual orientation, your outrage and pain were "relevant." However, if you had been attacked because of your gender or color rather than your gayness your concern belonged elsewhere. Woe betide those who had been assaulted for all three reasons or who didn't know exactly why they had been assaulted!

The conflicts in these queer groups stem from the way we constitute and designate our coming together. Any U.S. politics, no matter how coalitional its compass, that identifies itself in terms of gender and/or sexual orientation only ("lesbian separatism," "Queer Nation," "Lesbian and Gay Studies") will be a white-centered and dominated politics, since only white people in this society can afford to see their race as unmarked, as an irrelevant or subordinate category of analysis. "Women" means white women; "lesbian and gay" means white lesbians and gay men. When any marginalized subjectivity (i.e., gayness) becomes the basis for community, it will, in turn, create and enforce marginalizing prioritizations and exclusions. The notion of the gay community is conjured up to celebrate deviance in the face of a massive structure of compulsory heterosexuality, but also in order to reinscribe other relations of domination and to silence diverse queer voices.

This policing of identity was vividly illustrated to me in a 1993 issue of the San Diego "gay" newspaper *Update*,[2] in "Tribal Writes,"[3] the regular column written by Connie Norman, a white male-to-female transsexual HIV + queer AIDS activist.[4] I want to emphasize that I am discussing Norman's article because I think it represents prevailing attitudes not only among the lesbian and gay establishment, but also among many participants in more militant, non-assimilationist groups such as Queer Nation and ACT UP. In this particular article, Norman, quite appropriately in my opinion, rages against homophobic violence. But she begins her column as follows:

> All right folks, don't you think it is just about time that we started circling the wagons? And I don't really give a shit if "indigenous peoples" object to my use of the phrase "circle the wagons" or not. I don't give one whit if that phrase comes from the dominating white imperialist culture and therefore is racist in connotation and is the tool of language that western culture has used to dominate and oppress people of color and on and on and politically correct this and multiculturalism that, I'm just sick of it!
>
> When in the hell are we going to come together as a community and start fighting our real enemy, *homohatred!*

The community Norman invokes is a racist one; only queers who do not think that racism is as pernicious as homophobia are welcome in it. Her "we" assumes that all queers are white, since it is primarily white queers who can enjoy the luxury of constituting "homohatred" as the only "real" enemy; her "we" also erases the alignments and experiences of those white queers irrevocably committed to anti-racist work. Let me make this quite clear: I do not want to be a part of Norman's community, and I resent her and others' imputation that I am or should be a part of this community.

The problem with our identity-politics tradition and its current dissemination in political appointments, grassroots organizing, and trendy courses in academic institutions is its absolute inability to think beyond the either or's of the rigid categories that enable and define it. Angela Davis has described her schizophrenia in the sixties: in white-dominated feminist groups she was expected to be a colorless woman, while at male-dominated Civil Rights movement meetings she had to be an ungendered black person. Today, how often don't we hear the fashionable litany, "women, gays, and people of color," in discussions of discrimination and civil rights. In this formulation once again one can only be female, *or* gay, *or* a person of color. Multiple subjectivities don't fit the formula; neither do those subjectivities whose "combination" of femaleness, gayness, and/or coloredness constitutes a subjectivity that is something different in itself rather than an accretion of the elements of gender, race, and sexuality. Asian-American lesbians, for instance, don't exist.

I refuse to divide up and separate my political commitments, experiences, and identities. If being a party pooper means spoiling the kind of party that people like Connie Norman want to get going—keep going—then I say we should do everything in our power to ruin it. There is no time now to hierarchize oppressions, there is no time now to worry about airing dirty laundry in public, about protecting a false unity forged on the backs of others.

Such homogenizations as "the gay community" attempt to co-opt queer sexualities into a liberal pluralist paradigm by silencing the diversity of queer voices. For instance: I am repulsed by lesbian and gay efforts to become legally married; I am less than euphoric about the wave of domestic partnership policies currently being adopted by some business enterprises and academic institutions in this country; and I am enraged that many lesbian and gay activists are begging for admission into a U.S. military apparatus that executes genocidal cultural, economic, and political imperialisms all over the world. Should we celebrate the day it becomes legal for queers to kill? The placards I like read "cruise queers, not missiles," "extend the ban to heterosexuals," "demilitarize masculinity," and "ban the military." But public debate over queers in the military, queer marriage, and the recognition of domestic partnerships is framed in such a way as to allow for only two positions: either one is progressive and supports these supposed advances, or one is conservative and homophobic and opposes them. The terms of this binary logic erase undisciplined queer voices who do not fit into any of these two cozy positions, and, who, in fact, reject with contempt the binary frame itself.

The official framing of these debates is indicative of the ways in which the identity-politics tradition in this country can be used to construct single-issue political movements that will not account for multiple identifications and that refuse to recognize the interdependency of different regimes of domination. The recognition of this interdependency poses a deadly threat to liberal pluralism, which legitimizes its rule precisely by insisting that it permits oppositional voices and identities to exist (the myths of free speech, free enterprise, the melting pot, the American dream, and so on). Liberalism needs to produce and display these "oppositional" identities in order to rationalize its claim to dominance. What it has to mask is the fact that it only provides space for those voices that do not challenge the hegemony of liberal pluralism itself.[5]

Queers will be tolerated, but only on their terms, only if we insist that we are just like everyone else. The consequence of this kind of humanism is a society that is as relentlessly heterosexist as ever: if only straight queers are acceptable then nothing has changed—it's still only straight people who are acceptable, and queers are just the latest version of straights, just further evidence of how all-embracing straightness really is.

This new heterocentrism has been tellingly enacted in the recent spate of domestic-partnership policies adopted at college campuses around the nation, and the uncritical ecstasy with which most lesbian and gay academics have greeted them. These policies prove emblematic of a variety of processes of containment now being deployed against queer identities in the wake of the increased visibility of anti-homophobic activism. Most college campuses explicitly discriminate against queer students and employees in many ways; one component of this discrimination is the benefit packages that provide, for example, health coverage to the spouses of heterosexual employees but not to the partners of lesbian and gay employees. The domestic-partnership policies that recently have been adopted by some cities, corporations, and academic institutions allow lesbian and gay employees to enjoy some of the benefits that had previously been the exclusive province of their heterosexual colleagues—I use the words "lesbian and gay" very deliberately here because I maintain that these new benefits most definitely do not extend to queer employees; in fact, they are designed to domesticate and co-opt lesbian and gay employees as allies of the straight employees against their common enemy: the queer.

I now want to discuss in some detail the domestic-partnership affidavit that applicants are required to sign at the University of Iowa, which, amidst much fanfare in the gay press, was one of the first colleges to implement a domestic-partnership policy in 1992.[6] The Iowa policy is fairly representative, not only of domestic-partnership policies in general, but also of other conservative efforts to constitute, police, and delimit queer subjectivities.

A quick glance at this affidavit reveals that it does not appear to recognize the specificity and diversity of lesbian and gay relationships. On the contrary, it seems to attempt to force queers to conform to dominant heterosexual relationship models (and as we all know, those model heterosexual relationships have hardly been healthy or inclusive). For example, item 4 of the affidavit requires signatories to certify, "We are not related by blood closer than would bar marriage in the state of Iowa and are mentally competent to consent to contract" (University of Iowa). By enforcing the same restrictions against lesbian and gay couples that obtain for heterosexual marriages, the affidavit not only attempts to create domestic partnership in the image of heterosexual marriage but also, illogically, preserves the incest taboo designed primarily to safeguard the health of potential offspring for a couple who will not jointly produce biological offspring.[7]

However, this document actually goes further than merely attempting to create an equivalence between heterosexual marriage and domestic partnership: domestic partners are, in fact, deployed to embody the *fantasized* imperative of heterosexual marriage. To receive domestic partnership benefits, queers must live together, share expenses, have been together for twelve months, and commit themselves to monogamy and life together until death us do part: item 5 states, "We are each other's sole domestic partner and intend to remain so indefinitely and are responsible for our common welfare." Heterosexual couples, on the other hand, receive these benefits merely by marrying. They don't have to wait twelve months, they can be as adulterous as ever, they can maintain the divorce rate as is, they don't need to share expenses, they don't need to live together. Lesbians and gay men will be forced to fulfill the fantasy ideal of heterosexual marriage because heterosexuals won't or can't. How convenient that with the right-wing in this country be-moaning the loss of family values, lesbians and gay men can be used to appease the right by being forced to take on these destructive family values, while heterosexuals pay lip service to them but continue to violate them! Lesbian and gay couples become the stand-ins for the blissful delusion of heterosexuality that straight people never could ful-fill!

The final insult: queer domestic partners must certify that "we are not married to anyone" (item 2). Domestic partners may not participate in heterosexual marriage, but, not surprisingly, there is nothing to stop married heterosexuals from forming domestic partnerships (we all know about the married "straight" men who have sex with other men). Het-erosexuals may continue to enjoy the benefits of homosexuality (exotic illegitimate sex) while queers may not enjoy any of the benefits of heterosexuality (the privileges that accompany the institution of mar-riage). Item 2, in effect, prohibits queers from having queer sex. If, in this document, domestic partnership has come to signify heterosexual marriage, then it's heterosexual marriage that is the site of queerness.

By forbidding queers to be married, the affidavit makes its clearest distinction between queer, on the one hand, and lesbian and gay, on the other. Lesbian and gay equals fixed/stable/singular sexual orientation, whether homo or hetero. Queer equals shifting, multiple, slutty, con-structed, elusive. Guess which one gets the domestic partner benefits? Lesbians and gay men, of course, also participate in this shoring up of heterosexuality and its assimilationist lesbian and gay mirror image, and the concomitant scapegoating of queers. A recent issue of the "gay" newspaper *Bravo! Newsmagazine* synecdochally illustrates both pro-cesses interactively at work. A story on a picnic for "lesbian and gay families" ("Lesbian") is matter of factly uncritical of the ways in which familial discourses have produced homophobia and excluded a panoply of marginalized sexualities from their purview (see Warner). In the same issues of the newspaper, a story on a "commitment ceremony" for lesbian and gay couples notes, "The ceremony starkly disproved the common stereotype of the male and female homosexual as fiercely promiscuous. Instead onlookers saw same-sex couples enjoying their love for each other, often with their children" ("Out"). Here other lesbians and gay men disavow "promiscuous" queers as fervently as does the homophobic heterosexual religious right.

It is important to recognize that the Iowa policy excludes queers of all sexual orientations. Item 7 of the Iowa affidavit requires the signatories to certify, "We are of the same sex," thus explicitly excluding unmarried heterosexual couples from coverage. This is a common provision in these kinds of domestic partnership policies.[8] Now I would be the last to champion heterosexual rights, but I am greatly disturbed by these provisions: they illustrate that the debate over domestic partnership policies is not so much about lesbian and gay rights as it is about policing certain kinds of relationships, whether they be lesbian, gay, heterosexual, or anything else. Again the message is be married or act married. No queers allowed.[9]

What makes queers so threatening? Queer relationships are hard to pin down, hard to police. It's hard to tell their sex, and harder still to tell if and when they're having sex. Something that seems to be taken for granted in these domestic-partnership policies is the privileging of sex, what Michel Foucault referred to as the "monarchy of sex" ("End"). It is ironic that in a society whose dominant institutions pay lip service to a puritanical and moralistic sexual ethos, fucking relationships would enjoy the greatest privilege. This is implied but not explicit in the Iowa affidavit. MIT's policy is franker in stating in so many words that "roommates, parents and siblings will not be considered eligible" for domestic partnership benefits (Fairfield). Why should people qualify as domestic partners merely because they are fucking each other? (And who decides what constitutes fucking?) Why are fucking relationships considered better or more important than non-fucking relationships? We all know that this sex is a social fiction, anyway, and that there is no more guarantee of sexual activity in domestic-partner relationships than in many other types of relationships. It's a vicious circle: there is no way of differentiating between spouses, domestic partners, and other relationships, other than by the categories that supposedly identify the relationships, but that, in fact, construct them and misrepresent them. Many married couples and domestic partners do not have "sex" with each other, while many friends, roommates, and siblings do have "sex" with each other. Many married couples and domestic partners do not "love" each other and do not stay together very long, while love and longevity do exist in many relationships between, for instance, siblings, between roommates, between friends, and between parents and children. Foucault often pleaded for homosexuality to be seen and lived as an epistemology that invented, worked through, and affirmed a multiplicity of relationships and attachments, rather than delimited a reproduction of heterosexual sexual coupling ("Friendship"). More recently, Eve Sedgwick has invoked queer theory against a rigid and singular lesbian and gay politics in order to distinguish "those of us whose 'primary attachments' may be plural in number, experimental in form, or highly permeable" (294). This promise is betrayed by the heterosexualization of queernesses.

A recognition of the plurality of significant relationships in all people's lives would be a truly productive reassessment of family values. But this radical recognition is of course one that political and educational institutions in this country are not willing to make, given their commitment to a classist, racist, sexist, and heterocentric status quo—despite the rhetoric of change, inclusivity, multiculturalism, and so on. Even inclusive domestic-partnership policies would be discriminatory to the extent that they shore up the injustices of corporate capitalism. After all, they would only benefit privileged queers—homeless, unemployed, and poor queers who don't have connections with their upscale lesbian and gay "brothers" and "sisters" mostly will continue to be denied these benefits.

I am advocating, then, a double and contradictory understanding and embodiment of identity and activism, as conjured up by the queerzines that I invoked at the beginning of this essay. Firstly, we must insist on a scrupulously politicized delineation of queerness rather than its location as an indication merely of the materialities of a particular lifestyle or the identification of a simple sexual orientation. We must return to the radical roots of twentieth-century queer activism and its later political positionality in the 'zines, and the work of such people as Foucault and

Gloria Anzaldúa. Anzaldúa writes of the borderlands between the U.S. and Mexico, between and within cultures, between genders, genres, and languages, and within the self:

> The prohibited and forbidden are its inhabitants. Los astravesados live here: the squint-eyed, the perverse, the queer, the troublesome, the mongrel, the mulatto, the half-breed, the half dead; in short, those who cross over, pass over, or go through the confines of the "normal." (3)

As we insist on these transgressions, affiliations, and politicizations, we must refuse to allow for the queer to be appropriated by liberal pluralism. It is not OK that Queer Nation San Diego in 1991 refused to oppose Operation Desert Storm; it is not OK now for queers to march for marriage, domestic partnership benefits, or admission into the military.

The other element in my contradiction is the discomforting multiplicity in queer, the difference within itself. My title "Fuck Community" denotes, of course, the community whom I fuck as well as the "community" and the idea of community that I say fuck you to. It is the recognition of this division that impels me to confess the multidirectionalities of my rage. Judith Butler has written,

> The insistence in advance on coalitional "unity" as a goal assumes that solidarity, whatever its price, is a prerequisite for political action. But what sort of politics demands that kind of advance purchase on unity? Perhaps a coalition needs to acknowledge its contradictions and take action with those contradictions intact. (14)

Rather then the debilitating facade of unity, Butler calls for an articulation of difference. She emphasizes that this kind of action-in-contradiction is neither disabling nor apolitical—instead it calls for a rethinking of the political.

Furthermore, by saying that I support gay-bashing I decenter heterosexuality, taking for granted my rage at explicit homophobes and institutionalized heterosexuality. By attending to debates *among* queers I ignore heterosexuals and thus marginalize homophobic rhetoric. These internecine debates fragment and multiply queer identity. Not only do I want to make it impossible for homophobic rhetoric to construct a singular gay stereotype, but I also want to destroy destructive conceptualizations of unity and community. I reject the notion that this type of infighting would be kept from public view—that I should not be airing dirty laundry in front of breeders. I insist on refusing identity politics and its coercive imperative of political unity. We must reconceptualize our notions of politics and political action. We must recognize and say that we don't get on. I refuse to construct any one organic subject as the repository for my rage. Don't try to pin down my rage.[10]

NOTES

1. Johnny Noxzema and Rex Boy, quoted by Cooper, 31.

2. As I wrote this article I contemplated characterizing *Update* for readers who might not be familiar with this publication. Given my agenda of exposing the exclusions that undergird most political and cultural work that presents itself as "lesbian and gay," I could not honestly describe *Update* as "a San Diego lesbian and gay newspaper." It was tempting then to try to identify and articulate its focus and exclusions: I could have attempted to name the narrowness of its scope by referring to *Update* as "a middle-class white gay male newspaper," but even this is an imprecise generalization, given the important differences in political and religious affiliation, age, citizenship status, physical and mental ability, and so on, between middle-class white gay men. In fact, I realized that there is no finitely delimiting list of defining differences, and that my attempts to pin them down were symptomatic of the power of the politics of categorical unity that I am critiquing. I am no less drawn to the seductive promise of empowerment through communal identity than anyone else. So I have resisted the temptation to attempt to delineate *Update*'s constituency, instead leaving it with just that "gay" marker, with all the possibilities that gay and those quotation marks invoke and exclude.

3. The title of the column itself points to the problematic I am identifying. Both the words "tribal" and "rites" (which the "writes" alludes to) conjure up a fixed and self-contained community of identicality in the tradition of "Western" ethnographers and anthropologists who similarly reify and reduce "Third World" peoples and cultures. The title "Tribal Writes" in Norman's column constructs "the gay community's" uniqueness by erasing the identifications and traditions from, for instance, communities of color, and lesbian feminism that subjects might bring to queerness. This is a common conceit for many white lesbians and gay men, as the latest spate of books on "worldwide" lesbian and gay "cultures" and lesbian and gay "communities" in the United States attest. Frank Browning's recent book, *The Culture of Desire: Paradox and Perversity*

in Gay Lives Today, immediately comes to mind: even to ask the question, "Do the subculture and life-style of urban gay life in America . . . constitute an actual culture comparable to other ethnic and racial cultures . . . that make up the heterogeneity of modern American life?" (1), as Browning does to set out the agenda of his book, is to normalize middle-class white gay maleness and obliterate, inter alia, queers of color.

4. In describing Norman, I faced difficulties similar to those described in note two above in the context of characterizing *Update*. I have chosen to highlight those components of her identity that I feel are most pertinent to the present discussion.

5. See Rooney.

6. Iowa was also one of the first colleges in the United States to hire an openly queer academic couple as a couple.

7. There are also some revealing inconsistencies between the affidavit and Iowa's more detailed explanation of domestic partner eligibility (I don't know if these inconsistencies have been removed in later versions of the documents). For instance, the more detailed document requires that the "partners have been residing together for at least twelve (12) months," while provision 8A on the affidavit demands only that the relationship be in existence for at least twelve months. What if the "relationship" has been in existence for a year but the "partners" have only been living together for one week? What if the partners do not live together and have no intention of doing so? Or is the phrase "domestic partnership" to be taken to assume co-habitation?—a strange assumption, particularly in academia, where so many heterosexual academic couples do not live together because they work in different parts of the country. But this contradiction that requires that the partners live together while implicitly recognizing that they might not merely sets the pattern for the remainder of the document's trajectory of coercions and denials.

8. For instance, when MIT implemented a domestic-partnership policy, Vice President Simonides announced that health benefits eligibility would not be extended to unmarried opposite-sex couples, arguing that because "opposite-sex couples have the option to marry, the issue of access is less compelling" (Fairfield).

9. In her article "Thinking Sex: Notes for a Radical Theory of the Politics of Sexuality," Gayle Rubin delineated the hierarchy of socially legitimated sexualities and relationships to show that divisions are not always congruent with the opposition homosexuality/heterosexuality. For instance, married monogamous heterosexual couples, unmarried heterosexual couples, promiscuous heterosexuals, and long-term stable lesbian and gay monogamous couples all receive greater social sanction than bar lesbians, promiscuous gay men in the park, and transvestites, transsexuals, sadomasochists, pedophiles, and prostitutes of all sexual

orientations (282). It is the types of relationships and identities on the bottom of Rubin's hierarchy that I designate as queer, and it is these ones that today are the focus of the state's censure, and that are thus excluded from domestic partnership benefits. By this definition, then, some heterosexual relations would be queer, whereas some lesbian and gay relations would not be queer.

10. My thanks to the following for assisting me with this article: Donna White, Keven Kopelson, Javier Morillo-Alicea, S. J. Mitchell, Terry Allison, Renée Curry, Anne Shea, and Mónica Szurmuk. I am also grateful to OUT, the queer student group at Indiana University, Bloomington, for inviting me to present an earlier version of this paper at IU's 1993 Lesbian, Gay, and Bisexual Pride Week.

Works Cited

Anzaldúa, Gloria. *Borderlands/La Frontera: The New Mestiza*. San Francisco: Aunt Lute, 1987.

Browning, Frank. *The Culture of Desire: Paradox and Perversity in Gay Lives Today*. New York: Crown, 1993.

Butler, Judith. *Gender Trouble: Feminism and the Subversion of Identity*. New York: Routledge, 1990.

Cooper, Dennis. "Queercore." *Village Voice*, 30 June 1992, 31–33.

Davis, Angela Y. "The Personal and the Political: Reproductive Rights in the 1980's." Address sponsored by Women's Resource Center at University of California, San Diego, 9 May 1987.

Fairfield, Stephen. "Details on MIT Domestic Partners." E-mail message from E-directory of Lesbian, Bisexual, and Gay Scholars, 2 May 1993.

Foucault, Michel. "The End of the Monarchy of Sex." Interviewed by Bernard-Henry Levy. 1977. In *Foucault Live: Interviews, 1966–84*. Ed. Sylvere Lotringer. Trans. John Johnston. New York: Semiotext(e), 1989.

"Friendship as a Way of Life." Interview. 1981. In *Foucault Live: Interviews, 1966–84*. Ed. Sylvere Lotringer. Trans. John Johnston. New York: Semio-text(e), 1989.

"Lesbian and Gay Families to Picnic in Balboa Park." *Bravo! Newsmagazine*, 14 October 1993, 9.

Norman, Connie. "Tribal Rites." *Update*, 10 February 1992, A-16. "Out of the Closets into the Aisle." *Bravo! Newsmagazine*, 14 October 1993, 5.

Rooney, Ellen. *Seductive Reasoning: Pluralism As the Problematic of Contemporary Literary Theory*. Ithaca: Cornell University Press, 1989.

Rubin, Gayle. "Thinking Sex: Notes for a Radical Theory of the Politics of Sexuality." *In Pleasure and Danger: Exploring Female Sexuality*. Ed. Carole S. Vance. Boston: Routledge, 1984.

Sedgwick, Eve Kosofsky. "Gender Criticism." In *Redrawing the Boundaries: The Transformation of English and American Literary Studies.* Ed. Stephen Greenblatt and Giles Gunn. New York: MLA, 1991.

University of Iowa. "Affidavit of Domestic Partnership," "Domestic Partnership," and "Domestic Partner Eligibility." November 1992.

Warner, Michael. Introduction. In *Fear of a Queer Planet: Queer Politics and Social Theory.* Ed. Warner. Minneapolis: University of Minnesota Press, 1993.

"'Zine Round-Up." *Holy Titclamps* 9 (Winter 1991/92): n.p.

Artistic and Cultural Representations of Rage

CHAPTER 5

Whatup in the 'Hood?

The Rage of African-American Filmmakers

WILLIAM BRIGHAM

In his 1989 film, *Do the Right Thing,* Spike Lee imitated life by borrowing from the infamous Howard Beach incident where whites beat African-Americans for being in the wrong place at the wrong time. In the film, the protagonist Mookie (played by Lee) sets off the climactic burning and looting of Sal's Pizzeria by shouting "Hate!" and throwing a trash can through the window of Sal's store. Three years later, at the flashpoint of the Los Angeles riots, in a case of life imitating art imitating life, a home video camera captured a young black man tossing a metal sign through the window of a passing car at the now well-known intersection of Florence and Normandie. The rage depicted in each of these images speaks of ire directed toward the dominant white culture and to intense desire for self-preservation.

Between these two incidents, these two filmic images, little if anything changed for the better in relations between African-Americans and whites. Although over 40 percent of the looters were Latinos, and whites and Asians were involved as well, 50 percent of those arrested for riot-related offenses were African-Americans (Lieberman and O'Reilly A34) who were certainly reacting—on one level—to yet another set of images, arguably the most widely viewed and notorious of videotapes, that of the beating by Los Angeles police officers of Rodney King.

Finally, in an almost surrealistic closing of the circle, in his film *Malcolm X,* Spike Lee incorporated the Rodney King beating tape in one of the most inflammatory and condemning montages in American film, segueing to an American flag burning down to an emblematic X.

The rage which this montage bespoke might be seen as the zenith of the collective voice of African-American filmmakers raging at the American social structure, or conversely as the nadir in contemporary relations between the dominant white culture and that of people of color. In any event, in the past three to four years African-American film directors have gained some franchise in that most glamorous example of American monopoly capitalism, Hollywood. The level and breadth of rage at American society which characterizes the four films I will discuss here is striking in its forcefulness. How are we to understand why Hollywood (and New York, and Tokyo, and wherever else the money flows from) is willing to invest millions of dollars in motion pictures which rail against—or at least imply the evils of—racism, the American class system, and American social institutions? Let me dispense with this question at the outset. These films are distributed solely because they will return to their investors a profit. For example, *Do the Right Thing* and *Boyz N the Hood* each cost about $6 million to produce. Moviegoers bought $28 million worth of tickets for *Do the Right Thing* (Easton, "Good News," 6), and almost $60 million worth for *Boyz N the Hood* (Pacheco, 25). Videotape rentals and sales, as well as merchandising tie-ins, will generate even more revenue. In short, art, social criticism and justice do not enter into the capitalist equation which determines whether films made by African-Americans are ever released.

BLACK FILMMAKERS

In 1926, poet Langston Hughes called upon black artists to speak forcefully about their lives, culture, and state of oppression. "We younger Negro artists who create," Hughes said, "now intend to express our individual dark-skinned selves without fear or shame. If white people are pleased we are glad. If they are not, it doesn't matter" (694). Over forty years transpired from the time Hughes put out his call for black artistic honesty before Gordon Parks directed the first major American film by a black man, the 1969 autobiographical movie, *The Learning Tree,* and almost another twenty years before Spike Lee's independent production of *She's Gotta Have It* (1986).

Parks's studio-produced film—and the contemporary studio and independent productions under examination here—were preceded by the first wave of independent black filmmakers. Beginning in the late 1920s and continuing into the early 1940s, more than one hundred companies produced what were called "race movies," providing both employment for black directors, writers, technicians, and actors, and entertainment for the audiences of over seven hundred ghetto theaters around the country. The prolific Oscar Micheaux epitomized this group of film-makers, whose career spanned three decades from 1918–1948. How-ever, a confluence of events, including the influenza epidemic of 1923, the advent of sound in film and, most telling, the Great Depression, conspired to eliminate virtually all of the independent black production companies and many of the ghetto theaters. From the late 1930s—until the films of the late 1980s—white filmmakers and white-controlled production companies made films specifically for black audiences (Bogle, 101–16).

Post-World War II Hollywood social problem films began to address such issues as anti-Semitism (*Crossfire* 1947; *Gentlemen's Agreement* 1947) and, a few years later, racism. *Pinky* (1949) and *No Way Out* (1950), under the creative control of white writers, directors, and—in the case of *Pinky*—a white actress portraying a black woman, provided no substitute for the race movies which, in some cases, dealt quite bluntly with the lives of black Americans. Sidney Poitier's film debut in *No Way Out* was as a doctor who urged his more militant friends to turn the other cheek to racism and hate, a stance his filmic characters—created by whites, of course—would take for many more years.

A qualitative change occurred in 1960s films which featured black characters and/or themes relating to race relations, a change in concert with the sociocultural events unfolding and necessarily impacting popu-lar culture. Early in the 1960s, Poitier was *the* African-American male of Hollywood films, and he reigned at the beginning of the decade in roles and films which rather abruptly went out of vogue. Poitier's characters often represented an integrationist or assimiliationist sensibility; his con-trolled, measured style was non-threatening, and the characters he por-trayed were rather widely accepted by white audiences. Toward the end of the decade, in 1967, he portrayed a successful doctor engaged to the daughter of a white liberal in *Guess Who's Coming to Dinner?*, a film which grossly distorted the state of contemporary race relations. The interracial attraction, romance, or marriage of early 1960s films (*Shad-ows* 1961, *One Potato, Two Potato* 1964, *A Patch of Blue* 1965) became an insult to blacks by the end of the decade, and films like *Guess*

Who's Coming to Dinner? and *The Lost Man* (1969) enraged rather than entertained African-Americans. The twin forces of 1960s racial violence and black cultural nationalism (Reid) had brought about a self-awareness and sensibility among many blacks who eschewed the peaceful, integrationist notions of the early civil rights movement and its leader, Martin Luther King. When interracial "romance" returned in the black action films of the 1970s, it returned in the form of sexual conquest by the black man, not assimilation or integration.

Black writers and directors in the 1970s added an important facet to African-American filmmaking. During the 1970s black filmmakers enjoyed their widest exposure to date with films distributed by major studios. Melvin Van Peebles's *Sweet Sweetback's Baadasssss Song* in 1970 stands as the most strident film of that generation. Its focus on police brutality and black rage is, unfortunately, a timeless theme in America. *Sweetback* rejected both the dominant white culture and the black bourgeoisie. It celebrated black urban life, its rhythms, language, and dress. Both the black man's rage and his sexuality—the latter too long repressed in the many characters portrayed by leading black actor Sidney Poitier—emerged forcefully in Sweetback.[1]

For the entirety of the film, the protagonist Sweetback—so named for his sexual prowess, an unfortunate perpetuation of stereotype and/or braggadocio—runs throughout the Los Angeles ghetto trying to stay out of the grasp of whites whose only interest is in harming him. This microcosm of the relations between whites and blacks in America is reinforced by the actions of corrupt police and by dialogue which pulls no punches in its condemnation of white America. Sweetback is a man of few words and much action; the black action film was literally spawned from this character.

Almost lost amidst excessive efforts by Van Peebles to create a film with a hip cinematic look and sound is the explicit message he wants to convey: the black man will no longer suffer at the hands of the white establishment. *Sweetback* opens with a dedication to the "Brothers and Sisters who had enough of the Man" and includes soundtrack lyrics such as "I got my finger on this trigger, I want to get up off my knees."

Van Peebles's view in this film is toward a different future. He has a preacher thank Sweetback for protecting a young black militant from the police: "You saved the plant they were planning to pinch in the bud." Later, toward the end of the film, Sweetback has a chance to escape on the back of a friend's motorcycle but tells the friend to take the injured young militant instead: "He's our future. Take him."

Van Peebles wanted to make a film for the "unpoliticized" black filmgoer. He "wanted a victorious film . . . where niggers could walk out standing tall instead of avoiding each other's eyes" (Van Peebles in Reid, 76). Indeed, he was successful in giving voice to the emotions, particularly the rage, of many African-Americans, and in doing so attracted not only the expected audiences: "The fact that a black man met violence with violence and triumphed over the corrupt white establishment appealed not only to the mass black audience (particularly, the black young, who flocked to it) but to some young white audiences as well" (Bogle, 235).[2]

Many of the films made by African-Americans in the late 1960s and the 1970s reflected the black separatist ideas of the times (e.g., *Uptight* 1969; *The Lost Man* 1969), as well as the everyday struggles of life for blacks in America's large cities (*Bush Mama* 1976; *The Killer of Sheep* 1977). Most of these films have been criticized as "blaxploitation," and film historian Donald Bogle (1989) characterizes such films as *Shaft* and *Superfly* as the "urban buck dramas" of the 1970s (242). The urban buck or black action films added a new voice for African-Americans on the screen, that of unbridled strength, rage, and, in some cases, lawlessness. Black characters embodying this combination certainly grabbed the attention of white audiences, and black audiences flocked to the movie theaters in record numbers. Not since the halcyon days of the black independent filmmakers and the hundreds of ghetto theaters had black audiences been provided with such gritty fare. The commercial success of these films paved the way for a slew of low-grade sequels and rip-offs—most written, directed, and produced by white independent companies and studios. The further from the original source film, the more distorted the representations of black life in America became.

The decade of the 1970s did provide many opportunities for black directors, some of whom succeeded in reaching beyond Hollywood's formulaic approach to filmmaking. Parks's autobiographical *The Learning Tree* (1969) provided a historical perspective on the lives of black Americans in the early decades of this century and, one year later in 1970, Van Peebles's *Sweet Sweetback's Baadasssss Song* contemporized the urban existence of African-Americans and their relations with such institutional forces as law enforcement. Michael Schultz's *Cooley High*

(1975) provided an honest, low-key look at the days and nights of black teens in 1960s urban America. Still largely unknown and underappreciated today, Charles Burnett wrote and directed a low-budget look at the black working man in *Killer of Sheep* (1977), a film which provided an unvarnished look at life in the L.A. ghetto. The most popular films of this era, however, were the black action films featuring private eyes and cocaine dealers (e.g., *Shaft* and *Shaft's Big Score*, 1972, by Gordon Parks, Sr.; *Superfly* by Gordon Parks, Jr.). These films provided, in many respects, black versions of tired Hollywood formula films. The notable difference was that a black man prevailed at story's end.[3]

But just as the advances made by blacks in America were cut short by the economic downturn of the 1970s and the backlash and/or inattentiveness of the Reagan/Bush era, films in the 1980s offered a new look at African-Americans. The 1980s in film has been labeled by Bogle as the "era of tan" (267ff), wherein black actors and actresses had their distinctive ethnic edge toned down, often relegated to the cinematic background. In regard to the lives of American blacks, films in the 1980s reflected the inattentiveness of the Reagan/Bush administrations to domestic problems. A spate of buddy films, such as *Rocky II and III*, *Nighthawks, White Nights, Off Limits*, and the *Lethal Weapon* series, all exemplified the amalgamation of black and white into tan; a superficial and invalid melding of the races. And in a case of revisionism, the historical role of blacks was inexplicably diminished in the 1988 film, *Mississippi Burning* (Cha-Jua).

By the latter part of the decade, however, a new trend in films emerged. Although preceded for decades by the likes of Oscar Micheaux, Gordon Parks, Sr. and Jr., Ossie Davis, Melvin Van Peebles, Charles Burnett, and others, Spike Lee's independent production in 1986 of *She's Gotta Have It* signaled this trend. Somewhat regrettably, because of its misogynist storyline, this film must be recognized as the one which initiated a new generation of African-American filmmakers, writers and directors who have addressed over the last several years the serious plight of blacks in America. But it was Lee's third film, *Do the Right Thing* in 1989, which established the filmic parameters for the eye and voice of many African-American filmmakers who have followed Lee. In 1991, African-American males directed nineteen feature films, more than in the entire decade of the 1980s.[4] Many of these movies bespoke a renewed (on film anyway) anger and rage toward the dominant white culture but also an inner-directed rage, one which pointed to the best possible solution to the predicament of so many blacks in America—self-preservation.

RAGE IN AFRICAN-AMERICAN FILM

In *Do the Right Thing,* an argument between Mookie (Spike Lee) and Pino (John Turturro) about race relations serves as the jumping off point for an "in-your-face" diatribe of racial epithets from a variety of characters in the film.

> MOOKIE: Pino, all you ever talk about is nigger-this and nigger-that, and all your favorite people are so-called niggers.
> PINO: It's different. Magic, Eddie, Prince, they're not niggers, I mean, they're not black . . . they're black but they're not black. They're more than black.
> MOOKIE: Pino, fuck you, fuck your fucking pizza, and fuck Frank Sinatra.
> PINO: Oh yeah. Well, fuck you too, and fuck Michael Jackson.

Following to camera:

> MOOKIE: You dago wop guinea garlic-breath, pizza-slinging, spaghetti-bending, Vic Damone, Perry Como, Luciano Pavarotti, O Sole Mio non-singing motherfucker!
> PINO: You gold-toothed, gold-chain wearing, fried chicken and biscuit-eating monkey ape baboon big-thigh, fast-running, high-jumping, spear-chucking, 360 degree basketball-dunking . . . spade. Take your fucking piece of pizza and go the fuck back to Africa!
> PUERTO RICAN: You little slanty-eyed, me no speakee American own every fruit and vegetable stand in New York, bullshit Reverend Sun Young Moon, Summer Olympic 88 Korean kickboxing son-of-a-bitch!
> CAUCASIAN COP: You . . . bean-eating, 15 in a car, 30 in an apartment, pointy shoes, red-wearing, Menudo . . . Puerto Rican cocksucker! Yeah, you!
> KOREAN MERCHANT: It's cheap! I got good price for you, Mayor

Koch! . . . Chocolate egg cream-drinking, bagel and lox, Bnai Brith, Jew asshole!

Lee demonstrates here that racism is not the sole province of whites. African-Americans and Americans of Korean, Italian, and Puerto-Rican descent can and do rage against one another. But Lee also attempts to show that dominant whites dictate the zeitgeist. Hate and rage emanate from, or are caused by, the dominant race. But his protagonist Mookie is uncertain as to what to do; ultimately he opts for action and solidarity with his race, and incites a riot by tossing the trash can and echoing back to his oppressors the same hate characteristic of them.

In the film *Boyz N the Hood,* Singleton illustrates racism in yet another way. In one sequence, Tre (Cuba Gooding, Jr.) and Ricky (Morris Chestnut), innocent of any wrongdoing, are pulled over by the police. A black police officer threatens Tre with a gun and expresses his feelings toward young African-American males.

TRE: I didn't do nothing.
COP: Oh, think you tough, huh? (Pointing gun at Tre's head.) Scared now, huh? I like that. That's why I took this job. I hate little motherfuckers like you. Little niggers like shit. I could blow your head off with this Smith & Wesson and you couldn't do shit.

As with Lee, *Boyz* director John Singleton shows us that racism resides in some blacks also. But by situating hatred of blacks in the character of an African-American cop, Singleton illustrates the institutional embeddedness of racism in social institutions and roles. More to the point, it is not just racism, but "classism."

The real point of *Boyz N the Hood,* however, is to illustrate the self-destructiveness of gang violence. In the climactic sequence, Doughboy (Ice Cube) and his homies track down, ambush, and brutally murder the killers of Doughboy's brother, the college-bound football player Ricky. This kind of violence, of course, is not a filmic creation. In Leon Bing's revealing book about Los Angeles gangs, *Do or Die,* one gangbanger acknowledges that young African-Americans kill each other over gang turf because, he said, "You got to have somebody to fight with" (276).

Gang-related homicides in Los Angeles County have increased from 212 in 1984 to over 800 in 1992; these murders now account for 38 percent of all homicides in the county (Katz, A23). This tragic displacement of anger and rage is dramatically and effectively illustrated in the show-down at the end of *Boyz N the Hood.* The look on Doughboy's face after avenging his brother's murder suggests a complex of emotions not easily deciphered or understood.

In another film about L.A. gangs, *South Central,* gang leader Ray-Ray implicitly acknowledges that whites control some part of the lives of African-Americans, but that at least the gangs own the night.

> RAY-RAY: You don't control the day. The Man controls the day. But we will control the night. Now at night we take over the land, and that's the same as owning it. And shit don't go down in the 'hood less we say so. . . . And we're going to have to kill somebody to send out the message, Don't fuck with Deuce. . . . Control your 'hood.

Again, the theme is violence by blacks against blacks, a filmic repre-sentation of a real dynamic. In 1983, 94 percent of homicides committed against African-Americans were perpetrated by other blacks (Palley and Robinson, 59). The leading cause of death among black males 15–34 years old is homicide committed by other blacks (Dyson, 74). Ray-Ray acknowledges that "The Man controls the day." In other words, don't make the mistake of taking on the white man; give him his peaceful day. But, he says, "we will control the night." They will sell the drugs and protect their turf against other African-Americans who dare to intrude. Again, you've got to fight somebody, and you'll lose if you try to fight the white man. The result is blacks killing blacks.

In a fourth film, *Straight out of Brooklyn,* an enraged and inebriated father tells an imaginary white man just what he thinks of the life chances of African-Americans, and of what the father wants for his son.

> FATHER: Hey, white man! Remember me?! I'm the man you de-stroyed. Just like you destroyed my father. And his father. Now you're going to destroy my god-damned son! You had my father telling me I could be anything I wanted to be. A lawyer. Yeah, a

doctor. You even had him tell me I could be President. I believed that shit! You're afraid of me. You're afraid I'm going to take your woman. You're afraid I'm going to take your house. You afraid I'm going to start to think just like you . . . I don't want your woman. You know what I want. Know what I want.

What he wants is his rightful role in, and share of, the American dream—which for him thus far has been a nightmare. This film provides a somewhat rare filmic example of explicit and literal rage against white social forces. It attacks the false promises of America and the defeat of and beating down of one generation of African-Americans after another.

As Diawara (20) has pointed out, some of these films center on a rite of passage for their young protagonists. They have come to realize that the enemy is not just outside, but within; rage within themselves and their community is being misdirected at one another. With the possible exception of Mookie in the *Do the Right Thing,* these young men recognize that they are losing their family, friends, and self-identity (even Mookie rails against his sister's flirting with Sal). The ritual which brings about this epiphany is death; burying family and friends. What these African-American filmmakers are saying is that social structural factors have put blacks in dire straits, and that they are certainly living lives of desperation. But to turn against and kill one another is a self-destructive course of action which only they themselves can stop. This kind of cinematic or artistic plea has been called for before. In 1968, critic and poet Larry Neal said that the black nationalist movement required art "directed at problems within Black America . . . with the premise that there is a well-defined Afro-American audience. *An audience that must see itself and the world in terms of its own interests*" (quoted in Reid, 75; my emphasis). It is, quite simply and bluntly, not in the interests of the white power structure to stop this killing. Blacks must rage against the killing of brother by brother, not just against white police brutality or discriminatory hiring practices or inadequate governmental support for the poor. The future of African-Americans must be somewhat determined by their own actions. Paul Robeson said that "We . . . realize that our future lies chiefly in our own hands. On ourselves alone will depend the preservation of our liberties and the transmission of them in their integrity to those who will come after us" (quoted in *Songs of My People*).

SOURCES OF BLACK RAGE

Consider again the tormented and enraged face of Doughboy as he stands over the lifeless body of his brother's killer. This kind of image, this kind of rage, will continue to be projected onto movie screens because, first, to return to my earlier point, it is a profitable enterprise, and, second, because this rage emanates from social structural conditions not easily or quickly abated: such conditions as racism, unemployment, poverty, violence, substandard housing, illiteracy, infant mortality, teenage pregnancy, and other calamities of life for African-Americans.

The proportion of African-Americans living in poverty[5]—slightly more than 30 percent, triple that of whites—is no lower now than in the early 1970s (Brownstein, A38) when *Shaft* and *Superfly* supplied the most common filmic depictions of blacks. African-American males are unemployed at twice the rate of the national average and, in California, African-American teens have an unemployment rate of from 40–50 percent (Peterson and Hawkins, A24). Although blacks comprise about 12 percent of the U.S. population, they are only 4 percent of all college professors, 3 percent of physicians, and 2 percent of lawyers (Race, M2), and only slightly more than 1 percent of teachers in elementary grades are black males (Harris, A25). The 1989 median African-American family income was 59.4 percent of white family income, and was lower than it had been in 1970 (Brownstein, A38). African-American babies are twice as likely to die as whites (Scott, A24), and over 40 percent of African-American children lived below the poverty level in 1989 (Race, M1). Almost 50 percent of the homeless are black (Brigham, 18), and over 40 percent of African-Americans are functionally illiterate (Gaw, A1).

Mind-numbing statistics such as these provide a quite dismal snapshot of the diminished life chances of most African-Americans. One outcome is crime and violence: a relatively quick, definitive yet self-destructive way of getting some piece of the American pie. Consequently, in 1989, 23 percent of all African-American men aged 20–29 were either in jail or prison, or on probation or parole (Morganthau, 20).[6] The homicide rate for African-American black males between the ages of 15–44 is ten times that of whites (Palley and Robinson, 59). Since 1969, nearly 1,000 black male teenagers have died each year from gunfire (Hutchinson, F3). And in one of those surrealistic juxtapositions which social scientists and journalists are always creating, it has been determined that in California, African-American males are three times more likely to be murdered than to be admitted to the University of California (Harris, A1).

It is also instructive to examine the statistics regarding those arrested during the rioting in Los Angeles County in 1992. Over two-thirds of the African-Americans arrested were unemployed; of all looters, 60 percent were high school dropouts; and 87 percent reported income of less than $1000/month (Lieberman and O'Reilly, A34–5). If one is seeking a snapshot of the supposed underclass in America, he or she need only review the profile of those involved in looting and burning Los Angeles, a profile essentially unchanged since the Watts riot of 1965 (Lieberman and O'Reilly, A35).

CONCLUSION

Many of the black filmic dramas of the 1970s were characterized by a threatening tone. Not only were *Shaft* and *Superfly* the baddest dudes in the ghetto, fighting and dominating other blacks, they also dispatched with some ease corrupt and inept white cops and politicians. They spoke and acted out of a self-survival instinct, and as representations of the burgeoning black pride movement and the separatist ideology of some African-Americans at that time. The final graphic on the screen at the conclusion of *Sweet Sweetback's Baadasssss Song* read "A baadasssss nigger is coming back to collect some dues." This message targeted whites as well as blacks who were the more likely audience for the film. It was a message intended to cause fear in whites, and pride and solidarity in blacks.

Two decades later, a new generation of filmmakers and films have shown that most of the violence which has indeed resulted has been violence perpetrated by blacks against blacks. The message of the current films, by and large, is that this self-destructive rage and violence have to stop. The protagonist in *South Central* is shown by his Muslim mentor that he has three ways to deal with his rage: he can either kill his enemy and end up on death row, he can turn it in on himself and go crazy, or he can change. The final graphic at the conclusion of *Straight out of Brook-*

lyn reads "We need to change." And the coda on the screen at the end of *Boyz N the Hood* reads "Increase the peace," a message directed primarily to blacks, because the most fatalistic, yet pragmatic, interpretation of the American social arrangement is that the dominant white race is not sufficiently motivated to stop African-Americans from killing each other.

NOTES

1. However, *Sweet Sweetback's Baadassss Song* provided anything but a more progressive view of women. Its misogynist characterizations and plotting have regrettably been adopted by many contemporary black filmmakers. As a non-studio production, *Sweetback* has been offered as paradigmatic, as "the fatherwork of Black independent film . . . [but] it goes without saying, however, that practices of resistance are always deeply compromised by their willingness to make major concessions to other hegemonic conventions" (Wallace in Diawara, 260–61). Thus, *Sweetback*'s angry and violent retort to the racism of America is severely compromised by Van Peebles' stereotyped and demeaning characterizations of black and white women.

2. This same attraction is evidenced today in the case of rap music. One survey showed that 74 percent of all rap music sold in 1992 was purchased by white consumers, primarily teenagers (Philips, 76).

3. The black action film, with its focus on drugs and organized crime (ultimately supplanted filmically by urban gangs) would be revived in the early 1990s in films such as *New Jack City* (Mario Van Peebles 1991), *Juice* (Ernest Dickerson 1992), and *Deep Cover* (Bill Duke 1992).

4. Only three feature releases have been directed by black women: *Daughters of the Dust* (Julie Dash 1991), *Just Another Girl on the IRT* (Leslie Harris 1993), and *Love Your Mama* (Ruby Oliver 1993). In the 1960s, Shirley Clarke was active as an independent director and writer, producing films about the lives of blacks in urban America, such as *The Connection* (1961), *The Cool World* (1963), and a documentary about a teen male prostitute, *Portrait of Jason* (1967).

5. The Federal "poverty level," it must be noted, is approximately $14,000 per year for a family of four, a figure rooted in arcane formulae first developed in the early 1960s on the basis of nutritional needs. It is, of course, ludicrous to suggest that a family of four making even twice or thrice that amount could live in any degree of comfort.

6. This is not to say that the criminal records of blacks are attributable solely to lives of desperation and alienation. Considerable evidence is available which

illustrates the inequities in the judicial systems of America. Conviction rates for similar crimes are disproportionately higher among blacks and other people of color than among whites (Hacker, 179–98).

WORKS CITED

Bing, Leon. *Do or Die.* New York: Harper Collins, 1991.

Bogle, Donald. *Toms, Coons, Mulattoes, Mammies, and Bucks: An Interpretive History of Blacks in American Films,* 2nd ed. New York: Continuum, 1989.

Brigham, William. "Down and Out in Tinseltown: Hollywood Presents the Dispossessed." In *Beyond the Stars V: Ideologies in Popular Film.* Eds. Linda K. Fuller and Paul Loukides. Bowling Green, OH: Popular Press, forthcoming.

Brownstein, Ronald. "Beyond Quotas." *Los Angeles Times Magazine* 28 July 1991, 18+.

Diawara, Manthia, ed. *Black American Cinema.* New York: Routledge, 1993.

Dyson, Michael. "Growing Up under Fire: Boyz N the Hood and the Agony of the Black Man in America." *Tikkun* 6.5 (1991): 74–78.

Easton, Nina. "New Black Films, New Insights." *Los Angeles Times,* 3 May 1991, A1+.

———. "Good News/Bad News of the New Black Cinema." *Los Angeles Times,* Calendar, 16 June 1991, 5+.

Gaw, Jonathan. "Report Says Latino Education in Decline." *Los Angeles Times,* 22 September 1990, A1+.

Hacker, Andrew. *Two Nations: Black and White, Separate, Hostile, Unequal.* New York: Scribner's, 1992.

Harris, Ron. "NAACP Seeks Solutions to Crisis of Black Males." *Los Angeles Times,* 10 July 1990, A1+.

Hruska, Bronwen, and Graham Rayman. "List Growing, but Black Women Filmmakers Rare in Hollywood." *San Diego Union Tribune,* 7 March 1993, E8–9.

Hughes, Langston. "The Negro Artist and the Racial Mountain." *The Nation,* 23 June 1926, 692–94.

Hutchinson, Earl Ofari. "Film Ads with Guns Only Fuel Racial Fires." *Los Angeles Times,* 10 May 1993, F3.

Katz, Jesse. "County's Yearly Gang Death Toll Reaches 800." *Los Angeles Times,* 19 January 1993, A1+.

Lieberman, Paul, and Richard O'Reilly. "Most Looters Endured Lives of Crime, Poverty." *Los Angeles Times,* 2 May 1993, A1+.

Morganthau, Tom. "Losing Ground." *Newsweek,* 6 April 1992, 20–23.

Pacheco, Patrick. "Fighting the 'John Singleton Thing'." *Los Angeles Times,* Calendar, 12 April 1992, 25+.

Palley, Howard A., and Dana A. Robinson. "Black on Black Crime." *Society* 25.5 (1988): 59–62.

Peterson, Jonathan, and Beth Hawkins. "State's Jobless Rate Falls: U.S. Picture Mixed." *Los Angeles Times,* 3 August 1991: A1+.

Philips, Chuck. "The Uncivil War." *Los Angeles Times Calendar,* 19 July 1992, 6+.

"Race and Black America." *Los Angeles Times,* 8 September 1991, M1+.

Rainier, Peter. "Just Another Girl on the I.R.T. Moving in the Right Direction." *Los Angeles Times,* 2 April 1993, F4.

Reid, Mark A. *Redefining Black Film.* Berkeley: University of California, 1993.

Scott, Janny. "U.S. Slips Badly in Infant Mortality Fight, Panel Says." *Los Angeles Times,* 1 March 1990, A1+.

Singleton, John. "The Fire This Time." *Premiere,* July 1992, 74–75.

"Songs of My People." Display of photographs. San Diego Museum of Art, April-May 1994.

Selected Filmography

Boyz N the Hood. Dir. John Singleton. 1991.

Connection. Dir. Shirley Clarke, 1961.

Cool World. Dir. Shirley Clarke, 1963.

Crossfire. Dir. Edward Dmytryk. 1947.

Do the Right Thing. Dir. Spike Lee. 1989.

Guess Who's Coming to Dinner. Dir. Stanley Kramer, 1967.

Juice. Dir. Ernest Dickerson. 1992.

Just Another Girl on the I.R.T. Dir. Leslie Harris, 1993.

Learning Tree. Dir. Gordon Parks, Jr., 1969.

Lethal Weapon. Dir. Richard Donner. 1987.

Lethal Weapon II. Dir. Richard Donner. 1989.

Lethal Weapon III. Dir. Richard Donner. 1992.

Love Your Mama. Dir. Ruby Oliver, 1993.

Malcolm X. Dir. Spike Lee. 1993.

New Jack City. Dir. Mario Van Peebles. 1991.

Nighthawks. Dir. Bruce Malmuth. 1981.

Off Limits. Dir. Christopher Crowe. 1988.

Patch of Blue. Dir. Guy Green, 1965.

Portrait of Jason. Dir. Shirley Clarke. 1967.

Rocky II. Dir. Sylvester Stallone. 1979.

Rocky III. Dir. Sylvester Stallone. 1982.
Shadows. Dir. Tom Forman. 1922.
Shaft. Dir. Gordon Parks, Sr. 1971.
She's Gotta Have It. Dir. Spike Lee. 1986.
South Central. Dir. Steve Anderson. 1992.
Straight out of Brooklyn. Dir. Matty Rich. 1991.
Superfly. Dir. Gordon Parks, Jr. 1972.
Sweet Sweetback's Baadasssss Song. Dir. Melvin Van Peebles. 1970.
White Nights. Dir. Taylor Hackford. 1985.

CHAPTER 6

Rage and Remembrance

The AIDS Plays

D. S. LAWSON

As the incidence of Acquired Immune Deficiency Syndrome has spread, the literature dealing with or focusing on the disease has burgeoned. Ironically, at the same time that the virus is killing many men and women around the world, the body of literature surrounding AIDS seems to be growing with alacrity; as people sicken and die, the words flourish and live.

Early on in the plague, two plays—Larry Kramer's *The Normal Heart* and William Hoffman's *As Is*—established twin avenues of dramatic reaction to the situation. Borrowing terms from the subtitle of gay American composer John Corigliano's first symphony, I call these reactions rage and remembrance. Kramer's invective typifies the rage many feel at this microscopic killer and at the society that for so long ignored (and continues to ignore) the health and destiny of its gay brothers and sons and fathers and friends. Hoffman's nostalgic play defines a mode of remembrance, of sadness over freedom and innocence and pleasure lost; it is a wistful elegy for a world we can now only remember and hope to recapture. Of course, often these modes of dramatic reaction are mixed together in any given play, but I hope to show that many plays are primarily either rage or remembrance plays.

Since these two plays first attracted attention, many others have taken the epidemic and those it affects as subject matter—too many, in fact, for a coherent consideration in a short amount of space. Therefore, I

"Rage and Remembrance: The AIDS Plays" by D. S. Lawson. Reprinted with permission of Simon and Schuster from *AIDS: The Literary Response*, edited by Emmanuel Nelson. Copyright © 1992 by Twayne Publishers.

would like to trace the threads of rage and remembrance in a small group of plays that have had New York productions and were written by gay male American playwrights. Lest these boundaries seem arbitrary or capricious, I would hasten to point out that, in America at least, gay men have borne and are continuing to bear the brunt of the disease and that New York, along with San Francisco, has been the site where the epidemic began and where attention to it has been focused.

The notoriety of Larry Kramer's *The Normal Heart* was responsible for one of the earliest encroachments of the disease into the dramatic culture of the United States. Certainly Kramer is a very angry man with many axes to grind in his play; the anger (sometimes vicious, sometimes righteous) gives *The Normal Heart* its power. The anger of gay men— whether caused by their oppression, their marginal position in society, the physical danger they often face, or the immediacy of death by AIDS—is a deep vein of ore for a playwright to mine. The rage surfacing in contemporary protest groups (most famously in ACT UP) is already present in Kramer's play.

The prevailing ideology of our times is anti-gay; the centrality of family, patriarchy, bourgeois values, heterosexuality, of work and money in society cannot be denied. In his play, Kramer indicts various aspects of society that are responsible for maintaining and inculcating the dominant ideology. The then nearly helpless medical profession, the legal system, and the press all come under merciless critique. Even good, caring doctors cannot cure or ease the pain of men who only quite recently were young and healthy; the refusal of the main character's brother—a high-powered lawyer—to do pro bono work on behalf of gay causes reveals the failure of the legal process and the family to help those victimized equally by homophobia and by microbes; the "marriage" ceremony at the play's climax underscores our society's unwillingness to give sanction to same-sex relations; the refusal of the "newspaper of record" for the United States—the *New York Times*— to give early, timely, and thorough coverage to gay issues foregrounds a tendency to ignore and exclude homosexuals and the issues which they confront from the public discourse. The death of a *Times* reporter from AIDS at the play's end only serves to highlight how the official organs of society (in this case, the press) are ignorant of the situation and plight of gay men (even those whom they know directly).

The play shows the state functioning in a variety of ways that exclude and marginalize its gay citizens. A reader can easily see the play as accusing American society—through all the state apparatuses depicted in *The Normal Heart*—of being directly complicit in the deaths of so many gay men. Given the powerful sanctions society places against homosexuality, as portrayed in Kramer's play, the wonder is not that gay men are dying, but that there were ever any gay men in the first place.

From its very title *The Normal Heart* seeks to challenge the dominant ideology. In citing W. H. Auden (virtually a gay icon), the title holds up an image of homosexual men contrary to that shown by society to itself.[1] These men are compassionate, they suffer and love, they get angry and take action, they fail or succeed much as straight people would, and they live or die in very ordinary, nonthreatening ways. Only when their rage prompts them to battle those elements of society that try to define them negatively or oppress them do Kramer's characters threaten; significantly, they do not molest children, camp up the national culture, or weaken the morale of the armed forces—in short, they threaten, but not in any of the ways society typically expects of gay men. They threaten only in hopes of obtaining a "normal" life. Even the specious "freedom" from commitment or familial responsibilities so accusingly thrown at homosexuals is absent here; these men care about each other in enduring, formalizing ways and must, of necessity, become a family for each other as there is no other real family for them to appeal to for help, succor, celebration, advice, or any other of the myriad functions allegedly served by heterosexually based, typically patriarchal family units.[2] In the words of the title, Kramer depicts his gay characters as having normal hearts—not as the sex-driven monsters of ideologically based stereotypes.

The play also treats gay issues figuratively. The famous scene in which a carton of milk splatters accidentally to the floor and ruins a sack of groceries is a case in point. Read abstractly, this scene features prominently the wasting of valuable, necessary, nourishing resources. Certainly on one level this might represent the waste of human potential as society first ignores and then allows the deaths of a large group of men who have a lot to contribute. On the other hand, the scene also depicts the inability of gay men to find the nourishment they need to live. Either reading of the scene makes clear the motivation for anger.

Kramer's abandonment of conventional stage realism—of a trompe l'oeil set—serves his interests well. The isolation of his characters and their actions from a recognizable landscape both allows a Brechtian distancing, whereby the audience can react critically and objectively to the play and formulate a politically correct response to it, and projects an image of homosexual men as pariahs, outcasts from a world whose ideology is so well perpetuated in literary and dramatic realism.

In all Western literary genres the realist mode has long been the most popular one. In direct ways, the dominance of realism on the stage threatens gay people and inculcates homophobia. The middle class, the family, the workplace and the home, and the subjugation of persons other than bourgeois, white, Christian males have been the almost exclusive focus of realism on the stage. If audiences over and over again see plays that depict this way of life (even if some individual realist works critique that way of life), would they not conclude that this way of life is somehow the proper one, perhaps the only one to be considered, perhaps even the only one available? Kramer wisely jettisons conventional realism; since he wishes to indict the society in which he places his characters, he does not wish to support that society by using a set of dramatic conventions that have long served that very society's interests.

The rage created by the AIDS epidemic is also present in Alan Bowne's play *Beirut,* the production of which caused a scandal even greater than that of Kramer's play. Certainly *Beirut* tells us many unpleasant and frightening things about both ourselves and the society we live in. Otherwise open-minded and perceptive theater critics responded to the New York production of *Beirut* with incomprehension and accusations; one reviewer even deemed the play a danger to society.

Perhaps a critic strictly oriented to gay theoretical matters would find *Beirut* a disappointment: Bowne has transferred AIDS to a heterosexual context; the characters seem in no important way to resist or resent their imprisonment by society; and the play ends with a genuflection to traditionally romantic (and, hence, heterosexist, patriarchal, and homophobic) notions of the primacy of a man/woman commitment despite overwhelming odds.

In Bowne's play, the Lower East Side of Manhattan has been transformed into a prison for people suffering from a nameless, sexually transmitted disease. The main action of the play involves an illegal (and initially unwelcome) visit from Blue (an uninfected young woman) to her boyfriend Torch. The play exploits the stereotype that domestic violence is inherent in relations between lower-class, relatively uneducated people as Torch and Blue repeatedly scuffle and push each other, while constantly firing off barrage after barrage of vituperative insults filled with personal attacks and curse words.

Certainly the characters are undesirable types. The only other character to appear on stage is a sex-starved guard who attempts to watch Blue and Torch having sex and is finally frightened off by fear of infection. In the outside world, sexual relations have been prohibited: pornography is rampant, and reproduction is accomplished exclusively in test tubes. The guard is uniquely in a position where he could have direct, immediate access to human sexuality, and he attempts to exploit this situation at the first opportunity.

It seems germane to note that one early conservative response to AIDS was to propose quarantining those infected with AIDS. In the play, disease victims are even tattooed in a private place so that those who potentially would have sex with them will be forewarned; this extreme measure was also proposed as an appropriate reaction during the early days of the AIDS crisis.[3] Bowne's fantastic, dystopian play twists this frightening suggestion around, applying it to young straights. Rather than seeing the heterosexual context of *Beirut* as a sell-out, I view Bowne's purpose here as pointing an accusing finger at the dominant heterosexual culture, the ideology behind it, and the power it wields; Bowne is asking, "What if this were to happen to men and women and not to men and men?" The strategy here is counterattack; Bowne tries to make the heterosexuals face the possibility that it could happen to them (as seemed likely at the time the play was written).

Obviously the title links the AIDS crisis to the situation in Lebanon during the time the play was written: various middle eastern factions fought for control of a once beautiful and cosmopolitan but now ruined and dangerous city. At the time, the Americans were involved in Beirut variously with naval forces deployed off shore, with marines occupying part of the embattled city, and with hostages held by several of the battling factions within the city itself. In a way, the Lower East Side never adequately becomes literally like Beirut, but the figurative connection is powerful and meaningful. Just as decades of failed, misguided U.S. policy toward Arabs in the middle east (significantly, like homosexual men, a group usually despised by the American public and often given highly negative stereotypical portrayals in vehicles of popular culture) helped to create the mess in Beirut, years of oppression and ignorance and fear of gay men—all of which was reflected in public policy—helped to fuel the AIDS crisis once it began in earnest. Like Kramer, Bowne blames the government and the society whose interests it represents for the explosion of the epidemic. Although the title *Beirut* is in some ways sensationalistic (and in purely literary terms cannot be seen as a total success), it does help to serve Bowne's purposes here and is another means for Bowne to express his rage at society.

The play's ending is undeniably disturbing: Blue forces herself on Torch so that they cannot be separated in the future; as she will have been exposed to the illness, she thus must be quarantined. Her desire to stay with the man she loves, to experience him sexually, and to share her life (and death) with him reeks of a romantic sensibility. In the face of a widespread epidemic that is killing thousands of people annually, the implication that some people willingly contract it and others willingly spread it in significant ways serves the prevailing ideology that this play seeks so strenuously to subvert.

Unlike Kramer's play, *Beirut* in no way abandons conventional realism. One might legitimately ask whether a play that co-opts, uses, and projects techniques that for so long and so powerfully have served the bourgeois, phallocentric, heterosexist, patriarchal society could be a "gay" play. The best that can be said of Bowne's dramaturgy is that he attempts to use realism to accuse and to reject the type of culture and ideology that have made his work possible and necessary in the first place.

Joe Pintauro's *Raft of the Medusa* is another instance of the "rage" response to AIDS. Dramaturgically, the play is somewhat of a muddle, but undeniably it has important things to say about the crisis, those who suffer from it, and the society in which it is happening. The play suffers from rampant tokenism: there is one example of every kind of person likely to contract AIDS (a homosexual man, a prisoner, an intravenous drug user, a heterosexual woman with bisexual partners, a homeless person). Among Pintauro's characters there are men and women, Anglos and Hispanics, blacks and whites, middle- and lower-class people.[4]

Pintauro organizes his play around a support group for PWAs headed by a heterosexual psychiatrist. Ideologically, one might object to Dr. Rizzo as a representation of the patriarchy and, indeed, he functions in certain respects as the paterfamilias to this group. Despite these negative elements, however, he is presented as enlightened and compassionate. He gives clean needles to Nairobi, a homeless, deaf, black woman addicted to drugs and infected with HIV. Like the doctors in *The Normal Heart*, though, he is utterly unable to cure those he seeks to comfort and help.

The realism of the support group scene is violated, however, by an apparently gratuitous frame of a deathbed scene at the opening of the play featuring the death of one member of the group (whose lover will remain in the group) as his parents watch in helpless sadness and regret. The ghost of the young man will periodically appear in the early parts of the play, but he is quickly dropped from the scheme later on. Pintauro seems not to know what to do with this frame once he has established it; it seems to belong to an early conception of the play that might best be abandoned in favor of a strictly realist format based on one particularly dramatic meeting of the support group.

Although the anti-realist elements of Pintauro's dramaturgy would seem to serve the interests of a radically new, gay theater, in this particular instance they in fact weaken the play by confusing and obscuring the primary plot line and by pulling the audience in two directions at once as they try to integrate the surreal magic of the ghostly presence with the detailed realism of the support group. In this respect the play is hopelessly flawed. Notwithstanding these very real problems, *Raft of the Medusa* is a worthy addition to the "rage" plays.

Pintauro's rage, as might be expected, focuses on the society that permits (and even encourages) the epidemic. Among the group members is a man who contracted the disease in prison and a young woman who contracted it from her abusive, drug-addicted boyfriend. Certainly Pintauro means for the audience to connect the society's failure to deal with the problems of crime and drugs with the presence and spread of AIDS. Just as society's problems manifest themselves in a vastly overcrowded prison system and in violence against women, society's problems are also manifest in the AIDS crisis in which once again a small, relatively weak and helpless minority segment of society has been allowed to suffer while the majority refuses to help or even to acknowledge the problem.

As in Kramer's play, one character in *Raft of the Medusa* is a reporter. In this case, the reporter is merely posing as a person with AIDS to obtain information on a soap opera star who becomes a member of the group but who is not publicly out and whose antibody status is known to neither his fans nor his employers. Certainly this plot device is Pintauro's indictment of the media's attitude and response to AIDS; rather than informing and educating, the media in *Raft of the Medusa* seek to exploit and expose. Of course greed is the underlying motivation: "exclusive" news of the star's homosexuality and illness would sell papers in a way that reports on research or articles on safe sex would not.

When the reporter's true purpose for attending the group is revealed, in a genuinely effective and horrific scene Nairobi sticks him with a needle and allows him nearly to go mad with fear before acknowledging that she has pricked him with one of the clean needles just given to her by Dr. Rizzo. Is Pintauro here advocating or approving of extreme, potentially violent ways of forcing society to recognize and deal with the AIDS crisis? Certainly he condemns those who would exploit the epidemic, but his other purposes remain unclear.

Once again, the title of Pintauro's play is important. By citing the Gericault painting, Pintauro attaches his artistic response to a horrifying situation to another, more famous work of art with social significance. He may be arguing that art is a perfectly appropriate response to an ugly and deadly circumstance; also he seems clearly to hope that his art will awaken public awareness and raise concern for AIDS. Perhaps Pintauro also believes that his characters are like these people who were on *The Medusa*—adrift in an inhospitable world with precious little hope of survival.[5]

Another play that might aptly be described as a "rage" play is Ed Cachianes's *Everybody Knows Your Name*. Rather than directly attacking various "public" apparatuses in anger, Cachianes takes on the more difficult task of depicting the "private" rage of individuals whose lives are ended or disrupted by the epidemic. Most of the play's dialogue is written in a campy, "queeny" language utterly appropriate to the New York gay subculture. The language of *Everybody Knows Your Name* is one of its chief beauties and the main source of its power. Just as an anti-realist mode can help to reject the bourgeois culture that oppresses homosexual men, a gay dialect also rejects that culture by denying the power of its language to define and circumscribe discourse.

In fundamental ways, our language controls what we think since, after we acquire language in childhood, except for primitive and basic thoughts, most of our thought occurs in language. If the language of the prevailing ideology dominates the thought and discourse of those people whom that ideology rejects and oppresses, then, by using that language, the oppressed prop up the very society that is set on their destruction. Cachianes's use of gay dialect permits a radical dislocation of the dominant discourse and thus frees gay men to use gay language and not thereby contribute to their own oppression. Certainly it is not stretching the point to view the queening dialect as a manifestation of rage: men who consciously choose not to use the mainstream language might do so as a result of anger with the system that perpetuates and is perpetuated by it.

The characters' use of gay language is crucial in redefining themselves. When they feminize their names, call each other "girl," or puncture the balloons of those outside their private linguistic world, they not only redraw the boundaries of the discourse that delineates their lives, but they also impinge on that dominant, public world whose language they distort. Whenever they co-opt the language for their own purposes, or twist it into new patterns of meaning, or attribute new signifieds to its old signifiers, they build their own frame of reference that is beyond appeal to the language's standard use. Much as the sexuality of gay men diverges from the prevailing heterosexual mainstream, their language is part of a private world where the grounds of meaning and interpretation are different.

Cachianes also rejects conventional stage realism in favor of a more flexible dramaturgy. He is quite successful in presenting the narrative elements of his plot in a nonrealist mode. The play shifts between dreaming and waking states, between contemporaneous action and past memories, and between various locales—chiefly apartments and a hospital room. The characters not only include a man dying of AIDS, his friends, a New Age AIDS buddy, and a nurse, but also the man's long-dead mother who appears in the nonrealist guise of a stand-up comic.

Everybody Knows Your Name also uses surrealistic transformations of ordinary and mundane scenes to highlight the play's themes. Early on we see a dream of Andrew, a man in his mid-thirties who is dying of AIDS; in this dream he and his longtime friend Carl prepared for a night out in the preplague days. As they primp in front of the mirror and apply makeup, trashing mutual friends all the while, the transforming power of the dream begins to take effect. Recurrently in a voice-over above the diagetic dialogue we hear Andrew screaming for himself to wake up, thus introducing and subsequently reinforcing the notion that Andrew is having a nightmare. Later on, Andrew will incomprehensibly find his hands covered with blood and not be able to wipe the blood off his robe. The scene shifts into and out of disco music and dancing— presumably moving from "home" to "disco" at will.

Scenes such as this one and the later appearance of Andrew's mother with her rapid-fire and often cutting humor help to dismiss the realist mode from the stage in this play. When otherwise familiar and realistic characters are confronted with incongruous shifts of location, associative trains of events, and other characters who violate the rules of the realist conventions, the stage becomes ripe for presentations of action and theme that will fall as far outside the purview of realism as urban gay life falls outside the middle-class lives that realism depicts; similarly, the agonies and fears of AIDS lie far beyond the comfortable, insulated world of the bourgeois living room that so often provides the set for realist drama.

The rage of these characters manifests itself not only in how their actions are presented and in how they speak, but also in what they do and in what they say. Although the rage is caused by the circumstances of a minority population under attack from society, politics, and microbes, these characters vent their anger at whatever is at hand. They curse, they verbally attack each other, they torture themselves in nightmares and memories of the past—all as a result of anger over their helplessness at the hands of the dominant society and their powerlessness to alter the progress of the virus that is shattering their lives. Not only are Andrew's verbal assaults on his AIDS buddy Ray, on his overweight friend Ellison, and on his nurse often hilarious, but they are also usually quite frightening at the same time: Andrew is turning humor (and the language it uses as a vehicle) into a weapon, and thus we laugh at the same time that we blanch with fear.

Gay drama's other main response to the AIDS crisis has been remembrance, fond nostalgia and wistful longing for a return to a world that can no longer exist. The play that first defined this mode of response is William Hoffman's *As Is*. Certainly Hoffman's characters feel rage (as is demonstrated in the scene in which Rich is in the hospital and refuses to cooperate with his nurse and insults the Hispanic janitor), but the primary mood of *As Is* is one of regret.

The play follows two men, Saul and Rich, past lovers, who at the start of the play are dividing up their possessions because Rich has moved out to live with his new lover Chet. The scene serves to introduce the audience to the main characters, and it also contains Rich's announcement to Saul that he has tested positive to HIV and now has swollen glands.

Hoffman chooses to abandon the realist mode. The play has recognizable playing areas (a living room that is later transformed into a hospital room, and a bar) but the action shifts in and out of chronological sequence. One trick Hoffman often employs is shifting the action to some other locale whenever something that transpired outside the main playing area is remembered or discussed. In this way, we see Rich attempting to pick up men at bars, we see the past when he and Saul were lovers, we see him first meeting Chet, and we hear how news of his illness affects his friends and family. We see some characters merely identified with numbers, First Woman, PWA 5, Clone 2, and so on. These characters serve important functions in various scenes, but they are not individuated (for example, the clones' names all begin with "Ch"—Chad, Chuck, Chip—perhaps in a dig at the callow and selfish Chet for whom Rich leaves Saul; in the course of the play Chet dies of complications brought on by AIDS). They cannot be seen as characters in the realist sense of the word, and thus, they add to the abandonment of realist techniques.

One of the most beautiful moments in *As Is* occurs when Saul and Rich are remembering the past: public sex in a hotel window while crowds in the street below watch and cheer; late nights at famous New York City gay landmarks; orgies at the baths; trips to porno bookstores; a vacation in Morocco; simply talking dirty with other men. The past is presented as a kind of dream world of plentiful, pleasurable sex with little more to worry about than how to get rid of an undesirable partner tactfully. Hoffman also utilizes a scene in which various persons (some of whom are characters, some of whom are simply a kind of witness and never reappear in the play) remember when they first heard of AIDS. At the end of this dreamlike scene with its nondiagetic characters and overlapping dialogue, the actors simply recite a long list of male first names, implying that these people have died and are now part of that remembered past.

These strikingly nonrealist elements contribute to the mood of remembrance and show dramatically that the world being fondly remembered is patently not part of the "real" world of the play's here and now. Certainly this wistful remembrance of the past is meant to convey a positive gay image—a time when the gay men of New York were happy and more or less carefree. One is left hoping that somehow, miraculously, this world could return.

As Is ends with Saul and Rich's attempt to regain part of that lost world: they have sex for the first time since the onset of Rich's illness. The question of whether having sex will help resolidify their troubled relationship is left unanswered, but their attempt to have some sort of intimate, sexual life in the troubled times of *As Is* is admirable. Indeed, the ending of the play is hopeful and optimistic: yes, the past is irretrievably gone and the present is frightening and dangerous, but we must take the present and those in it "as is" if we are to find any pleasure, any way of life with meaning and value.

In contrast to the rage plays, the anger in Hoffman's play is subordinated to an overwhelming nostalgia. In the rage plays we see the characters as the victims of many wrongs—only one of which is AIDS. In the remembrance plays, on the other hand, the presence of AIDS is seemingly the only thing that prevents gay men from being happy and leading fulfilling lives. Perhaps this is a bit reductivist given the richness of the remembrance plays, but none of them takes on societal and political wrongs wholesale in the direct and confrontational manner of the rage plays.

Harvey Fierstein's three short plays grouped together under the title *Safe Sex* are best seen as part of the remembrance mode as well. The plays are linked by a shared set of themes: love and loss, the potential health risks of sexual activity, the nature of enduring relations between gay men (both with each other and with the "outside" world). The first two one-act plays, "Manny and Jake" and "Safe Sex," are definitely part of an anti-realist stage practice appropriate to gay subject matter.

"Manny and Jake" features dialogue that is almost poetic in its rhythmic progress and often elliptical subject matter. The play depicts two handsome young men who might have had sex together in the past. Jake is willing, but Manny is not. Manny meditates on his life, on the world situation, and mostly on the past. He looks forward to a new world, without the specter of AIDS, in which he will know what to do because he will *remember* it from before. At the breathtaking end of the play,

Manny rhapsodizes about a future time when he can return to spontaneous sex with as many partners as he pleases and promises to have learned nothing during the plague—rejecting overtly, that anything of value could come from something so deadly, so unfair.

The second play of the trilogy, "Safe Sex," concerns two lovers, Mead and Ghee, who interrupt themselves in the middle of making love because their passion has tempted them to be unsafe. The interruption sparks a conversation about what is possible for gay men to do together and what is necessary for their survival psychologically; after all, if gay men cannot or will not have sex, how can they be overtly gay? They may certainly continue to exhibit many of the signs of being gay, but they stand to lose a defining characteristic of homosexuality—the desire for and commission of sexual acts with other men. The play takes on the fear of loss of selfhood and identity if sexuality is lost or too long denied. Through Ghee, Fierstein accuses some gay men of using AIDS to avoid sex, for what they are afraid of is not disease, but homosexuality itself.

As Ghee and Mead rehash past grievances with each other, they remember a world without AIDS. They remember sex as fun, as dirty, as something they actually did. They remember worrying about herpes, or the clap, but not about dying. The world has transformed itself into a hostile, dangerous place where everything must be checked against the safe list, where intimacy is a potential source not only of argument and frustration or of pleasure and satisfaction, but also of horrible death.

The set of "Safe Sex" is a giant seesaw or teeter-totter—which is utterly appropriate as a set for the action of two men arguing and making up, trying to balance their needs and desires against what is possible and safe. The teeter-totter's potential for large swings might also represent the radical shift in the lives of gay men. Certainly Mead's standing on the edge of the board at the play's end and his daring and coaxing Ghee to do the same is meant to demonstrate the nature of "danger" and the necessity to face it and come to terms with it. The anti-realist stage practice of this play is brilliant: the seesaw works on a symbolic level in addition to being an original alternative to the living room or kitchen set of the realist mode.

The final play, "On Tidy Endings," features a man, Arthur, whose lover, Collin, has recently died of AIDS. As he packs to vacate their apartment, Arthur must deal with the man's ex-wife, Marion. The play is basically a domestic comedy in which the characters solve some serious problems (surviving the loss of a beloved, sorting out their feelings, negotiating a relationship with each other) while trading a stream of one-liners. In high realist fashion, the living room of the apartment is the set.

"On Tidy Endings" is the longest, most fully developed and ultimately most disappointing of the three plays. The play's only gay character, Arthur, exhibits unswerving loyalty to heterosexually based modes of behavior. He and his late lover have had a sort of marriage and family that even included the lover's eleven-year-old son, Jim, who called Arthur "Uncle."

Not only does the action of "On Tidy Endings" ideologically mirror prevailing, heterosexual notions of human relations, but Fierstein's realist stage practice also reinforces that ideology. A critic oriented to theoretical matters might term the play a sellout to the dominant ideology in both theme and technique. Arthur is presented throughout the play, however, with compassion, understanding, intelligence, and humor. Although the end of the play (a presumably continuing connection with the ex-wife and child of his beloved) reeks of bourgeois heterosexuality, Arthur maintains his wit and dignity throughout the action. On the other hand, the ex-wife gets all the perquisites, benefits, and problems of a relationship with Collin: she is selling the apartment; she has his son; her name was mentioned in the newspaper obituaries; she was surrounded by friends and family at the funeral; and even she, not Arthur, is HIV positive. Though the play itself is meant to be critical of the society that has displaced a man's male lover at such a difficult time, the techniques through which that criticism is presented tend to reinforce the values of that society.[6]

Victor Bumbalo's *Adam and the Experts* can also be classified as a remembrance play. It, too, however, contains a generous amount of rage, especially from Eddie (a PWA friend of the title character) who vents his fury with the system (particularly with the politicians) in one especially memorable and effective scene. Nevertheless, the central mood of the play is remembrance. Adam has reacted to the AIDS crisis by retreat and retrenching. He has put his sex life (and with it parts of his emotional life) on hold indefinitely. He is frequently assailed by The Man, a nondiagetic character who is an embodiment of all those things Adam has denied or repressed himself. The Man is a visual reminder of all that used to be in Adam's life and, as a result of AIDS, is no longer there. As such, The Man constitutes the chief vehicle for remembrance in *Adam and the Experts.*

The Man is by turns hilarious, demanding, and wistful. By the end of the play, Eddie has died and Adam has come to a sort of reconciliation with The Man—acknowledging his need for a whole life, even in the time of plague. Thus, as in *As Is,* there is a faint element of hopefulness at the end of *Adam and the Experts* that some happiness and pleasure can still be salvaged from this world. The note of sad remembrance for the past in Bumbalo's play is extended by inference to the present and the future; toward the end of the play The Man speculates on what might have happened if Eddie had lived and met a nice young man at a party who might have been his lover. Bumbalo's characters are not merely remembering a lost past but mourning a future never to be.

Obviously through employing a device such as The Man, Bumbalo departs from realist practice in his play. The play's set is flexible and contains several locales important to the action, but it is not overtly designed to represent any of them with realist detail. Like Hoffman, Bumbalo uses a small group of actors to double all the minor roles. The action shifts back and forth from location to location and some of the characters (particularly a priest and two ersatz maharishis) are treated with a great deal of often funny satire, which renders them frankly nonreal. Bumbalo's dramaturgy helps to reinforce the thematic material of his play. Ultimately, *Adam and the Experts* is one of the most satisfying of the remembrance plays.

Jean-Claude van Itallie's *Ancient Boys* uses a gathering of the friends of the late Reuben, an artist who has recently died, as the basis for its nonrealistic plot. The friends remember Reuben (who essentially kept them separate from each other), and their memories are acted out and interspersed into the relatively thin main plot of the "memorial ceremony" itself. Van Itallie's achronological treatment of his material is a great strength in *Ancient Boys,* for we see Reuben at various stages in his life and can put together for ourselves a holistic picture of him.

Van Itallie's use of a continuing series of projected slides (scenes from Reuben's life, famous works of art, pictures of the characters in amusing situations) further violates the realist stage and thus solidifies this remarkable play's wholesale rejection of the realist mode. By the end of the play the stage is dominated with a large example of Reuben's art, which serves as a powerful reminder of the great potential wasted by this man's death.

Reuben himself is a problematic character. At times he seems to succumb to homophobic notions about the nature of AIDS, arguing that the thymus glands of people who have died of AIDS are often shrunken; since the thymus is located near the heart and plays a role in the onset of puberty, Reuben concludes that gay men are misusing their heart energy—their love—and suffer health consequences as a result. At one point he even says he is tired of being gay and actually prefers women to men. In one scene, Reuben imitates his mother and remembers the comforts of her garden and her telling him that the world outside the garden was a terrible place. It is not stretching it to read this as hetero-sexist ideology: if you stray from the idyllic garden, you face utter nothingness and might as well end your life.

On the other hand, Reuben offers positive images of gay people when he argues that gay native Americans were usually the powerful and respected medicine men of their tribes; he even goes so far as to compare the gays to the Jews as a group of God's chosen people. Reuben's dichotomy is quite real: he clearly rejects his mother and her ideology, but he is marked for life by it and has co-opted and internalized various elements of the very ideology that seeks to thwart his happiness.

Part of what is going on in *Ancient Boys* is an exploration of Reuben's problems (of which AIDS is the most life threatening, but not the only one): his compartmentalization of his life, his partial retreat from or denial of his artistic abilities, and finally his inability to accept himself fully. Certainly Reuben in these regards is typical of many gay men, but ideologically this portrait (and its equating disease with certain stereotypical elements of gay male psychology) is disturbing.

The ending of the play is troubling as well. Reuben opts for suicide rather than living through a horrible and depersonalizing death. One could easily imagine a play in which this kind of decision was treated as a positive, self-affirming act, but *Ancient Boys* is not such a play. Reu-ben's final words (directed to his mother who is not physically present at the time) indicate that, rather than feeling that he is taking a positive step, he thinks he is doing something shameful or naughty, something for which he needs his mother's forgiveness.

In *As Is* at one point Rich asked Saul to get him enough depressants to kill himself. Saul goes to buy the drugs and ends up throwing them in the gutter when he has the realization (on an unpleasant street in ugly weather) that there is still beauty in the world; the idea that there could still be beauty in life even with AIDS is obvious. Reuben in *Ancient Boys* is never afforded a parallel kind of realization and thus cannot find any reason to deny himself a suicide.

One further play—Craig Lucas's *Prelude to a Kiss*—warrants consideration here and seems most nearly to fit the remembrance category, so I have included it as a sort of epilogue to my discussion. The play is lyrical and magical; it has a great deal of beauty in it, but its relation to the themes discussed herein is ambiguous. AIDS is in no overt way the subject of the play; *if* the play is about AIDS, it is only in a figurative sense.

The action of the play consists of the heterosexual courtship, marriage, and minor marital problems of a young, urban couple, Peter and Rita. At their wedding, Rita is kissed by a mysterious old man whom no one knows, and somehow the two exchange souls. Peter, who had married a young, beautiful, healthy person, finds himself instead in love with a sick, dying old man (whose body contains the soul and personality of his beloved). Certainly a symbolic representation of AIDS can be seen here: in the gay world many men like Peter fall in love with someone young and healthy only to have HIV turn their lover into a dying old man.

If this reading is accepted, then *Prelude to a Kiss* is a remembrance play, since Peter expends so much energy trying to recapture the world he thought he had won. Peter relentlessly tries to understand what has happened and attempts to undo the change, to reorient the souls into their proper bodies so that his life can continue on as he had envisioned it. Certainly many gay men feel the desire to be able magically to return the world to what they had hoped it would be.

Dramaturgically the nonrealistic plot devices are reinforced by a nonspecific stage setting that shifts through various locations including apartments, a suburban home, a honeymoon vacation spot, a bar, and so on. Ideologically, the thematic material of the play is thus underscored by the dramatic techniques used on the stage. As is the case with Bowne's *Beirut,* one might object to the heterosexual context in which Lucas places his action, and one might also see the fairy-tale motifs that he employs (the magic kiss, the Prince Charming, the lonely maiden, the happily-ever-after ending) as serving a homophobic ideology. Although

Lucas does not overtly take on the AIDS epidemic in his play, *Prelude to a Kiss* does have connections with the plays I have been discussing and thus must be seen as at least a cousin of the family of plays considered here.

AIDS plays continue to be produced in increasing numbers. Several plays have gone beyond New York to touring companies, or to local productions throughout the United States, or to West End productions in London. Early on in the history of dramatic representations of AIDS written by gay American men for the New York stage, two broad categories of response to the crisis—rage and remembrance—were codified by important productions. In their ground-breaking plays, Kramer and Hoffman defined the parameters for treating AIDS on the stage that would be used in many later plays, not just those plays discussed here. The response to AIDS in both of these initial plays is coupled with a radical departure from realist stage practice, which, as I have argued, is appropriate, given that the plays are highly critical of the prevailing ideology and, in fact, place much of the blame for the AIDS epidemic and the deaths of thousands of gay men squarely on the shoulders of the society that perpetuates itself through the dominant ideology. Whether raging against the lot of gay men in the contemporary world or sadly remembering the free and beautiful past, those plays are most successful that reject the theatrical techniques of dramatic realism and strike out into territory unknown on the popular stage; in very real ways, gay men in their lives have been abandoning the familiar and exploring the new throughout human history. It is only appropriate that theater that celebrates them or mourns their passing or erupts with anger over their situation should itself break new ground.

NOTES

1. The quotation from Auden might also be seen as providing a positive gay image, a reference point for gay men who wish to find reassuring reinforcement from a culture they created.

2. One frequently held homophobic belief is that gay men threaten society merely by virtue of being outside the family—that often cited foundation of western society and culture. The theory goes that the freedom of gay men threatens society by presenting an alternative (one often defined as selfish or egocentric or immature) to the commitment, responsibility, and stability of creating and maintaining a family. I might hasten to point out that the nuclear

family in our time and day is suffering from a wide number of ills, very few of which could be legitimately placed at the door of homosexuality. Also, the function of the family in suppressing "difference" (especially sexual difference) is noteworthy and the family is often seen as providing in microcosm a model for the functioning of society as a whole—one in which the interests and behaviors of individuals are subordinated to the power of a male leader or father figure.

3. The parallels to Nathaniel Hawthorne's *The Scarlet Letter* here are quite obvious and are probably intentional on Bowne's part but inadvert but on the part of those conservatives who in real life proposed this step. At any rate, this connection reveals a fundamentally American response to those who break gender and sexual rules: brand them so that the "innocent" and morally upright elements of society can be protected from their real or imagined contagion. Also Hawthorne's equation of religion and law in his short novel probably also plays a role in the measures proposed to mark those infected with HIV.

4. Perhaps Pintauro's inclusion of the entire spectrum of Persons with AIDS is a reaction to criticisms of the Norman Rene film *Longtime Companion,* which featured only middle-class, white males as its afflicted characters.

5. I might also note that in the Gericault painting a nude man with a beautiful body and visible genitalia is present in the foreground. Perhaps this painting might be seen as a sort of homosexual icon and thus as doubly appropriate as a partial inspiration for a gay work of art.

6. Fierstein's tripartite structure here and his movement from lyrical, antirealist practice to domestic comedy duplicate exactly the form of his Tony Award–winning Broadway success *Torch Song Trilogy,* which was criticized in some gay circles for its parallel deference to heterosexually based models of behavior. The final play of *Torch Song Trilogy* is very similar to "On Tidy Endings," because both feature a gay man trying to reestablish a "family" after the death of a male lover. Significantly, both plays end with the main male character alone on stage, seemingly catching his breath after having worked through many of his familial problems to create a "family" unit based in obvious ways on a heterosexual paradigm.

CHAPTER 7

The Aesthetic Politics of Rage

CLAIRE KAHANE

In *Jane Eyre* Charlotte Bronte, in a sudden textual turn from narrative to argument, interpolates a passage on the need for action in women's lives:

> It is vain to say human beings ought to be satisfied with tranquility; they must have action; and they will make it if they cannot find it. . . . Women are supposed to be very calm generally; but women feel just as men feel; and it is narrow-minded in their more privileged fellow-creatures to say that they ought to confine themselves to making puddings and knitting stockings, to playing on the piano and embroidering bags. . . . It is thoughtless to condemn them, or laugh at them, if they seek to do more or learn more than custom has pronounced necessary for their sex.
>   When thus alone I not unfrequently heard Grace Poole's laugh. (112–113)

Most of us recognize this text: it was cited by Virginia Woolf as an example of narrative rupture, caused by an eruption of Bronte's rage into her story. While many feminists have reproached Woolf for her criticism and justified Bronte's digression on narrative grounds, there is a break; from an eloquent and passionately felt feminist appeal in essay form, the text, almost as an afterthought, returns clumsily to Jane's story. For Bronte as a novelist, an imaginary derisive and significantly

Reprinted by kind permission of Gordon and Breach Science Publishers, Inc., from *Literature, Interpretation, Theory*, vol. 3, 19–31. Copyright © 1991 by Gordon and Breach Science Publishers, Inc.

male laugh created a division within the narrative voice, the effect of an interference: of rage manifest in the rupture of story-line, and of outrage, which provoked the narrator to leave the circulation of voices and fasten onto her social object: male injustice. I want to delineate very briefly the relation between rage, outrage, and the body and explore their effects on literary voice.

Psychoanalytic theory describes rage both as an infantile response to separation and loss, and as a primal aggressivity against the maternal body, the most ambivalently constructed other who bears the illusory traces of self.[1] Yet because the violence of this archaic affect has as its goal not only the destruction of the object, but re-union with it, it destroys the subject as well. Certainly we all have had some body-knowledge of rage. We see red, or experience some other somatic disturbance—stammering, stuttering, or in more extreme cases, the conversion symptoms of hysteria. Experienced as psyche turning into soma, rage disempowers us as subjects, making us subject to *its* regressive vicissitudes.

Although the experience of rage silences the subject—like unconscious desire, it can never be directly expressed—once objectified as part of the symbolic Other, it can have a very creative life, assuming discursive shape as scenarios of obliteration, apocalyptic narratives, or as their more distanced kin, wit and caricature. Displaced into language, rage is sublimated through the subject's identification with a patriarchal symbolic discourse rather than confined to the body, and language recuperates the objects of the obliteration it represents. Yet even sublimated as a discursive event, rage is locked into a scenario which can only repeat the violence of its fantasmatic origin. The experience of rage is powerful, but not political. However, when it remains repressed and unsublimated, it leads to the invalidism that pathologized a generation of women in the late 19th century, and that continues to wreak havoc on the female body today.

If the violence of rage demands repression and a barring of the subject, the violence of outrage demands expression in a voice claimed by the subject. Outrage, the word itself cues us into the difference: unlike rage, outrage—"a violence affecting others" according to the Office of Educational Development—is in a sense transitive, requiring an object. A socialized and mediated form of rage, outrage is directed toward identifiable and bounded others in the external world, and is thus less threatening to the self. Indeed, while still tied to the repetition compulsion of its origin, outrage fastens onto an object and cannot let go until it has achieved its aim: transformation of the object. Unlike rage, outrage by its very nature is a force for change, is political. I want to propose a broad generalization here, one which inevitably oversimplifies but still provides a skeletal anatomy for speculation; that for women in the 19th century, repressed rage led to conversion hysteria, displaced rage to hystericized fiction and poetry, and outrage to feminism and essays. This cutting up of rage should not obscure the fact that all three vicissitudes could, and did, exist within one subject, and that the effects of each were manifest in its textual productions.

Certainly there was sufficient cause for both rage and outrage among hysterics in the 19th century: Freud's and Breuer's *Studies in Hysteria* noted that hysterical girls were more intelligent and more ambitious than most, more "masculine" according to the boundaries of gender that patriarchal definitions had established. Yet once these gifted middle class adolescents began menstruation, they were confined in a social identity—"femininity"—that demanded dependence and fostered passivity. As Elaine Showalter notes,

> Physical activities, traveling, exercise, and study were curtailed or forbidden. While their brothers went away to school, most middle-class girls were educated at home, their social life . . . restricted to a few safe contacts. . . . A girl's growing awareness of this social dependence and constraint . . . may well have precipitated an emotional crisis. (957)

Indeed, if, as the psychoanalyst Alan Krohn suggests in *Hysteria: The Elusive Neurosis*, the hysteric utilizes the dominant myth of passivity in his/her culture to represent a conflict about passivity, the very nature of the feminine self as constructed by 19th-century discourse and the passive desire that purportedly constituted it was enough to provoke hysterical effects. Such symptoms as aphonia (loss of speech), absences of consciousness, and partial paralyses were the all too common effects of an ambivalence about the feminine position that Freud located as the nucleus of hysteria.

For Freud this ambivalence was a matter of interpersonal desire: the hysteric was caught between an unacknowledged passive desire for the father—the core fantasy of the conventional female oedipal complex—and an unacknowledged identification with him that took the mother as object of desire (1908). Beyond this oedipal scenario, as Freud was to discover later, was a more primal figure of conflict, a maternal fantasm whose inevitable loss and social devaluation persisted as a burr in the psyche of hysterical daughters (1931). Yet whatever the actual relations between daughters, mothers, and fathers, as Lacan's expansion of the field of desire suggested, the daughter's paternal identification concerned not merely the actual father but the Symbolic father, the discursive locus of intellect, ambition, and privilege. Since the Word flowed from Him, who would not inherit the Father's estate? Adolescence, however, confirmed the daughter's exclusion from that paternity, and menstruation in particular became the corporeal signifier both of her future place in the Symbolic order as maternal body, and of her discursive impotence. The disjunction between the daughter's identification with the Symbolic father, which legitimated her as patriarchal subject and the subject of language, and a body that compelled identification with the mother, often provoked an excess of aggressivity impossible for daughters to express. Thus the hysterical symptoms of Victorian daughters typically expressed a rage turned punitively against themselves, a kind of biting of their own tongue instead of using it aggressively against the other in both its maternal and paternal forms. Unable to assume the post-oedipal lineaments of femininity, the female hysteric remained suspended at the oedipal moment in all its ambiguous potential, miming in her body the script that had entrapped her.

Alice James is a case in point: although she had no public presence during her life nor was she a writer by profession or identity, she is an interesting figure precisely because, unlike her famous brothers, who inscribed themselves magnificently into public discourse in spite of their hysterical symptoms,[2] Alice James, invalided from the age of nineteen, became primarily the good patient, her body the medium through which she could covertly represent the problematics of her being.[3] When shortly before her death, she took up the pen to write, her writing took the form of a diary, a private voice, to be acknowledged only after her death.

That James intended her *Diary* to be read is clear from several entries in which she tellingly addresses her imaginary reader as male, an inflection especially bizarre given that the better part of the *Diary* was dictated to her female companion and amanuensis, Katherine Loring. Yet in this gendered address James's text speaks the very contradiction of the hysteric: the imaginary ear to the listener/reader belongs to a male subject even when she is literally speaking to a woman. James herself comments upon this paradox in her entry of January 1891, shortly before her death:

> I am as much amused, dear Inconnu (please note the sex? pale shadow of Romance still surviving even in the most rejected and despised by Man) as you can be by these microscopic observations recorded of this mighty race. (166)

Such amused acerbic observations pervade James's text, although usually she directs her barbs at others. Indeed, though James writes in that most personal of literary forms, the diary, the actual passages of introspection are few. When she does turn her eye on herself, her text resonates with suggestive ambiguities, as in this well known and self-revealing passage[4] in which she describes the after-effects of her own first hysterical attack:

> As I lay prostrate after the storm with my mind luminous and active and susceptible of the clearest, strongest impressions, I saw so distinctly that it was a fight simply between my body and my will, . . . Owing to some physical weakness, . . . the moral power pauses . . . and refuses to maintain muscular sanity, worn out with the strain of its *constabulary* functions. As I used to sit immovable reading in the *library* with waves of violent inclination suddenly invading my muscles, taking some one of their myriad forms such as throwing myself out of the window, or knocking off the head of the benignant pater as he sat with his silver locks, writing at his table, it used to seem to me that the only difference between me and the insane was that I had not only all the horrors and suffering of insanity but the duties of doctor, nurse and strait-jacket imposed upon me, too. Conceive of never being without the sense that if you let yourself go for a moment . . . you must abandon it all, let the dykes break and the flood sweep in, acknowledging yourself abjectly impotent before the immutable laws. When all one's moral and natural stock in trade is a temperament forbidding the aban-

donment of an inch or the relaxation of a muscle, 'tis a never-ending fight. (149, italics mine.)

The two forms of her violent inclination, self-destruction or the destruction of the father—and here a particularly archetypal father, the "benignant pater" writing—and the totalistic either/or syntax speak a deeply regressive desire to break down the boundaries between self and other, here self and father, a retaliatory desire rooted in rage. Not surprisingly the scene of this melodrama is the library—the repository of patriarchy, where the daughter can read the script but not write it, a scene repeatedly invoked in late 19th- and early 20th-century texts. Think of the provocative Maggie in *The Mill on the Floss*—a character James loved—reading her father's books, or Dora in Freud's case history dreaming of reading a big book in her father's library.

But if Maggie outdoes her brother in intellectual prowess, James's leading symptom is an intellectual inhibition. "Cerebration is an impossible exercise and from just behind the eyes my head feels like a dense jungle into which no ray of light has ever penetrated" (149), she writes of her inability to study or think concentratedly without great anxiety. Given the phallic marking of intellectual activities—activities in which her particularly brilliant brothers excelled—it is not hard to loosen the knot of meanings in this inability to think, by which she avoids the domain of her brothers and performs a conventional femininity she also despised. "How sick one gets of being 'good,' " she writes, "how much I should respect myself if I could burst out and make every one wretched for 24 hours" (64). In a very real sense, Alice was "sick" of being 'good.'

This restriction of language and consciousness—a form of defense against knowing—was no doubt fostered by Alice's relation to William, who as Jean Strouse points out, played the flirtatious male with his sister, his letters provocatively sprinkled with erotic double entendres (52–55). Erotic ambiguities between brother and sister were a staple of 19th-century discourse, encouraging fantasies of transgression and reactive denials, as well as figuring a narcissistic identification with the male other to which women were especially subject. Certainly it was such an intermingling of desire and rage that George Eliot represented in the climactic brother-sister *Liebestod* of Maggie and Tom drowned in an embrace in *The Mill on the Floss,* a novel especially dear to Alice James. Indeed, its final image is echoed in James's articulation of her own struggle to contain "the flood" within her—a trope of excess that her body somatized and her discourse inhibited. Thus not surprisingly the *Diary* seems restricted in its scope of inquiry and attention, and even in her comments on her reading—a space where her observations would have transcended the limits of her environment—her thoughts are not allowed the expansion of significant reflection. Her remarks are crabbed, or conversationally elliptical, her voice relieving its excess in caustic commentary.

In this regard it is especially striking that the most acerbic rupture of the chatty surface of James's prose is provoked by her reading of George Eliot's letters, letters which elicit a vigorous reaction:

> Read the third volume of George Eliot's Letters and Journals at last. I'm glad I made myself do so for there is a faint spark of life and an occasional remotely humorous touch in the last half. But what a monument of ponderous dreariness the book! Not one burst of joy, not one ray of humour, not one living breath in one of her letters or journals, the commonplace and platitude of these last, giving her impressions of the Continent, pictures and people, is simply incredible! Whether it is that her dank, moaning features haunt and pursue one thro' the book, or not, but she makes upon me the impression, morally and physically, of mildew, or some morbid growth—a fungus of a pendulous shape, or as of something damp to the touch. I never had a stronger impression. Then to think of those books compact of wisdom, humour, and the richest humanity, and of her as the creator of the immortal *Maggie,* in short, what a horrible disillusion! Johnnie seems to have done his level best to wash out whatever little colour the letters may have had by the unfortunate form in which he has seen fit to print them. (40–41)

The image by which she characterizes Eliot here is singularly repulsive. What is it about Eliot that gives James the impression of a fungus, of something damp to the touch? If we follow the logic of the imagery, the morbid growth, the mildew and fungus all share the quality of a repugnant parasitic dependence. Certainly James's words, "I never had a stronger impression," suggest some very affective root has been tapped, and what follows next is a radical exposure:

On the subject of her marriage it is of course for an outsider criminal to say anything, but what a shock for her to say she felt as if her life were renewed and for her to express her sense of complacency in the vestry and church! What a betrayal of the much mentioned "perfect love" of the past!

This sequence of association, from Eliot as a damp fungus to her remarriage, suggests that what repulses James is Eliot's indulgence of the sexual body, an indulgence that remarriage signifies and reveals. Indeed, James repeatedly censures second marriages both as an infidelity, a betrayal of an imagined "perfect love"[5] and as an unworthy craving for sensation.

January 23, 1891: How surprised and shocked I am to hear that Ellie Emmet, whose heart, I had been led to suppose, was seared by sorrow, is contemplating marriage again. . . . 'Twould seem to the inexperienced that one happy "go" at marriage would have given the full measure of connubial bliss, and all the chords of maternity have vibrated under the manipulation of six progeny, but man lives not to assimilate knowledge of the eternal essence of things, and only craves a renewal of sensation. (172)

As with her response to Eliot's remarriage, James here criticizes remarriage as a "renewal," criticizes these women for their indulgence of the body against which she was engaged in an ongoing war.[6]

If the body as enemy is a pervasive trope of the *Diary*, indulging it makes remarriage a virtually "criminal" transgression, as the following passage intimates:

The women seem to do here constantly what so rarely happens at home, marry again. 'Tis always a surprise, not that I have any foolish young inflexibility about it, for I am only too glad to see creatures grasp at anything, outside murder, theft or intoxication, from which they fancy they may extract happiness, but it reveals such a simple organization to be perpetually ready to renew experience in so confiding a manner. (102)

This sardonic juxtaposition or remarriage with murder, theft and intoxication, is followed by a startling synecdoche in which the moral integrity of the woman who remarries is analogized to the female flesh having been torn, with its connotations of sexual violation:

As they do it [remarry] within a year or two the moral flesh must be as healthy as that pink substance of which they are physically compact, the torn fibres healing themselves by first intention, evidently. The subjective experience being what survives from any relation, you would suppose that the wife part of you had been sufficiently developed in one experiment, at any rate that you would like to contemplate the situation a bit from the bereft point of view—but, no, they are ready to plunge *into love again* at a moment's notice—as if 'twere quantity, not quality, of emotion that counted. (103)

The trope of the daughter as a potentially torn fibre occurs again in her retelling of a familiar narrative paradigm, a daughter who dies from grief at her father's remarriage, "a little maid" who "passed with peaceful joy from amidst the vain shadows. Will there be no stirrings of remorse in her father's bosom for the brutalities which rent that delicate fibre?" (195–96). James's representation of the daughter as a delicate fibre torn by the father's brutalities recreates a perverse Gothic family romance in which the consequence of the renewal of paternal desire is imagined as a violation of the daughter.

Given this context of the inimical, vulnerable, or criminal body, it is provocative to find that when James represents her own parents' marriage as ideal, she frames it by an allusion to her own body's vulnerability. Having just remarked on her "devilish headache," she alludes to the danger of microbes from the influenza epidemic invading her chamber. But immediately James transmutes the body into discourse, the invasive materiality of illness to "ghost microbes"—old letters from her parents which have a profound effect upon her, as she writes, "one of the most intense, exquisite and profoundly interesting experiences I ever had" (78). Although her metaphor "ghost microbes" implies an infection by the past, the text quickly transforms this representation of the past as illness to the past as a fountain of perpetual nurturance:

It seems now incredible to me that I should have drunk, as a matter of course, at that ever springing fountain of responsive love and bathed all unconscious in that flood of human tenderness. The letters are made of the daily events of their pure simple lives, with souls unruffled by the ways of men, like special creatures, spiritualized and remote from coarser clay. Father ringing the changes upon Mother's perfections . . . And Mother's words breathing her extraordinary selfless devotion as if she simply embodied the unconscious essence of wife and motherhood. What a beautiful picture do they make for the thoughts of their children to dwell upon! How the emotions of those two dreadful years, when I was wrenching myself away from them, surge thro' me. (79)

While her parents are represented as "remote from coarser clay," the physicality of the image of her mother "breathing" selfless devotion is striking, especially if one recalls that the very dress of women in mid-19th century bound their respiration unnaturally. Certainly James seemed stifled in relation to her mother's image, for aside from the above passage, there is oddly no anecdotal recall of her mother in the *Diary*. While her father and brothers are frequently remembered in writing, her mother remains an absence, the maternal voice and figure virtually effaced from representation. In its place are substitute women, including herself, women who by virtue of their bodies can in no way approach the disembodied mother as ideal.

If her mother's voice is silent in the *Diary*, her father's is not. While in the above passage James recollects her father's voice ringing the changes on maternal perfection, one of the last entries is a more disquieting memory of her father's voice, this time ringing the changes on her own character, in a manner that perhaps accounts for her earlier impulse to smash the paternal pate.

After remarking on the quality of her moral judgments and sharp wit, she recalls the disapproving

ring of Father's voice, as he anathematized some shortcomings of mine in Newport one day: 'Oh, Alice, how hard you are!' and I can remember how penetrated I was, not for the first time, but often, with the truth of it, and saw the repulsion his nature with its ripe kernel of human benignancy felt—alas! through all these years, that hard core confronts me still. (192)

Since this "hard core" (the imaginary antithesis of the wandering womb that hysteria signifies) contains precisely those qualities that are her strengths, she is paradoxically confronted with an image of self that negates her; her very core identity becomes a wound induced by internal-ization of the condemnatory paternal voice. Close upon this recollection of paternal judgment is another memory which further elucidates her father's place in her internal script: a joke, in which Emerson, a friend of her father's, asks another friend about her:

> "And what sort of a girl is Alice".... "She has a highly moral nature".... "How in the world does her father get on with her?" (193)

The punch-line, so to speak, is the difference between her and her father, a moral difference in her favor that she denies by literally erasing herself as signifier in the next sentence: "But who shall relate that long alliance, made on one side of all tender affection, solicitous sympathy and pater-nal indulgence!"

Finally, it is a disturbing conflict about self-erasure in the name of the Father that lurks in the gaps of James's prose—a self-erasure which would also erase the body while paradoxically inducing a rage that could only be articulated through the body.[7] To undo that erasure, she makes herself a writing subject; she writes the *Diary* but writes herself out of it as its primary object. Only as the *Diary* closes on her last year, assuming what she called "a certain mortuary flavor," does she write about herself with more sensitive self-reflexivity. "I would there were more bursts of enthusiasm, less of the carping tone through this, but I fear it comes by nature" (218). References to the body she could no longer ignore increase, while at the same time she continues to disclaim its significance:

> If the aim of life is the accretion of fat, the consumption of food unattended by digestive disorganization, and a succession of plea-surable sensations, there is no doubt that I am a failure, for as an animal form my insatiable vanity must allow that my existence

doesn't justify itself, but every fibre protests against being taken simply as a sick carcass . . . for what power has dissolving flesh and aching bones to undermine a satisfaction made of imperishable things. (183)

Even as she approached the end and allowed herself to be the object of her writing, she distanced her body by assuming the stance of pure percipient of its outline. "Of what matter can it be whether pain or pleasure has shaped and stamped the pulp within, as one is absorbed in the supreme interest of watching the outline and the tracery as the lines broaden for eternity" (232). In spite of this self-representation as passive observer, the lines that broadened were the lines she herself penned in the *Diary*, her manipulation of the materiality of language giving her the only outline she still historically retains—as writer of the *Diary*. Not surprisingly then, James continued to make manuscript corrections to the last, as if more than her life depended upon her words, and as Katherine Loring wrote, "although she was very weak and it tired her much to dictate, she could not get her head quiet until she had it written: then she was relieved" (232–33). While one must be very cautious in attributing psychological causality to physical events, cautious, that is to say, about privileging the Imaginary as source of the Real, especially given the very real illness which Alice James and so many 19th-century women suffered, it remains an uncanny piece of James's history that she ultimately succumbed to breast cancer, a final physical symptom that exceeded the limits of the Symbolic in a death she welcomed with relief.

If the voice of Alice James was inhibited by rage, the voice of Florence Nightingale who like James was also bedridden for much of her life seems to have been projected into her time by outrage. Like James, Nightingale was invalided for most of her life, but unlike James her illness did not prevent her from exerting an influential public voice. The youngest of two daughters, Nightingale grew up in a divided family constellation, in which she was allied with her father, who had himself rigorously educated her, against the more conventional social expectations of her sister and mother. This family friction took its toll: in her autobiographical writings she describes the dreamlike trances and religious hallucinations of her childhood, her sense that "she was a monster," and the voices she heard at traumatic moments in her adolescence calling her to a special destiny (Showalter, 62).[8] Defying her mother's strong censure for not marrying, Nightingale chose nursing as a vocation. Yet after her success in the Crimean War, she returned to London with a host of symptoms—including heart palpitations and an extreme nausea when presented with food—and at the height of her reputation, she retired to her bedchamber for almost half a century. That her illness was a hysterical one is dramatically rendered by the fact that after about forty years of invalidism, Nightingale, shortly after her mother's death, apparently recovered. Even invalided, she was one of the most influential women in Europe, writing prolifically on issues of public health care and constituting nursing as a respectable profession for middle-class women.

The figure of the nurse has dominated histories of hysterics, from Anna O.'s nursing of her father, which was followed by her own need to be nursed, now inscribed as a contemporary myth of the origins of psychoanalysis, to Freud's remembered relation to his nurse constructed as an origin of his own hysterical proclivities.[9] That Nightingale ultimately chose nursing as her field—and literal battlefield—of action, concerned as it is with mastery of the vulnerable body, but through the pain of the *other,* seems certainly overdetermined. Certainly one should note that Nightingale thought of herself not as a practicing nurse but as an administrator, as fabricator of the nursing-system, a role more attached to the masculine executive functions than the feminine nurturing ones. Yet in constructing the figure of the modern nurse and becoming that figure for her time, as well as a life-long patient, Nightingale acted out in her own bifurcated life a split identification with a powerful maternal imago, the nurse, and its impotent antithesis, the nursed dependent child, a split that as with Alice James, also problematized Nightingale's writing voice.

Writing is not what we associate with Nightingale, yet she was always writing, and wrote to excess. Among her papers is the fragmentary prose piece *Cassandra* which began as an autobiographical novel but which she seemed unable to complete as a fiction; eventually, after many revisions, it metamorphosed into a long and fractured essay, part of which has been published by the Feminist Press.[10] I am not surprised that the polemical essay was more congenial to Nightingale than fiction. Clearly the 19th-century fictional paradigm of a woman's life, ending with a marriage in which the heroine finds her pleasure as object of desire, went against Nightingale's fierce but ambivalent embrace of the subject position. Nor surprisingly, in the early fictional version of *Cassandra*, her heroine, unable to live out her desire, dies, a scene Nightingale retained at the conclusion of the essay as well, and one which was not uncommon to the 19th-century heroine's text.

But there were other reasons for Nightingale's dis-ease with fiction, a distrust *Cassandra* frequently suggests, perhaps most markedly in her reiterated disparagement of fantasy, which she represents as a dangerously seductive substitute for action; "We fast mentally, scourge ourselves morally, use the intellectual hair shirt, in order to subdue the perpetual day-dreaming, which is so dangerous!" (27). Why was it so dangerous? While there are references in the essay to "the evils of dreaming" that allude to sexual fantasizing, more importantly, dreaming requires a submission to interiority, a passive yielding to the monstrous Other, or to those other voices in the psyche to which Nightingale could not submit. Fiction requires the ability to let go of the first person singular, to identify with the voices of the Other in a multiple circulation of agents and objects, and this Nightingale seemed unable to do. In the essay, however, a form which foregrounds the subject's voice, Nightingale could retain more control, could circumscribe the space of fantasy in the unconscious, and thus more readily vent her outrage at her object: the psycho-social conditions that predisposed women to invalidism, conditions to which she was subject and about which she wrote with the clarity of a great passion.

Even as argument, however, *Cassandra* bears all the marks of a symptomatic discourse, digressive, fragmentary, inconsistent in its subject position, characteristics which caused J. S. Mill to describe it as a "cri du coeur" even though it had been very much "written." In this context Nightingale's process of revision of the early manuscript novel is revealing. In its first version *Cassandra*, although framed as a third person narrative, is primarily told in the first person voice of its tragic heroine Nofriani, a Venetian princess who complains of her situation as a woman to her brother Fariseo in a sequence of long dramatic dialogues with little action. When at the end she dies, her brother recounts her final words: "Free, free, oh! divine Freedom, art thou come at last? Welcome, beautiful Death!" In the essay version, these words are attributed to some anonymous dying woman, and the quotation marks of Nofriani's earlier dialogue are removed thus transforming a private voice into a third person public voice of argument.[11] In an intermediate stage, however, Nightingale excised the specifically feminine narrative voice altogether; the voice vacillates between a masculine first person narrator, Fariseo, the brother who tells his sister's story, and an anonymous third person narrator. Ultimately both Nofriani and Fariseo are absorbed into the narrative voice of the published essay, but here too, in its final version, the voice inconsistently shifted between a defeminized, disembodied omniscient third person, and a first person plural "we" which identifies with a generalized female plight.

Not surprisingly, *Cassandra* almost obsessively articulates the danger of passivity, and is perhaps most vividly represented through the trope of the voice in Nightingale's description of being "read aloud to," which she calls "the most miserable exercise of the human intellect."

It is like lying on one's back, with one's hands tied and having liquid poured down one's throat. Worse than that, because suffocation would immediately ensue and put a stop to this operation. But no suffocation would stop the other. (34)

The violence of the metaphor in which listening to the voice of the other is the equivalent of being force-fed and its oral site points to a familiar infantile fantasy of an intrusive maternal body, and one recalls Nightingale's symptomatic nausea, the most primal rejection of that intrusion.[12] Just as psychoanalysis describes the oral stage of infantile development as a prototype of a later femininity in which orality is the privileged mode of conflict, so Nightingale's text represents the feminine position of listening rather than speaking as an oral danger provoking her rage. Being compelled to listen to the voice of the other becomes the ultimate threat to the self.

The issue of the maternal voice is a familiar one to contemporary critical discourse,[13] one of its more uncanny features being its transgression of the boundaries of inside and outside. As Kaja Silverman writes,

Since the voice is capable of being internalized at the same time as it is externalized it can spill over from subject to object and object to subject, violating bodily limits. (80)

It is this spilling over, this violation of not only her bodily limits but her psychological integrity that makes the voice of the other so menacing for

Nightingale, and that prompts her to propose an antithetical image of desire: the daughter's passionate desire to talk. While mothers taught their daughters that women were not passionate, Nightingale writes, on the contrary, passion swells their imaginations. But given the straitjacket of femininity, it is displaced into a passion for sympathetic conversation. Thus Nightingale represents the fantasy of a vocal interchange with an imaginary male double—recall Alice James's "Inconnu"—as the fulfillment of the daughter's desire:

> That, with the phantom companion of their fancy, they talk (not love, they are too innocent, too pure, too full of genius and imagination for that, but) they talk, in fancy, of that which interests them most; they seek a companion for their every thought; the companion they find not in reality they seek in fancy, or if not that, if not absorbed in endless conversations, they see themselves engaged with him in stirring events. (26)

Romantic fiction, Nightingale suggests, appeals to women for the same reason: it encourages a fantasy of liberation through conversation with a sympathetic male other.

> What are novels? What is the secret charm of every romance that ever was written? The first thing . . . is to place the persons together in circumstances which naturally call out the high feelings and thoughts of the character, which afford food for sympathy between them on these points—romantic events they are called. The second is that the heroine has generally no family ties *(almost invariably no mother)* or, if she has, these do not interfere with her entire independence. (28, italics mine)

Note the barely disguised wish to eliminate the mother as a figure of constraint, which most 19th-century novels by women did. Just as in this passage, the mother is displaced by the imaginary counterpart with whom she can share "food for sympathy" rather than be force-fed, so in her own life Nightingale displaced her mother with actual counterparts, significant figures upon whom she depended for sympathy and whom she ruled as narcissistic extensions of her will and desire. When ultimately the exigencies of life caused an intimate to leave her, she responded with rage and symptoms.

It seems prophetic that in *Cassandra*—written in 1852, before she took to her own bed—Nightingale recognized that invalidism was a perverse form of aggressivity which corrupts not only the individual life, but impoverishes the symbolic order as well. In one of her formidable insights into the paralysis induced by rage she writes: "The great reformers of the world turn into the great misanthropists, if circumstances . . . do not permit them to act. *Christ, if he had been a woman, might have been nothing but a great complainer*" (53, italics mine). The paradox is rich: If Christ had been a woman, he would only have complained rather than acted. But also, if Christ had been a woman, his discourse would have been impotent; his audience would have heard and dismissed his message as only a complaint. Christ would have been Cassandra, the enraged prophet-daughter who speaks but is destined not to be heard, whose voice is stripped of any claim to authority. Like a number of women in conflict with patriarchal femininity, like Alice James hearing her father's voice, her brother's voice, writing to her male Inconnu, Nightingale establishes the discursive potency of the male voice, and finds her imaginary counterpart, her ego ideal, in Christ, the prophet-son, who is empowered to speak as a woman never is.

Thus it is especially telling (and prophetic, for Nightingale's "cri du coeur" was not heard until recently) that Nightingale chose Cassandra as her voice (she referred to herself as "poor Cassandra" in her letters and notes, the mad prophet-daughter). More resonantly, Nightingale's own proper family name—a name her father assumed in order to claim an inheritance—alludes to a myth—the rape of Philomela—in which a woman's complaint is silenced by cutting out her tongue and changing her into a nightingale. Did Nightingale hear herself as Philomela as well as Cassandra? The excision of the woman's tongue is meant to destroy the female voice as logos, as meaning.[14] The voice of the woman in patriarchal discourse must remain the voice of the nightingale, a vocal image of pleasure rather than knowledge, sound without meaning, without pain.

But if the myth of the nightingale conventionally represents silence as the form as well as consequence of women's suffering, through the first person plural Nightingale's Cassandra gives suffering a communal voice and makes pain a spur to social action:

Give us back our suffering, we cry to heaven in our hearts—suffering rather than indifferentism, for out of nothing comes nothing. But out of suffering may come the cure. Better have pain than paralysis! (29)

Although Nightingale herself refused the label feminist, in *Cassandra* her outrage turned the complaint to political account, enabling an identification with women that was ultimately empowering.

NOTES

1. For psychoanalytic discussions of rage, see especially Klein, "Early Stages of the Oedipus Conflict" (1928), "A Contribution to the Psychogenesis of Manic Depressive States" (1935); Freud, "The Ego and the Id" (1923), *SE* XIX; and Lacan, "On Aggressivity" in *Ecrits* (1977).

2. It is well documented that both Henry and William suffered from physical ailments and effects no less mysterious and hysterical than Alice's. See especially Jean Strouse, *Alice James* (New York: Houghton Mifflin, 1980).

3. It is fascinating to note that in the months after her mother's death, Alice James was suddenly no invalid, but rather, herself nursed her demanding and depressed father until he starved himself to death less than a year after his wife's death.

4. In that passage, she discusses Binet's idea of hysterical "contractions of the field of consciousness," instances of "absences" of consciousness common to hysteria which allow the ego to disavow unacceptable impulses.

5. Writing of a suffering English lady who was the first married to a handsome cavalry officer by whom she had one daughter, and who then married, after his death, a stodgy curate by whom she had nine children, Alice approvingly notes that she was berated by her daughter for her second marriage, and by her sister for having so many children and setting a bad example (146–47, Oct. 12, 1890); also, see the story of the daughter dying because of father's remarriage, a story which Henry James used as subject of "The Marriages" (105, April 22, 1981).

6. In this way one can understand why her criticism of Eliot's remarriage is immediately followed by her unforgiving censure of Eliot's articulation of her pain:

What an abject coward she seems to have been about physical pain, as if it weren't degrading enough to have headaches, without jotting them down in a row to stare at one for all time, thereby defeating the beneficent law which provides that physical pain is forgotten. If she related her diseases and her "depressions" and told for the good of others what armour she had forged against them, it would be conceivable, but they seem simply cherished as the vehicle for a moan. (40–42)

7. Paradoxically, she welcomes her illness as giving her substance; when she finally discovers that she has a tumor, she is elated to be able to name her problem as real.

Ever since I have been ill, I have longed and longed for some palpable disease, . . . but I was always driven back to stagger alone under the monstrous mass of subjective sensations which that sympathetic being "the medical man" had no higher inspiration than to assure me I was personally responsible for. (207)

8. See the informative introduction to *Cassandra* by Myra Stark (New York: Feminist Press, 1979); also, Donald R. Allen, "Florence Nightingale: Toward a Psychohistorical Interpretation" in *Florence Nightingale: Saint, Reformer or Rebel?* edited by Raymond G. Herbert (Malabar, FL: Robert E. Krieger Publishing Co., 1981); Showalter, *The Female Malady,* op.cit.; Mary Poovey, *Uneven Developments* (Chicago: University of Chicago Press, 1988).

9. See Jim Swan, "*Mater* and Nannie" for a full discussion of this complex maternal imaginary in Freud.

10. I first learned of the nature of this document in conversation with Elaine Showalter, who described *Cassandra* as a very long digressive work, very much in the character of a hysterical prose piece. Subsequently, Katherine Snyder, who is writing a book on Nightingale, generously provided me with a copy of the original manuscript. I am greatly indebted to her transcription of Nightingale's first version of *Cassandra,* and her insightful reading of manuscript changes in an unpublished paper, "Self-Revision, Self-Construction: The Manuscript of 'Cassandra.'

11. Snyder notes such other alterations as Nightingale's excision of details that were autobiographical or too conventionally romantic, and her shortening of the heroine's fantasies.

12. Prophetically, the figure of being forced-fed became a violent reality for a host of militant suffragettes decades later. Also, it was her father who read aloud to her, not her mother.

13. For Julia Kristeva the voice is a pleasurable maternal enclosure, and the primordial listening experience a prototype for subsequent auditory pleasures. Other theorists insist on the negative dimension of the voice as an experience of maternal entrapment. For Lacan the voice is a fundamental object of desire—one of the first to be distinguished from the subject's own self and to be introjected. See Kaja Silverman, 84–85.

14. Psychoanalytically speaking, cutting out the tongue is a castration, in particular, an excision of the power of language. Its relation to the nightingale myth was reinforced for me recently when Professor Lia Lerner, of the Department of Spanish and Comparative Literature at Fordham University, called my attention to one of Boccaccio's stories in which a woman is holding a nightingale which suddenly is transformed into a penis. Thus Silverman writes that the "female voice provides the acoustic equivalent of an ejaculation," *The Acoustic Mirror*, 68.

WORKS CITED

Bronte, Charlotte. *Jane Eyre*. New York: New American Library, 1960.

Freud, Sigmund. *Standard Edition of the Complete Psychological Work (SE)*. Ed. James Strachey. London: Hogarth Press, 1961.

———. "Studies in Hysteria" (1895), II, 19–135.

———. "Hysterical Phantasies and their Relation to Bisexuality" (1908), IX 157–66.

———. "The Ego and the Id" (1923), XIX, 3–63.

———. Female Sexuality" (1931) XXI, 223–43.

James, Alice. *Diary*. Hammondsport, Middlesex: Penguin, 1982.

Klein, Melanie. "Early Stages of the Oedipus Conflict" (1928), "A Contribution to the Psychogenesis of Manic Depressive States" (1935), in *Selected Papers*, ed. Juliet Mitchell. Hammondsworth, Middlesex, England: Penguin, 1986.

Krohn, Alan. *Hysteria: The Elusive Neurosis*. New York: International Universities Press, 1978.

Lacan, Jacques. *Ecrits: A Selection*. Trans. A. Sheridan. New York: Norton, 1977.

Nightingale, Florence. *Cassandra*. New York: Feminist Press, 1979.

Showalter, Elaine. *The Female Malady: Women, Madness, and English Culture, 1830–1980*. New York: Pantheon, 1985.

Silverman, Kaja. *The Acoustic Mirror*. Bloomington: Indiana University Press, 1988.

Strouse, Jean. *Alice James*. New York: Houghton Mifflin, 1980.

Swan, Jim. "*Mater* and Nannie: Freud's Two Mothers and the Discovery of the Oedipus Complex." *American Imago* 31 (1974): 1–64.

CHAPTER 8

"All Anger and Understanding"

Kureishi, Culture, and Contemporary Constructions of Rage

TERRY L. ALLISON and RENÉE R. CURRY

Hanif Kureishi commits himself to the representation of rage as vital narrative force when depicting oppression in film and in literature. Since Kureishi works both in film and in literature and presents rage as a multi-issue, multicultural concern, he provides an exemplary representation of the current artistic engagement with rage. Kureishi describes the particular rage about belonging that a man raised in England by an English mother and a Pakistani father experiences upon his return from a trip to India:

> I read in the paper that a Pakistani family in the East End had been fire-bombed. A child was killed. This, of course, happens frequently. It is the pig's head through the window, the spit in the face, the children with the initials of racist organizations tattooed into their skin with razor blades, as well as the more polite forms of hatred.
> I was in a rage. (*London Kills Me*, 34)

However, the artistic predicament of displaying rage on a screen or on a page proves difficult and multifaceted because rage, by definition, is an unchecked intensity of anger, and because the behaviors often described as rage more accurately display the manifestations of a rage.

Rage, the emotion, serves as catalyst to the volatile or violent actions we often (mistakenly) call rage. Any attempt to represent rage in forms of art becomes an attempt at containing, understanding and formalizing an emotion that eludes shape and control. Nevertheless, a long history of representing rage exists in the literary and performing arts. This chapter does not attempt to gather all research about fictional representations of rage, but rather to focus on late-twentieth-century fictional texts. By surveying briefly other current fictional texts on rage, we will situate Kureishi among a coalition of filmmakers and writers for whom the issue of rage, its structural challenges, and its cultural significance constitutes a catalyst for artistic endeavor.

Although this chapter will address methodically all three of these aspects of rage in fictional texts, we must first address the particular problematic associated with asserting the cultural significance of any work of art. In accounting for the fact that filmmakers and literary artists feel compelled to record the experience of rage in fictional terms, regardless of its structural challenges, viewers and readers automatically leap to the assumption of a social and cultural meaning that lurks as backdrop to these creations. However, critics in cultural studies range in their assessment regarding the cultural "meaning" of any given artwork. Joseph Grixti asserts that because fictions constitute social and cultural productions, "they form part of the symbolic structures which we use to make sense of and ascribe meaning to our existence" (xii). Mukerji and Schudson warn against any such "simply stated relationships" between artistic products and their cultural context particularly because we live in "highly complex, differentiated, plural societies" that undermine any attempt to make direct correspondences between products and their producing societies (30). While avoiding a simply stated relationship, we interrogate the particular cultural significance of Kureishi's representations of rage. Furthermore, we argue that he participates in a powerful and rapidly forming coalition of rage production aimed at threatening and prophesying the possibility of increasing manifestations of rage in the world beyond the screen and the page.

Before discussing Kureishi's work, we want to outline both the critical tradition and to name the coalition participants who help elucidate Kureishi's relationship to rage representation and to a particular broader culture. Like most screenwriters, Kureishi had to find a film director willing to deliver his work to the screen. Kureishi chose Stephen Frears as his collaborator, and the union proved strategic, *simpatico,* and profitable for both artists. Similar in political and artistic vision, the two men produced the profound cultural mosaics, *My Beautiful Laundrette* and *Sammy and Rosie Get Laid.* These films launched Frears's directorial career and brought international fame, via an American Academy Award nomination for best screenplay *(My Beautiful Laundrette)*, as a writer to Kureishi.

Before the two worked together, Frears had made thirty-plus films for British television and two commercially unsuccessful genre films, *Gumshoe* (1971) and *The Hit* (1984) (Giannetti and Eyman, 454–54). *My Beautiful Laundrette*, Kureishi's first screenplay, afforded Frears an opportunity to shift away from formulaic cinematic constructions and to move toward a livelier fusion of relationship issues with political contexts. Their compatibility stems from a mutual sense that film image and written image, wedded by cinematic technology, can form a powerful union. Frears's films since his collaboration with Kureishi still maintain this linkage with the written image in that he predominantly adapts novels to the screen. Although successful, Frears's subsequent work, financed by the American film industry, "lacks the liveliness of Frears' collaborations with Kureishi" (Giannetti and Eyman, 454). Likewise, Kureishi's one solo foray into film directing *London Kills Me* (1992) lacks the technical prowess and cinematic depth of both Kureishi/Frears collaborations.

Besides taking part in a two-person collaboration, Kureishi and Frears also take part in a peculiar grouping of directors bent on delivering rage to the contemporary film screen. Our rendering of this group does not propose to be interpretive, but rather to be suggestive of a likeness in creative production and impetus.

At first glance, the following directors, working in the last two decades, and their products, seem unlikely compatriots; however, they share an interest both in prophesying about rage as well as in managing strategies for depicting the unrepresentable emotion. This coalition includes, but is not limited to, Marleen Gorris (*A Question of Silence*, 1983), Spike Lee (*Do the Right Thing*, 1989), Bill Bixby (*The Death of the Incredible Hulk*, 1990), Ridley Scott (*Thelma and Louise*, 1991), Julie Dash (*Daughters of the Dust*, 1991), Alison Maclean (*Crush*, 1992), and Joel Schumacher (*Falling Down*, 1993). The filmmakers and their films range in type from mass media popular culture to Hollywood blockbuster to independent arthouse film to foreign fare. These coalition members may never have spoken to one another; however, their films speak many tongues about the same issue: rage, its structural challenges, and its cultural significance.

Although the made-for-television movie, *The Death of the Incredible Hulk,* succeeds Gorris's and Lee's landmark films, the Marvel comic strip and the long-running television series both serve as predecessors to big screen rage. The Incredible Hulk, a large green muscle-bound man who alternately growls and roars, serves as the original manifestation of onscreen rage. Bill Bixby's *The Death of the Incredible Hulk* clarifies the exact relationship between rage and the Hulk. In a rare moment of revelation, David Banner, former Princeton and Harvard scientist, speaks about his transformations into the Incredible Hulk:

> I have a mutation near the rage center of my brain. And during moments of anger or fear, it secretes a hormone, and I become a mutant thing, a beast, until the rage ends. It's not human.

In this discourse, rage becomes an inhuman emotion. Yet the manifestation of rage on the screen, although primitive, is clearly human. The visual construction of rage on the screen thereby belies the narrative discourse associated with it. In this contradiction, we read a particular cultural inability to embrace feelings of rage as human, as normal.

The most interesting aspect of the rage constructed in the Incredible Hulk is the human obsession with viewing rage as a uniquely personal problem, and as a physical transformation of the self, rather than as a societal response to injustices against the self-system. In the Hulk, rage becomes an unnatural emotion. As Michael Lewis reminds us, enforcement of rage as unnatural and inappropriate induces shame and actually fuels the creation of rage:

> Anger is a simple bodily response, whereas rage is a process. This process involves moving from shame to rage, which leads to more shame, which leads to more rage. ("The Development of Anger and Rage," 159)

Bill Bixby's construction of rage as a primitive human form codifies a particular cultural message about rage: rage is monstrous, unjustifiable, and wrong. In Bixby's version, rage prophesies death and hideous transformation to the self.

Post-Hulk filmmakers working on rage redefine rage along Lewis's lines as a "natural emotion" (148) and thereby reassert its place as that emotion aimed at protecting the self from shameful injustices. In Dutch filmmaker Marleen Gorris's *A Question of Silence,* three ordinary women kill a male shopkeeper in reaction to a lifetime of shame induced by daily doses of gender-based injustice. Gorris constructs rage's unrepresentability by dividing the manifestation scenes into a tension-building, three-part flashback that utilizes a stalking camera and that addresses contemporary theoretical cinema issues, such as Laura Mulvey's theory of the gaze. The shopkeeper's last words, "Now look here ladies," ironically signal the women to make eye contact with each other and to then look upon him as a patriarchal representative. This film threatens the symbols of patriarchal order and prophesies to a culture the power of ordinary women with directed gazes to manifest their rage.

In *Do the Right Thing,* Spike Lee frames African-Americans' rage against the continuous disrespect white people demonstrate toward African-American discourse and accomplishment. Lee's signifying techniques used to depict rage, canted shots and extreme facial close-ups, enable him to produce a tilted, off-center, jarring onscreen world, a world which viewers must literally and figuratively turn their heads to view. These techniques allow him to layer a series of head-turning, escalating manifestations of rage. Lee prophesies a powerful systemic destruction as possibly the only means of maintaining self-respect even if it results in self-destruction.

In *Thelma and Louise,* director Ridley Scott anticipates Lani Guinier's premise that people resort to unsystematic and destabilizing means of attaining justice when they foresee no just future (5–7). This film's rage emerges from women's inability to fathom a just future for themselves. Louise tells Thelma's rapist: "In the future, when a woman is crying like that, she isn't having any fun," to which the perpetrator Harlan replies, "I should've fucked her." Louise, recognizing in Harlan's words evidence of an ongoing unjust future, kills him. Scott constructs this rage through framing devices that detach the gun, symbol of rage manifestations, from Louise's hand and devices that separate the frames housed by Louise and Harlan. They exist in different worlds. The cultural significance of this film lies in its death prophesy to those who threaten a safe future. In "Poem About My Rights," June Jordan further reiterates the cultural threat posed by women who have been raped:

and I can't tell you who the hell set things up like this
but I can tell you that from now on my resistance
my simple and daily and nightly self-determination
may very well cost you your life (104)

Rape causes another filmmaker to discern methods for displaying rage
on the screen. In *Daughters of the Dust,* Julie Dash situates turn-of-the-
century African-Americans fighting among themselves about the move
North and its particular meaning to African-American women. To construct this rage, Dash juxtaposes Eula's volatile discourse against the
rapid and gyrating movements of Eula's pregnant body. The particular
cultural significance of this depiction once again rests in the revelation
of a rage discourse based on women's relationship to rape. Eula rages:

If you're so ashamed of Yellow Mary 'cause she got ruined. . . .
Well, what do you say about me? Am I ruined too? . . . As far as
this place is concerned, we never enjoyed our womanhood. . . .
Deep inside, we believed that they ruined our mothers, and their
mothers before them. And we live our lives always expecting the
worst because we feel we don't deserve any better.

Here Eula speaks the unspeakable and thereby warns of a culture of
women who have been made to feel ashamed.

Alison Maclean's *Crush* also portrays a rage that bursts from within a
group of seemingly homogeneous people. This film, and its rage, breaks
down the myth of white woman's sisterhood for the purpose of demon-
strating that some of the rage against patriarchy stems from the way
women have been socialized to treat each other. Maclean's camera
studiously frames women's facial agony—the face of rage. She locks this
face in the frame at the exact moment before its manifestation which
results in one woman killing another. The cultural significance of this
film resides in its dark humor. The film laughs at the myth of women's
nurturing capabilities and allows women to "see" each other as complex
characters capable of multiple rages.

Joel Schumacher's *Falling Down* divorces rage from the disenfranchised, yet it continues the thematic of freedom and injustice. In this
film, a defense engineer, William Foster, turns his white rage onto the

surrounding community. Schumacher frames his seething rage in seven instances, each instance reflecting and reversing the celebrated rages of disenfranchised and reactionary groups: Koreans, Latinos, teenagers, women, homosexuals, the homeless, supremacists, and the elderly. Schumacher represents rage mostly through its manifestations and through third-person narrative accounts of Foster's problems. When Foster is finally arrested and says, "I'm the bad guy? How'd that happen? I protect America," the cultural significance of the film becomes clear. The film prophesies the advent of a white male rage that builds as defense against being everybody's bad guy. Whereas the other films concentrate on a singular and particular outburst, white male rage threatens everyone in its bent on preserving the ultimate good-guy image.

The constructions employed by filmmakers to represent an uncontainable emotion within a clearly defined frame include devices that range from special effects to narrative expressions. These devices include transformation of bodily form *(Hulk)*, tension-building scene division *(Question, Falling)*, stalking camera *(Question)*, redefined "gaze" *(Question)*, canted shots *(Right Thing)*, manifestation layering *(Right Thing)*, framing the face of rage *(Right Thing, Crush)*, fragmented frames *(Thelma and Louise)*, and image/discourse juxtaposition *(Daughters)*. In each case the filmmakers design a relationship between rage as subject matter and rage as filmic representation to varying degrees of success. The difficulty always stems from film's overwhelming ability to depict action over emotion, to depict manifestations rather than the precipatory rage.

Hanif Kureishi's and Stephen Frears's *Sammy and Rosie Get Laid* (1987) provides an important successful example of rage representation in cinema. This film, a dark comedy set in contemporary East London, situates a progressive married couple, Sammy and Rosie, against a backdrop of riotous events both literal and figurative. The visit of Sammy's father, a heartless political fugitive from an unnamed Asian country, provides opportunities for Sammy and Rosie to confront the race, class, and gender-based rage bubbling within their relationship as well as the rage stemming from their political values.

Kureishi and Frears employ a wealth of cinematic practices aimed at allowing the rage in *Sammy and Rosie Get Laid* to emerge from between various apparati attempting to contain it. This team seems particularly adept at synthesizing strategies to provide a pervasive sense of rage throughout their film narratives.

In the making of this film, Kureishi and Frears talked "frequently about the shape of it, of pressing it experimentally all over to locate the bones beneath the rolling fat" (*London*, 184). This discussion of experimenting with the shape of films describes a concept that Inez Hedges names "frame-breaking" (xiv-xv). The cinematic practices employed by Kureishi and Frears aim to break the conceptual framing of rage by refusing to mummify it or to preserve it with form. They design space from which rage might emerge; they do not frame rage in some type of falsifying form. Their techniques for encouraging a reading of rage include juxtapositions of violent scenes, vacillations between dialogue and dramatization, and layering and refocusing of arguments.

At first viewing, the rage in *Sammy and Rosie* seems never to come to fruition. Upon studying the film, this curbing of fruition proves deliberate; the directors want to distinguish between rage and its manifestations. The camera often cuts away, refusing to dwell on any particular violent, outrageous, or horrifying event. Kureishi and Frears seem to safeguard the audience from a concentrated violence. But in fact, the numerous images and discussions of violence in the film linger in the mind, and the overall tone of the film emits an ever-threatening, ever-growing, never-to-be resolved sense of rage. Kureishi and Frears attack the scopophilia—the pleasure in looking—of the film in order to reconstruct what their audience looks at. In Laura Mulvey's terms, such reconstruction attacks formation of pleasure and allows these filmmakers "to make way for a total negation of the ease and plenitude of the narrative fiction film" (16). Kureishi and Frears deliberately avoid constructing the pleasure that stems from watching and understanding a well-formed, thorough, encapsulated, and contained scene of violence. Instead they juxtapose scenarios that both provoke and suggest rage, but that stop short of depicting it. To depict the results of provocations would move the scenes into the realm of manifestations. To dwell too long on any one attribute of the rage would be to familiarize it to the audience and to make it comfortable and patterned.

Sammy and Rosie opens with just such a narrative juxtaposition. One scene involves an armed police raid of a black woman's house. As they intrude into the home, fill her hallway and grab for her son, she hurls a pan of boiling fat at them. A young cop then shoots her. The film immediately cuts away to a young man outside the house, then to the ensuing chaos building toward a riot in the streets. Kureishi and Frears juxtapose the two scenes—that of the woman being shot and that of the chaos in the streets—to establish for the viewer both a cause and an effect. The juxtaposition of the two types of chaos provides a narrative friction. This rub ignites the rage. The camera does not hover long enough to familiarize either the shooting or the rioting; it simply catches the igniting rage and allows the chaos—in the shape of the street riots—to linger throughout the film.

Rage about gender relations further complicates *Sammy and Rosie.* In one scene Alice tells Rafi how bitterly she suffered when, so many years before, he had promised to elope with her but then jilted her. The camera does not simply report Alice's face nor simply her words because the framed face of rage and the language would have served as containers for the expressed anger. Kureishi and Frears have Alice take Rafi into the basement, the symbolic horror setting for killings and for revelations of hidden evils. In fact, a ghost from Rafi's past follows Rafi into the basement, a ghost that only Rafi and the viewers prove able to see. In this basement, the camera follows Alice as she dramatizes the situation of her waiting period. She shows Rafi the years of journal entries she made to him, the suitcase packed and ready to go, complete with rotting elopement garments, shoes and a perfume bottle. The camera, rather than simply displacing the rage onto the objects, creates a vacillation between dialogue and object so that the tension evokes a sense of rage. The audience reels between the sound of the bitter words that encapsulate feelings, the oppressive sensation of the basement, and the sight of the objects that represent the pain. A simultaneous pulling of the objects and a releasing of the words enacts an alternative marriage of anger, shame, and dashed hope which produces rage as its offspring.

Kureishi and Frears also practice the narrative strategy of layering situations to exacerbate the rage of a political argument. In the dinner scene among Rafi, Sammy, and Rosie, Rosie confronts Rafi about his government activities, about the torturing and murdering, about the hanging of mullahs upside down on skewers. The argument becomes increasingly loud and volatile. The camera flash-focuses on a table of young adults waving to the manager to tone down the argument. The camera refocuses on the manager attempting to speak with the arguing table, but his voice lacks the volume needed to penetrate the scene. The camera then turns to a group of women musicians who scuttle over to the table in an attempt to drown out the argument. The filmmakers do not design this particular construction by juxtaposition or cutaways or camera vacillations. As the entire mise-en-scène contains and recenters each of the attempts to control the argument and to curtail the rage, the composition becomes more layered and the three complex forces feeding the rage—the gentility represented by the complaining couple, the authority represented by the manager, and the competing, non-threatening, melodic arts as represented by the musicians—become part of the tensions that prove catalysts for the creation of rage.

Through the use of narrative juxtaposition, vacillations, and layering in the films, techniques used to a lesser degree in *My Beautiful Laundrette*, and to a less political degree in the recent *London Kills Me*, directed by Kureishi alone, this filmmaker welcomes a complex rage to his film. At the end of *Sammy and Rosie*, the title characters embrace each other in consolation for Sammy's father having killed himself. They hold onto a quivering bond, an English woman and a Pakistani-English man; they hold onto the image of a marriage that threatens to crumble. However, this image does not imply that the marriage bonds have been reformed, but rather that connections ever-bound by raging issues of gender, class, and race continue. These forces, as prophesied in the image of the crying Rosie and Sammy, remain knotted together by tears and bound by an inconsolable pain.

If we consider how *Sammy and Rosie* depicts contemporary England as corrupt, dangerous, racist, sexist, a place where a systemic injustice which manufactures rage prevails, we might easily expect that other contemporary creative artists in similar societies share Kureishi's interest in representing rage. Similar to how we have placed *Sammy and Rosie* within a contemporary cinematic coalition, we would like to place Kureishi's novel on rage, *The Buddha of Suburbia*, within a fairly broad historical literary practice of rage. We then will examine more narrowly how Kureishi's novel represents and narratively constructs rage, then how it participates in a contemporary transatlantic "queer" conversation about rage.

In the last one hundred years or so of English and American literature, rage, when written by male writers, sometimes earlier appeared as an uncivilized thing, to be avoided in order to safeguard genteel traditions of behavior or traditional manly values. In one of the few critical analyses of rage in fiction, Margaret Diane Stetz claims that in *A Passage to India*, E. M. Forster seeks to create a philosophical understanding of the imperative to stifle rage. To Forster, loss of control of emotion might lead to loss of control over art (300). According to Donald Pease's critique of *The Red Badge of Courage*, Stephen Crane creates a thematic opposition between rage and courage. To Crane, rage enacts the loss of what may never be possessed and thereby serves as a mere ineffectual substitute for the courage required to face loss (169). For Forster and for Crane, rage signifies only impotence and loss. Both of these writers, though potentially outsiders due to their literary expressions of homo-erotic desire, nevertheless create characters, who like *Falling Down*'s William Foster, belong to the powerful white male authority structure for whom loss of power or agency could provide a primary incentive to rage.

As a male, English writer, Kureishi clearly must come to terms with this traditional male treatment of rage. Since males in most societies are deemed to have agency, potency, power, it appears unjust to them when they do not possess these qualities. Neither Kureishi nor most of his central novelistic or cinematic characters can fully assume this male prerogative as they are "black," working class, and to varying extents queer. Where previously males who wrote were primarily those who possessed agency, contemporary writers such as Kureishi, marginalized, hybrid subjects, have embraced rather than denied rage.

Kureishi's writing follows more in the tradition of women writers who design narrative disjunctions aimed at negating the silencing of rage. According to Mary Helen Washington, Gwendolyn Brooks's *Maud Martha* describes the character's family situation as a fairly happy one, yet Maud Martha's outward contentment conflicts with the terse, truncated sentences of her delivery, thereby creating a contradiction between content and form and a betweenness from which rage may be read (455). Greta Gaard argues that Louisa May Alcott strives to repress anger in *Little Women* (12), when, in fact, Alcott displays the promise of an inherent danger in a repressed rage. Her character, Jo, asserts: "It seems as if I could do anything when I'm in a passion; I get so savage, I could hurt anyone, and enjoy it. I'm afraid I *shall* do something dreadful some day" (Gaard, 12). The emphasis on *shall* betrays an admission to the inevitable uncontrollability of rage—that no matter how one tries to suppress it, the future *shall*, in fact, witness the unleashing of rage. Alcott creates a disjunction between desire for control and the fear of expression.

Though outwardly it may appear that current writers share no such constraint in their willingness to confront rage, they still employ familiar literary narrative tensions and constraints which prophesy or threaten rage. By surveying the texts of a particularly outraged group of current queer writers, all who actually use the word, rage, we will elucidate a range of narrative techniques effective in building rage that we broadly define as cyclical. This group of writers (who, though "queer" in practice, do not necessarily rally around a common rage; they form a conversation, not a literary school) often employs a name, an event, a circumstance, or a metaphor whose repetition signals another twist of the knife, another turn of the screw in a tightening circle of rage. The narrative's cyclical quality functions as a locomotive pulling away from a station, the wheels chugging at ever closer intervals building towards an inevitable scream of rage. Though the writers employ similar narrative techniques to create rage, they do so with distinct finesse, using variations such as stockpiling, echoing, retelling, returning, and interrupting.

One of the most obviously outraged writers, David Wojnarowicz, interrupts his frequently disjunctive book-length reportage, *Close to the Knives*, with two pages in bold print, the only bold-printed passage in the book, thus creating an immediately visible text within the text. Wojnarowicz writes a bold-faced diatribe disguised as a poem against the smugness of the U.S. public and politicians who wish that AIDS would disappear quietly along with all the HIV-infected people:

and I wake up every morning in this killing machine called america
and I'm carrying this rage like a blood-filled egg and there's a thin
line between the inside and the outside a thin line between thought
and action and that line is simply made up of blood and muscle and
bone . . .

there's a thin line a very thin line and as each T-Cell disappears
from my body it's replaced by ten pounds of pressure ten pounds of
rage and (161–2)

Through constructing a single two page run-on sentence connected with repeated "ands," Wojnarowicz exacerbates the sense of outrage expressed in the words' meaning. The "ands" stockpile one outrage upon another until finally at the end of the passage, Wojnarowicz writes "all I can feel is the pressure and all I can feel is the pressure and the need for release" (162). The passage energetically returns to key metaphoric phrases, the thin line, the pressure, the egg, that build a narrative cycle which somehow must come to an end. Both the contents of the passage, with its HIV infected blood threatening to splatter, and the narrative structure with its relentless hammer of the "and," prophesy more outrage, promise and threaten eventual relief.

Dorothy Allison builds the final chapters of *Bastard out of Carolina* around a painful question to which the narrator already has the answer, "Where was Mama?" (300). The first-person narrator, Bone, wonders how her mama, Annie, could fail to remain at her side; after interrupting her husband's brutal rape of his stepdaughter, Bone, Annie drops off her daughter at the hospital and disappears. Bone's aunt Raylene tells her:

> "Your mama . . ." She stopped and I looked back at her. "Your mama loves you. Just hang on, girl. Just hang on. It'll be better in time, I promise you."
> I promise you, she said. My mouth twisted. I stared at her hate-fully.
> Raylene looked at me as if my rage hurt her, but she said nothing. (301)

The phrasal repetitions create an echo which suggests the throb of pain and rage in Bone's head, still pounding from the rape. Later, when Mama does return, the echo effect resumes as she repeats, "I know," "I never thought," and "I just loved him." The repetitions enrage Bone as she must ask herself what her mother knew, why she did not think, and how she could still love a repeatedly sadistic rapist. In *A Passage to India,* the echo in the cave releases hysteria; in the raging present's *Bastard out of Carolina,* the echoing phrases release and exacerbate rage.

The echo in Dale Peck's *Martin and John* extends throughout the text as Peck recycles the "same" characters, John, Martin, John's father, Henry, and mother, Beatrice, to tell repeated stories of the son's desperate love for the father who abuses both John and Bea, interrupted by interludes of solace with Martin. Peck's reworking of the similar stories and characters creates an inevitability to abuse and injustice, building to an eventual self-realization of the narrator, John, that he can feel only "love and hate, rage and joy, terror and numbness" (227). Several book reviewers (Barclay, Kaufman, Texier) describe the novel's structure as fugue-like. *Martin and John* builds towards a climax, retreats, builds towards a similar climax, then varies the theme once again, manufacturing a music of rage.

Irish writer, William Trevor, creates a quite different mood in his short story, "Torridge." The character, Torridge, functions as an oft-repeated joke for three "Old Boys," friends from the same public school. Trevor establishes a simultaneous comfort with the old joke of Torridge, which he countervails with the inevitability that the punch line of the joke will finally arrive with his own punch. When Torridge does appear, he mysteriously introduces and reintroduces into the conversation the name of a fellow schoolmate, Fisher. Each time, however, Torridge deliberately withdraws from the name and seemingly returns to trivial politeness, establishing a falsely peaceful interlude from which his rage eventually seeps.

When Torridge finally tells his truths, that Fisher hung himself over spurned love from one of the "Old Boys" and that Torridge himself "perform[s] sexual acts with men," he leaves one of the men "quivering with rage" (262). Torridge's suave delivery contrasts with the catalog of shame and rage of the others present at the dinner party. "Torridge" effectively unveils the hypocrisy of "Old Boys" who wish to forget their own implication in boyhood homoeroticism and romance. At the same time, the story's building of tension through polite interlude effectively reproduces the simmering rage of a sincere boy whom, child or adult, the "in crowd" treats only as a joke.

Jeannette Winterson's post-modern novel, *Sexing the Cherry*, combines many of the narrative techniques that the above authors employ. Winterson recycles many bits of history, mythology, and folklore to reread them through women's rage against the patriarchy. The entire novel contains an echo effect as characters in both the sixteenth and twentieth centuries may be imagining or hallucinating each other. Winterson aims these characters' rage, particularly that of her Rabelaisian Dog Woman and her modern counterpart, against the hypocritical rule of the patriarchal puritans and capitalists.

However, at the greatest moments of rage, Winterson interjects humor. Comic interruption provides a particular challenge to the narrative structuring of rage, as it may easily undermine a gathering mood of rage.

In an already disjointed narrative, which does not attempt to sustain a particular mood, such as *Sexing the Cherry*'s, the humor may actually deflate rage. For example, Dog Woman surprises her hypocritical puritan male opponents just as they ready to disport with each other in a brothel, dressed as Brutus and Caesar. Dog Woman appears as an executrix, saying "I came to bury Caesar, not to praise him," then further, "quoting from a playwright whose name I can't remember" (96). Later, Dog Woman's contemporary counterpart, a chemist, seeks to end global economic problems by rounding up the board of the World Bank and tossing them all into a sack, though she "throw[s] in a few calculators so they won't be bored" (138).

Winterson's comic interruptions may serve as black humor, the laughter that gets stuck in the throat, providing a disjuncture from which rage may emerge. For example, in another episode, "Fortunata's story," the narrator flatly describes Orion's rape of Artemis and her retribution. "Orion raped Artemis and fell asleep. She thought about that time for years. It took just a few moments, and her only sensation was the hair on his stomach matted with sand. Her revenge was swift and simple. She killed him with a scorpion" (151–52). The juxtaposition of prosaic language with brutally swift revenge contrasts with Dog Woman's comic killing of the puritans, creating the possibility for multiple readings of the rage. The fragmented method of narrative and the recycling of other stories, combined with an often ribald humor present possibilities both of constructing and deconstructing rage. In a discussion of Kureishi's novel, *The Buddha of Suburbia*, we will further pursue the problem of comedy's intersection with rage.

Kureishi's novel, *The Buddha of Suburbia*, reenacts many of the multifaceted tensions at play in his first two screenplays. The novel depicts a series of racist, sexist, classist, and homophobic outrages against the novel's hero, Karim Amir, and against his fellow first- or second-generation South Asian immigrants to Britain. The frequently comic interruptions of these outrages may diminish or enhance the novel's reproduction of rage. By providing comic narrative disjuncture, Kureishi may invite the question, "What am I laughing about?," a question which may intensify a reading of rage. Though episodic and somewhat cinematic, Kureishi's narrative may fill in threatening gaps with an overriding comic mode. Kureishi employs some of the structural techniques which heighten rage in the other fictions, but the novel cyclically inflates, then deflates the rage, with the chance of explosion substantially diminished. The rage still emerges from the text, but sometimes with a splutter, not a bang.

The Buddha of Suburbia tells the story of Karim Amir, half English, half Pakistani, "a funny kind of Englishman" (3), as he moves through a series of picaresque adventures which carry him from the South London suburbs to the London stage, on to the United States, and finally back to London and a British television series. In Thatcher's Britain, Karim's hybrid ethnicity, his bisexuality, and his lower-middle but upwardly mobile class status repeatedly cause him to suffer constant insult and thus to experience an ongoing rage. Kureishi relies on traditional thematic constructions of male rage, particularly around agency and impotency, while he also parodies them.

Karim becomes an actor in the novel, but one without agency. He enacts on the stage, on television and in his relationships the stereotypical roles of "native" of the subcontinent, immigrant taxi driver, and passive Oriental. That Karim studies, observes, and analyzes, in other words, intellectualizes these roles before performing them, doubly distances him from his agency, thus under the traditional male thematic of rage, should exacerbate his rage. Instead, Karim's first person narrative reports his own hypocrisy. Karim thus implicates himself rather than others in his own lack of agency. He rages not solely against the systems of injustice, but feels saddened and chastised by his own inability to recast himself out of non-stereotypical roles.

Karim uses his limited agency to parody these roles, not to rage against them. For example, he transforms Mowgli's exaggerated colonized Indian accent into a South London one, questioning the audience's Orientalist reading of *The Jungle Book*. Karim only plays at the margins. His own inability to represent fully his own reading of what he calls "The Jungle Bunny Book" frustrates him and manufactures rage within the novel. Many times when such frustration threatens to explode into rage, however, the narrative bursts into comedy or conciliation.

Kureishi does not always retreat from the rage through comedy. For example, when Karim's director, Matthew Pyke, literally sticks it to him on stage and off, Kureishi's narrative structure recalls that of *Maud Martha,* with a competing staccato forming a disjuncture with the capitulation of Karim's statements. "So despite what he'd done to me, my admiration for him continued. I didn't blame him for anything. I was prepared to pay the price" (217). Karim's martyred acceptance of abuse works in counterpoint to the terse narrative, creating a possibility of emerging rage. However, this passage remains atypical of *The Buddha of Suburbia*. Three other scenes exemplify Kureishi's softening technique of exposing, then retreating from rage.

In the first scene, Karim stops by to see Helen, whom he has just met at a party. When Helen's father, whom Karim calls "Hairy Back," notices that Karim is "black," he pulls Helen back into her room, charges to the front door and unleashes against Karim a string of racist obscenities as well as a Great Dane. Karim, who has muttered clever wisecracks in response to the verbal attack, contemplates vandalizing Hairy Back's automobile, when he suddenly realizes the potential threat of the Great Dane. He quickly determines to escape when the dog "attacks" him.

> My soft words obviously affected the dog, for suddenly there was a flurry and I felt something odd on my shoulders. Yes, it was the dog's paws. The dog's breath warmed my neck. I took another step and so did the dog. I knew by now what the dog was up to. The dog was in love with me—quick movements against my arse told me so. Its ears were hot. I didn't think the dog would bite me, as its movements were increasing, so I decided to run for it. The dog shuddered against me. (41)

Kureishi juxtaposes Karim's impotency and inaction against the Great Dane's pursuit and sexual potency. Though Karim immediately becomes "fucking bad-tempered" after the scene, the physical residue of the dog's actions and not Hairy Back's vicious racism infuriate Karim. He transfers his potentially explosive rage from the father to the dog, from rage against political stances to anger against the libidinous actions of the dog. The pun on potency may greatly undermine, even parody rage. However, another reading of the same scene might suggest that Karim becomes even more enraged as it becomes clear to him that he does not even possess the power of an animal. Thus the comic interruption introduces an unstable reading of rage which may either diffuse or refocus the rage.

In a second scene, Karim's "uncle" Anwar flies into a rage against his son-in-law, Changez. Anwar has forced his daughter, Jamilla, to marry this mail-order groom from Bombay but becomes angry when he finds Changez partially disabled and pathologically lazy. Like the narrator, Karim, Anwar directs his fury against himself but admits this to none of the other characters.

After some time of not seeing Changez, Anwar spots him and his Japanese mistress on the street. When he spies Changez, Anwar lets out a war cry heard for several neighborhoods. Anwar does not hold back this time "No; the disappointed father-in-law was intending to crack his son-in-law over the loaf right now—and possibly club him to death" (210). Changez, grossly fat, still manages to avoid Anwar's attempted blow and smacks Anwar with a large, knobby dildo he has just bought in a sex shop.

Kureishi counters Anwar's rage at his impotency in controlling Changez, in turning the fat lump into a hard working, grandson-producing, son-in-law, with a dildo. Changez parries the usual thrust of masculine rage by its parody, a fabricated symbol of male potency. Kureishi stages rage, cleverly playing with symbols of male rage, but in creating these satisfying ironies, Kureishi's novel ultimately may neither prophesy nor threaten rage. Laughter may fill in where the pulse could quicken.

In the third example, contemplation, not comedy, interrupts the scene of impotence-producing rage. Karim would like to seduce fellow actor, Terry, whom he has known for some time. However, their meeting begins in rage. Karim denounces Terry's party-line diatribes: "Sometimes I feel disgusted by your ignorance. Your fucking stupid blindness to things" (240). After more conversation, then narrative in which Karim reveals that he "hate[s] the flood of opinion, the certainty, the easy talk" (241), Karim deflects his rage against monolithic political structures towards Terry as a sexual object.

When Karim begins to touch Terry, he asks Karim to stop. Karim continues, even more aggressively, then does stop as he looks Terry in the face: "However angry I was with him, however much I wanted to humiliate Terry, I suddenly saw such humanity in his eyes, and in the way he tried to smile" (241). By appealing to a universal humanism, Kureishi tames his rage as deftly as E. M. Forster might. In this scene, Kureishi tames not his sexual urge, but the urge to humiliate another, to belittle him, to reduce another's humanity through manifesting his rage. When Karim looks in Terry's face he sees not a reflection of his own impotency, despite the failed seduction, but a reflection of his shame. Kureishi constructs the seemingly self-effacing Karim as at least potentially superhuman, able to recognize and withdraw from his action, to acknowledge his shame without expressing it as rage that could harm others.

We do not cite these comic or conciliatory passages in order to dismiss Kureishi's comedy or even his humanistic stance, but to demonstrate the particular problem of either threatening or prophesying rage through comedy. Five pages from the end of the novel Kureishi still seems to prophesy a continuing state of rage: "Maybe you *never* stop feeling like an eight-year-old in front of your parents. You resolve to be your mature self . . . but within five minutes your intentions are blown to hell and you're babbling and screaming in rage like an angry child" (280). Yet, the novel's final sentence, "I thought of what a mess everything had been, but that it wouldn't always be the same" (284), invites readings both of a future when there will be no messes and of a future when the "mess" of rage will simply shift, rather than subside. Where *Sammy and Rosie* supplied a clear invitation to rage, *The Buddha of Suburbia* suggests a continuing rage, but also promotes comedy, irony, and parody as means of deflecting a mounting rage.

Although his cinematic constructions prove more amenable to creating an uncontrolled rage than does his written narrative, the growing body of work reflects an interrogation of suffering that Kureishi credits to James Baldwin. During a particularly "frightened and hostile" time in his life, Kureishi turned to a picture of Baldwin for consolation:

> On the cover of the Penguin edition of *The Fire Next Time*, was James Baldwin holding a child, his nephew. Baldwin, having suffered, having been there, was all anger and understanding. He was intelligence and love combined. As I planned my escape I read Baldwin all the time. (*London*, 8)

When Kureishi works alone in writing his novel, he may, through comedy, soften the threat of rage. However, his particular interest in exploring a multi-inflected rage correlates with his cinematic work. Kureishi's fictional work on rage distinguishes itself from other current writers who consider rage largely around a single issue, such as AIDS, child abuse, or the patriarchy. Kureishi's work becomes remarkable as he struggles to present the many dimensions of rage which a single, fictional character may face.

Kureishi's and Frears's filmmaking, although situated within a wide alliance of other filmmakers working to represent rage on the screen, stands out as particularly interested in diversifying and problematizing the multicultural cause. In their complicated rendition, they distinguish themselves as interested in posing difficult questions about the "culture" within multiculturalism and the monolithic denotations that the word, culture, carries with it. This particular theoretical project aligns Kureishi and Frears with such postcolonial critics as Homi Bhabha, who designates these types of artists as those who "demonstrate the contemporary compulsion to move beyond; to turn the present into the 'post'; or, . . . to touch the future on its hither side" (18). Kureishi and Frears immerse themselves into a post-celebratory, post-identity politics mode of creation. They prophesy a future that exists for the many, but only on the hither side of an ever-threatening rage.

WORKS CITED

Allison, Dorothy. *Bastard out of Carolina*. New York: Dutton, 1992.
Barclay, Steven. "Escaping from Pain in Private Fictions." *San Francisco Chronicle,* 28 Feb 1993, Sunday Review, 4.
Bhabha, Homi K. *The Location of Culture*. New York: Routledge, 1994.
Crush. Dir. Alison Maclean, 1992.
Daughters of the Dust. Dir. Julie Dash, 1991.
Death of the Incredible Hulk. Dir. Bill Bixby, 1990.
Do the Right Thing. Dir. Spike Lee, 1989.
Falling Down. Dir. Joel Schumacher, 1993.
Gaard, Greta. "'Self-Denial Was All the Fashion': Repressing Anger in *Little Women*." *Papers on Language and Literature* (Winter 1991): 3–19.
Giannetti, Louis and Scott Eyman, eds. *Flashback: A Brief History of Film*. Englewood Cliffs, N.J.: Prentice Hall, 1991.
Grixti, Joseph. *Terrors of Uncertainty: The Cultural Contexts of Horror Fiction*. New York: Routledge, 1989.
Guinier, Lani. *The Tyranny of the Majority: Fundamental Fairness in Representative Democracy*. New York: Macmillan, 1994.
Hedges, Inez. *Breaking the Frame: Film Language and the Experience of Limits*. Bloomington: Indiana University Press, 1991.
Jordan, June. "Poem About My Rights." *Naming Our Destiny: New and Selected Poems*. New York: Thunder's Mouth Press, 1989.
Kaufman, David. "Heroes With a Thousand Faces." *Nation,* 15 March 1993: 347–349.

Kureishi, Hanif. *The Buddha of Suburbia*. New York: Penguin, 1990.
———. *London Kills Me: Three Screenplays and Four Essays*. New York: Penguin, 1992.
Lewis, Michael. "The Development of Anger and Rage." In *Rage, Power, and Aggression*. Ed. Robert A. Glick and Steven P. Roose. New Haven: Yale University Press, 1993.
Mukerji, Chandra, and Michael Schudson, eds. *Rethinking Popular Culture: Contemporary Perspectives in Cultural Studies*. Berkeley: University of California Press, 1991.
Mulvey, Laura. *Visual and Other Pleasures*. Bloomington: Indiana University Press, 1989.
My Beautiful Laundrette. Dir. Stephen Frears, 1985.
Pease, Donald. "Fear, Rage, and the Mistrials of Representation in *The Red Badge of Courage*." Ed. Eric J. Sundquist. *American Realism: New Essays*. Baltimore: Johns Hopkins University Press, 1982.
Peck, Dale. *Martin and John*. New York: Farrar, Straus, Giroux, 1993.
Question of Silence. Dir. Marleen Gorris, 1983.
Sammy and Rosie Get Laid. Dir. Stephen Frears, 1987.
Stetz, Margaret Diane. "E. M. Forster: *Abinger Harvest*, Anger and the Letter 'C'." *The South Atlantic Quarterly* (Summer 1987): 296–311.
Texier, Catherine. "Loves of a Young Hustler." *New York Times Book Review*, 28 February, 1993, 7:12.
Thelma and Louise. Dir. Ridley Scott, 1991.
Trevor, William. "Torridge." Ed. David Leavitt and Mark Mitchell. *The Penguin Book of Gay Short Stories*. New York: Viking, 1994.
Washington, Mary Helen. "Taming All That Anger Down' Rage and Silence in Gwendolyn Brooks's *Maud Martha*." *Massachusetts Review* (Summer 1983): 453–66.
Winterson, Jeannette. *Sexing the Cherry*. New York: Vintage, 1991.
Wojnarowicz, David. *Close to the Knives: A Memoir of Disintegration*. New York: Vintage, 1991.

CHAPTER 9

The Psychohistory of Jewish Rage and Redemption as Seen through Its Art

MOSHE DAVIDOWITZ

Jews are people. Whatever the psychodynamics of people may be can be applied to Jews as well. This is pretty obvious, but the most difficult thing to see is the obvious. As deMause suggests, "Psychohistory is more a rediscovery than a discovery—it is a process of finding out what we already know and act upon." [1]

A good deal of the Jewish historic experience of the last few hundred years in Europe has been fraught with trauma and hatred. That, too, is obvious and is what we already know. But how did Jews act upon this powerfully negative environment in which they lived? What was their reality? Ebel writes that "Reality is terribly hard to bear, since its uncertainties threaten our imminent and often painful demise, and the prime function of the human institutions and cultural artifacts we call 'group-fantasies' is therefore to put reality under a fantasy control." [2]

How did European Jews of the Middle Ages deal with the reality of their persecution, and what group-fantasies did they create to let them live with some semblance of sanity in such a hostile environment? Whenever an individual or a group is persecuted and hated, there is a reaction of anger and rage at the tormentor. But how can you deal with that anger when to state it in an obvious way could cause a pogrom or more restrictive laws against you?

If you can not express it to the external world, you can at least express it to your internal community who share much the same emotional

Reprinted by kind permission of *The Journal of Psychohistory* 6 (Fall 1978): 273-84.

tension as you do. The anger can be expressed in words, but that can be dangerous, since anything in writing—in print or in manuscript—can and often is held against you, proving your "perfidious nature."

But there was a way in which Jews could express their emotions in a way that was relatively safe: in their art. Upon occasion, the Jews used their visual symbols as a group-fantasy to deal with their anger and rage. One case in point to illustrate this is a series of full page illuminations in a manuscript Passover Haggadah executed in fifteenth-century Germany.

The Passover Haggadah can be seen as a group-fantasy that organizes history along the basic theme of freedom from oppression. It views history not only as a series of chronological events but rather adds the "why" to the "what, when, and who" of standard historical writing.

The Haggadah is not an historical text, although there is some history in it. It is primarily a psychohistorical text written from a very specific point of view that concretized the collective mythos of the Jewish historic consciousness.

The narrative of the Haggadah sets up an historical model on three basic planes: (1) the heroes—the Jews, (2) the oppressor—Pharoah, and (3) the Controller and Mastery of history—God. While the text tells us little about the actual historic events it purports to describe, it indicates a tremendous amount about how the normative Jewish mind perceived those events.

The focus of the Seder theme is twofold. The first is to view the Exodus on an historical plane of an event that happened there and then—thousands of years ago, and thousands of miles away. But also it focuses on the significance of the event as a here-and-now experience, for Jews are asked to adjust their own personal fantasies as if they themselves were slaves and participated in the Exodus. The ritual system is designed to establish a mythic time of rediscovering the events of the past in the present and a re-experiencing the distant place within one's own home. The narrative also allowed for historic transpositions of the continuing repressions in any given generation.

How does one deal with the demonic, the shadow in life? You can attempt to destroy it if you can. But if you can not—then what? In addition, you can only destroy an external demon. How do you cope with an imploded internal demon?

One possible way was through historic analogies. To the Jews of

Medieval Europe their oppressor was not the Pharoah of Ancient Egypt but the then present Christian antagonism and persecution. The theme was that, just as Pharoah was destroyed by the wrath of God, so too the contemporary Christian tyranny will be destroyed by the wrath of God.

Indeed, modern Jewry did and does exactly the same thing. The Haggadah was and is responsive to the historic experience of the present context. In the modern editions of the Haggadah sections were added to the text dealing with the Holocaust under the Nazis, the creation of the State of Israel, and the plight of Soviet Jewry. In all probability, the Passover Haggadah is the most popular and widely used psychohistorical text of the Jew.

The Darmstadt Haggadah, of the German rite, was executed in the Middle Rhine in the second quarter of the fifteenth century. It is a manuscript written by Israel ha-sofer ben Meir of Heidelberg. We do not know whether the scribe also did the illuminations. It is probable that they were done by several artists of the same school of fifteenth-century mid-Rhine with either Italian or Netherlandish Gothic influence.[3] We will deal with three illustrated pages to explore one of the group-fantasies of the Jews of the period.

The most widely known illustration of this text is the picture of twenty young women being taught by an elderly male teacher set within a classic Gothic architectural framework (figure 1). It is reasonable to infer that this manuscript was executed for a woman as this type of illustration is rare and unusual. On the bottom of the page is a "Seder" scene (see figure 2). The Seder scene is clearly designed to illustrate the Last Supper of Jesus. We can see the youthful Jesus in the center of the table pointing to a person wearing a "Judenhut"—a Jewish hat, an obvious reference to Judas. There are only nine persons at the table, perhaps the full complement of the twelve Apostles would be much too obvious for safety. The text in the center of the page is an interesting one. It is the Hebrew text of "Shefoch Hamatcha," the section read at the Seder when the door is opened to let Elijah the Prophet enter into the home as the harbinger of the Messianic Age. The largest letter is the initial letter of the text, a large "Shin." This letter "shin" is also the first letter of the most commonly used name of God—"Shadai." The text in this page is a mosaic composite of Biblical verses which translate as follows:

FIGURE 1

אִשְׁ...יִשְׁ לֹא יָדְעוּךָ ... וְעַל מַמְלָכוֹת אֲשֶׁר בְּשִׁמְךָ

FIGURE 2

Pour out thy wrath upon the nations that do not know You and upon the kingdoms that do not call upon Your name; for they have eaten Jacob and laid waste his dwelling (Psalms 79:6, 7). Pour out your wrath upon them, and may the fierceness of Your anger overtake them (Psalms 69:25). Pursue them with anger and destroy them from under the heavens of the Lord (Lamentations 3:66).

This juxtaposition of such a powerful text with the illustrations conveys a significant aspect of Jewish consciousness of the period. An historical note is in order. This period was rather close to the last of the memories of the Crusades where Jewish communities were systematically destroyed along the Rhine Valley. Jewish communities had a very precarious tenure by virtue of a special invitation of some local rulers. They were always subject to the waves of unreasoning violence so especially characteristic of Germany. War, civic disturbance, the activities of some envenomed apostate, the disappearance of a Christian child, continued to be regarded as ample cause for assault and massacre, sometimes followed by expulsion.[4] Jews were legally considered as chattel, property of the local ruler, and not even considered as being really human.

If the outside world does not accept your as human, at least you can accept yourself as human and create a fantasy establishing your own self-validation. It may be that the issue here was not the development of a countervailing power but rather of maintaining a group-fantasy that allowed for sanity.

One way to deal with your rage was to focus it on the historic past where you were the victor, namely the story of the Exodus as told in the Passover Haggadah. But how can you do that if you use an ancient text that has no correlation with your present historic situation and where you would not alter the received text? You can substitute pictures for words and establish visual analogies that use art as one vehicle to let out the inner tensions and anxieties of fear and anger. This art, then, can become a synergy of an historic text and contemporary art that in effect deals with the tradition in a psychohistorical manner in addition to the straight interpretation of history.

This section of the Seder is an interesting one. Classically the home is established as a sacred space, a space which is organized and ordered along the mythic models you set up that separate the outside world of chaos from the inside space of cosmos.[5] If the external space is hostile and murderous, then the inner space is especially sacred. At this point in the Seder, the door which separates the two domains is opened to allow Elijah to enter. This signifies the entrance of the presence of the promise of God of the Covenant to enter one's historic present. Elijah brings with him, as God's messenger, the spirit of the sacred myth of Jewish redemption. For Elijah heralds the coming of the Messiah when Jewish oppression will end and the Jews' full humanity will be accepted both by the outside world, and more importantly, by the Jew in his inner world. This indeed is perhaps one of those occasions where a profound psycho-historic event is experienced, not only written and spoken about.

The kinesthetic system used where one must walk to the door, open it, all the participants rise, a special larger-than-life goblet of wine is filled, and all recite and chant those powerful and damning phrases, would seem to be psychohistory in action and psychohistory as ritual—an event where psyche becomes myth. Elijah is the instrument of power in the journey of the hero as Jew. Through patience, faith—helplessness is transformed into salvation.

At that moment of reciting the words, "Pour out Your wrath upon the Gentiles who do not know You," the fantasy and the historic myth are enacted: If I can not be safe now, if I can not destroy my persecutors now; then God indeed can, and will—when the time comes.

Seeing the picture of the symbol of their arch persecutor—the church—and of "Jesus," in whose name so many Jews were killed, the myth of the fantasy is experienced and the art becomes a channel for the emotional discharge of so much negative energy.

This was not a late fantasy, either, for the Bible also can be seen as manifesting similar sentiments. While there is a great deal of the traditional positive expressions of hope and love, of sweetness and light, of peace and goodness, there is also the complement of anger and rage in the biblical texts as well.

The obvious is that the Bible as a book of Life and living deals with all forms of emotional expression. Just to mention a few clear examples of this are the following:

The prophet Nahum writes: "the Lord is a jealous and avenging god, the Lord avengeth and is full of wrath; the Lord taketh vengeance on His adversaries, and He reserves wrath for His enemies," (Nahum, 1:2).

The theme of a jealous and avenging God is an echo of this concept in Exodus 20:5, 34:14, and Deuteronomy 32:21. And, of course, the last chapters of the Book of Esther describe in avid detail the rage and destruction wrought by the Jews on their enemies in ancient Persia. Another powerful statement is found in Psalms 137 verses 7–9:

(7) "Remember, O Lord, against the children of Edom the day of Jerusalem; who said: 'Raze it, raze it, even to the foundation thereof.' "

(8) "O daughter of Babylon, that art to be destroyed; Happy shall he be, that repayeth thee as thou hast served us."

(9) "Happy shall he be, that taketh and dasheth thy little ones against the rock."

In his introduction to this Psalm, Rev. Cohen, the editor of the Soncino Bible, writes in 1950:

The feelings which moved the writer of this Psalm will best be understood if we think of him as an exile recently back from Babylon, viewing with horror the havoc wrought in the city he dearly loved . . . Critics writing in comfort and security, usually deplore the bitter vindictiveness of the imprecation which ends the Psalm. Refugees from the continent, when they return and see how their native city has been turned into masses of rubble by the Germans, will share the mood of the Psalmist.[6]

And A. MacLaren, a Christian Hebraist, in reference to verse 9 muses that: "Perhaps, if some of their modern critics had been under the yoke from which this Psalmist had been delivered, they would understand a little better how a good man of that age could rejoice that Babylon was fallen and all its race extirpated."[7]

Yet, with all of the apologetics, anger and rage are as much a part of living as is any other emotion. The issue is: How does one deal with it? How does a community allow for the safe expression of the power and energy of this feeling flow, and how does it organize its group-fantasies around it? An explosion of such emotional energy was not only dangerous in relation to the external hostile world but it can also be a severe threat to one's own psychic world. Communal implosion often leads to a collective depressive state. Rituals such as this, augmented by the power of the visual images that focuses the emotional impact, mitigated some of the negative energy of the imploded anger and rage.

But the group-fantasy did not end here and neither does the Haggadah. The text ends with the sentiment of "Next year in Jerusalem," a psychohistoric fantasy of the time if ever there was one. For the imploded rage can end on a note of salvational historic mythos. The Covenant and its psychological implications are sublimated to a positive hope that helped sustain sanity and a valued self image of being a member of a chosen people. After the text ends there are two more full page illustrations that further emphasize the psychohistoric fantasy of the covenanted relationship of the members of the community of Israel.

The illustration that follows immediately after the conclusion of the text is unique in the iconography of Hebrew manuscript illumination (see figure 3). Here is depicted a rather obvious symbol borrowed from the Christian environment: "the Hortus Conclusus"—the enclosed garden—a symbol of the virgin Mary, who while closed as a virgin yet gave birth to the Christian Savior—the central flowering tree. The artist took this theme and pictured a specifically Judaic fantasy in it. Within the garden scene is the figure of Elijah riding on a white horse blowing a shofar—heralding the coming of the Jewish Messiah. This Messiah is

FIGURE 3

about to save the deer—a symbol of Israel—which is enclosed within the garden fence and can not escape. However, the deer has its head turned looking at its redeemer, Elijah.

This scene is also of a secular activity—a stag hunt. But in Jewish symbol systems of the period it is a commonly used allusion to the

FIGURE 4

persecuted Jewish nation. To the community of Israel, this seems to be a clear example of a psychohistoric group-fantasy that is encoded visually in artistic pictorial symbols. Any member of the inner community could decode its meaning and significance. This seems to lead to the next illustration which concludes the visual presentation of the group fantasy.

This last scene depicts a fountain of youth (see figure 4). One sees old and crippled men and women climbing the steps of the fountain and coming out healthier and younger. The mythic system continues but now closes as it reaches its full circle. Every mythic journey ends where it begins. Here it is with the life-giving nature of water. The Exodus story begins with the saving nourishing water of the Sea of Reeds—in a distant historic past. But it concludes in the saving waters of a fountain of youth and eternal salvation. Water is the often used symbol of birth-death and re-birth. To die and to be reborn is no easy matter. Yet the rewards are many. Also, the pictorial format of the hunt chase scene is confined and closed in. The tree is growing but it is fenced in. For in the historic present all one can do is look in hope toward Elijah for the future salvation.

In the final illustration of the fountain, the pictorial element is vertical without any fences and no constraints—the salvation has come.

Interestingly, the first illustration of the Seder scene (figure 1) is also in the design of a Gothic tower, but there, one sees a border that encloses it. The border in the original is red—the symbol of blood. However, in the last scene (figure 4) the tower is open—with no fences and no borders, with its spires pointing toward Heaven.

It is interesting to speculate as to whether the idea of the union of body-mind is to be found here. Since Reich, we are aware of the many ways in which emotional states are stored in the musculature and skeletal systems of the body. The very thing which is transformed in this panel is the body. The armoring, the muscle tensions that produced the cripple who enters is psychologically and spiritually healed through his participation in the ritual of a profound group-fantasy in action—the Passover Seder.

Psychohistory uses the historic documents of the past—textual records of words upon which it can illuminate the psychological "why" of the historical "what." It would seem that the medieval German Jews who created this document used their artistic talent as another focus of doing much the same thing. Many archetypal symbols of which Jung speaks so much of are evident in these panels which use such emotionally charged images depicting some of the group-fantasies that dealt with such tremendous amounts of psychic energy and allowed the inner community a focus to discharge some of the stored negative energy of fear and rage. In some small way it mitigates some of the anger that is bound to be imploded and depressive, and then to transform some of the energy into the positive, ego maintaining of fantasies of a time of safety and peace, and salvation.

NOTES

My sincere appreciation goes to Mr. Peter Ehrenthal of Moriah for allowing me to use his copy of the Darmstadt Haggadah for the illustrations for this article.

1. Lloyd deMause, "The Independence of Psychohistory" in *The New Psychohistory*, Lloyd deMause, ed., The Psychohistory Press, New York, 1975, p. 25.

2. Henry Ebel, "The New Theology: Star Trek, Star Wars, Close Encounters, and the Crisis of Pseudo-rationality" in *The Journal of Psychohistory*, Vol. 5, No. 4, Spring, 1978, p. 488.

3. Bezalel Narkiss, *Hebrew Illuminated Manuscripts*, Keter Publishing, Jerusalem, 1969, p. 126.

4. Cecil Roth, *A Short History of the Jewish People*, East and West Library, London, 1959, p. 255–56.

5. Mircea Eliade, *The Sacred and the Profane*, Harcourt, Brace and World, A Harvest Book, New York, 1959. See especially chapter 1.

6. A. Cohen, ed., *The Psalms*, Soncino Press, London, 1950, p. 447.

7. Ibid., p. 448.

CHAPTER 10

Aborted Rage in Beth Henley's Women

ALAN CLARKE SHEPARD

Beth Henley's tragicomedies study the effects of the feminist movement upon a few, mostly proletarian women in rural Mississippi, who are more likely to read *Glamour* than Cixous and Clement's *The Newly Born Woman*.[1] We are invited to sympathize with isolated heroines whose fantasies demonstrate the difficulty of conceiving female subjectivity while entrenched in patriarchal epistemes, whose resilience is expressed in their canny, survivalist compromises with the codes of passive southern womanhood.[2] Their compromises may be precisely located in the recurring imagery of homicide and suicide that pervades Henley's scripts. Take Elain in *The Miss Firecracker Contest* (1979),[3] for example, an aging beauty queen in flight from a suffocating marriage and motherhood. When her estranged husband worries that she may kill their children in a fit of fury, Elain answers him by quashing the idea of her repressed rage spiraling murderously out of control: "Oh, for God's sake, Franklin, no one's going to bake them into a pie!"[4] Franklin, borrowing from classical tragedy, baits Elain to circumscribe, even to annul her anger and her flight. One subtext of his inflammatory trope of filicide is that Elain's bid for greater autonomy threatens to incite a domestic "tragedy" (50). Yet the word "tragedy" is Elain's own assessment of impending doom. Though Franklin makes her "ill" (24), without him she is "feeling nothing but terror and fear and loneliness!" (50). And so, after a few minutes of "reckless" infamy under the wisteria bushes with an alcoholic carnival hand, she expects to return to her "dreary, dreary life" (101). No Medea she, Elain occupies the periphery

Reprinted by kind permission of *The Journal of Psychohistory* 6 (Fall 1978): 273-84.

of *Miss Firecracker,* but the arc of her brief rebellion illuminates a paradigm of female surrender running through Henley's plays. The southern heroines populating her tragicomedies frequently erupt in anger toward those (including themselves) who engineer or sustain the emotionally impoverishing circumstances of their private lives; and just as often, they retreat from the schemes of violence bred by that anger. They relish murderous and suicidal fantasies, then repudiate them. The problematics of their rage is my subject.

The shadow of violent death is diffused across Henley's landscapes. At times it is treated with the *sprezzatura* of black comedy. Accidents of nature abound, wacky in their studied randomness: Carnelle's father has died chasing "the Tropical Ice Cream truck" (*Firecracker,* 1), her Uncle George fell "to his death trying to pull this bird's nest out from the chimney" (12); Popeye's brother has been fatally bitten "by a water moccasin down by the Pearl River" (12); Lenny's horse Billy Boy has been "struck dead" by lightning;[5] Jamey Foster has been fatally "kicked in the head by a cow";[6] an orphanage has burnt, blood vessels burst, cars and pigs exploded. Katty observes that "life is so full of unknown horror" (*Wake,* 8).

But at other times the half-baked threats of homicide and suicide swerve toward the rant of revenge tragedies. Unlike accidents of nature, these threats have knowable if not justifiable causes, reactions to betrayals and injustices made visible as the plays unfold. Yet the fantasies of murder entertained by these heroines signify no commitment to the principle that drives revenge tragedies, namely that revenge is an heroic prerogative of the wronged party, for traditionally revenge has been a masculine mode, from which these heroines mostly draw back. The fantasies secreted in Henley's texts are indeed not so much retributive as palliative. They are strategies of coping with the residual scars of emotional abandonment, or with a fresh crisis of the same, a recurring motif in Henley's art. Consider those of the widow Marshael in *The Wake of Jamey Foster* (1982). Estranged from her husband Jamey, who eventually dies from being filliped in the head—by a cow—during a pastoral tryst with his mistress Esmerelda, Marshael is abandoned a second time in a thunderstorm by family friend Brocker Slade, to whom she has turned in her grief, as they are travelling home from the hospital bed of her then-critically-ill husband. Slade later surfaces at Marshael's house to launch a half-hearted campaign to cajole her into forgiveness, cooing,

"God, M., honey, . . . I'm about ready to run jump into the Big Black River." To his self-pity she replies coolly, "Well, don't forget to hang a heavy stone around your scrawny old neck" (47–48). But recommending his suicide is as far as Marshael's rage goes. It rapidly devolves into despair, with Marshael vesting herself in the role of invalid. The particular stresses of earlier days, inscribed in the "purple and swollen" (20) ulcers on her gums, the rash on her knuckles, have now become general and overwhelming: she is, she says, "sick of betrayal! Sick!" (47), echoing Elain's sentiment in *Miss Firecracker* that her husband Franklin makes her "ill." Yet as in *Firecracker,* again it is a man who is both the source and the cure of a heroine's disease. *The Wake of Jamey Foster* ends in a tableau of Slade soothing Marshael to sleep with the lullaby "This Old Man Comes Rolling Home," in whose refrain (of the same words) Marshael takes comfort from its implicit promise of Slade's enduring paternal presence.[7] He is redeemed, no longer a "scrawny old neck," but an "old *man*" (my emphasis). As the cure suggests, then, Marshael's rage against betrayal is not a liberating or even die-breaking action signalling her escape from heterosexist oppression, but a conservative, paradigmatic strategy for recuperating an emotionally dysfunctional man.

The embryo of this pattern of repudiated rage appears in *Am I Blue* (1972), the first of Henley's plays to be staged. *Am I Blue* investigates the pressures of gender relations, specifically of sexual initiation, felt by two adolescents, Ashbe and John Polk (or J.P.). They meet in a seedy New Orleans bar, return to the apartment Ashbe shares with her always absent father, and, compromising, agree to dance until dawn. Against our gendered expectations that men are always the sexual aggressor, it is the younger Ashbe who presses J.P. to have intercourse. When he refuses, fearing that Ashbe would "get neurotic, or pregnant, or some damn thing,"[8] she retaliates—she feigns having poisoned his drink dyed a suspicious blue: impulsively she hypothesizes his murder, only to recant the fiction immediately, then internalizes her anger, which, though tied to J.P.'s refusal, speaks of larger rejections and wounds.

Yet more striking than Ashbe's threat of the mickeyed highball are the fantasies of murder entertained by both teenagers. En route to the apartment, Ashbe, scooping up a stray hat from the street, wonders aloud whether it might not have been "a butcher's who slaughtered his wife or a silver pirate with a black bird on his throat"; J.P. fears that she "probably [has] got some gang of muggers waiting to kill me" (12). While he registers the practical risks of picking up a stranger in a bar, she romanticizes murder; the pirate Blackbeard roams the interstices of her imagination. In Ashbe's terms, a pirate's violence both creates and signifies his autarkic self; and Ashbe, virtually alone in the world, vicariously produces one, too, through her well-developed fantasy life, which privileges the swashbuckler mode, where violence is glamorous, sovereign, and artificial. But other fragments of her fantasy life belie her pose of nonchalance toward violence. They show Ashbe grappling with feelings of inexplicable rage, inexplicable to her because she possesses only an adolescent, even nascent, sense of herself as an autonomous being. For example, she describes visiting a grocery to smash bags of marshmallows (14), an act of rage comically diverted from its true object; she claims to have stolen ashtrays from the Screw Inn (it discriminates against the helpless, she says pointedly), and to have practiced the passive-aggressive art of voodoo against a clique of schoolmates. From all this, J.P. avers that Ashbe is "probably one of those people that live in a fantasy world" (17). In the most bizarre flight of fancy, she holds out hope of having sex with J.P. so that she might conceive, then travel to Tokyo for an abortion, explaining that she is "so sick of school I could smash every marshmallow in sight" (24). Mary Field Belenky and others have observed that oppressed women who are reconstituting themselves as autonomous subjects sometimes use "the imagery of birth, rebirth and childhood to describe their experience of a nascent self."[9] But Ashbe's struggle to develop as a subject results only in the cross-eyed impulses to smash marshmallows and to conceive only to abort. The latter mirrors the pattern of repudiated rage: she imagines internalizing, then expelling not only a fetus, but also the pressures of conventional commitments imposed upon young women to reproduce; to please and serve men, whatever the cost (recall Ashbe's imaginary butcher who slashes his wife's throat); to disavow the aggression typically associated with the masculine sphere. In the end, however, like Marshael, Ashbe abandons her resistance and, encircled by J.P.'s arms, dances to Billie Holiday. Relinquishing the murderous power of a blue mickey for "the blues" as soon as a man's company is even provisionally secured, Ashbe goes passive toward her own pain. Even the play's interrogative title serves notice of her surrender to the external regulation of her own feelings: *Am I Blue?*

Henley's heroines who have passed beyond adolescence do not similarly romanticize the murder and mutilation of women in later texts,
where the playwright explores relationships between men's abuse of
women and women's surprising, apparent diffidence or even absence of
rage in return. Breaking the conspiracy of silence that surrounds domestic abuse, a conspiracy once silently tolerated, then contested, by Babe
in *Crimes of the Heart* (1981), for example, whose medical history
narrates the injuries inflicted by her husband, Zackery, these texts map
out the cycle of emotional and physical battering. The abuse comes first;
and though bids for greater subjectivity sometimes follow a sudden
escalation of the abuse,[10] enduring, transformative rage seldom does, for
that is largely a privilege of "autarkic selfhood,"[11] about which Henley's
women, like Ashbe, seldom more than fantasize. If it is true, as George
Mariscal has said, "that all forms of subjectivity are conceived in a bitter
struggle for power and hegemony,"[12] then the absence of rage or its
diffident expression by Henley's abused women invites us to study the
strategies by which the men organize, control, even amputate the heroines' "bitter struggle."

Key moments expose the violence against women inscribed in the
situations of marriage and motherhood in Henley's plays. Two marriages near the brink of collapse—one peripheral, one central to a plot—
illustrate their strategies. In *The Wake of Jamey Foster* Katty and Wayne
Foster arrive to mourn Jamey's sudden death. The wake itself Henley
depicts humorously; it is the spectacle of Wayne's treatment of Katty
that transforms comedy into tragicomedy. Like Delmount in *Miss Firecracker,* who dreams at night of women's bodies dismembered (100),
Katty and Wayne live in a violently phallic universe. Wayne, who calls
Katty a "twat" (*Wake,* 36), sexually harrasses his sister-in-law Collard,
confident that men are entitled to control women's bodies: calling her
"Charlotte," imposing his preference for her "proper name," he lifts her
chin, marking her as his sexual property. Collard protests: "Lifting my
chin up like that—you're making me feel like some sort of goddamn
horse— . . . Oh, so you do like your women dirty?" (49). Katty witnesses this exchange, and immediately moves to protect her own claim
to Wayne's twisted affections: "Just because I lose those babies is no
reason to treat me viciously—no reason at all! You know I can't help
it!" (50)—as if it might be possible ever to justify such abuse. Falsely
blaming herself, Katty fails to see, as Collard does, how he is titillated

by dehumanizing women into chattel. Yet what Katty has seen precipitates a household crisis. She barricades herself in shame in an upstairs bath, emerging much later to announce, in sorrow and frustration,

> I hate the me I have to be with him. If only I could have the baby it
> would give me someone to love and make someone who'd love me.
> There'd be a reason for having the fine house and the lovely yard.
> (57)

Of course the same impulse that has driven Katty to mold herself to Wayne's desire for a submissive wife keeps her from reconfiguring her life. She remains committed to their marriage, answering Marshael's inquiry into her next move with numb resignation: "Why, nothing. That's all I can do. I don't have children or a career like you do. Anyway I don't like changes" (58). Katty takes refuge behind the "incompetency 'demands' of the conventional feminine role." [13]

What makes Katty interesting as a specimen of rage repudiated is not her response to Wayne's cruelty but a childhood experience she confides during an intimate talk with the other women, who have congregated in Marshael's bedroom to comfort and cheer her as she mourns. The lights go up on them in the midst of their trading stories of the cruellest thing they have ever done. The segue to Katty's story suggests its dramaturgic importance:

> KATTY *(Pulling at her hair with glee.)* Oh, it's so awful! It's too
>   horrible! You won't think I'm sweet anymore!
> COLLARD We don't care! We don't care!
> PIXROSE No, we don't care! Tell us! (54–55)

Collard and Pixrose function as a Greek chorus. They deliver the judgment of a community of women—"We don't care! We don't care!"— that sharply contrasts with the conventional commitment to sentimentality imposed upon women by the male characters in these texts. Moreover, it is possible to hear in Pixrose's "Tell us" a resemblance of a similar moment in *Portrait of the Artist* in which Joyce may be punning on the Greek noun *telos*.[14] Like Stephen Dedalus, who is engaged in challenging the authority of the Roman Catholic Church to establish the ultimate purpose of life, Katty challenges with her story of girlhood violence the authority of men to establish the *telos* of women:

KATTY One Easter Sunday I was walking to church with my maid, Lizzie Pearl. Well, I was all dressed to kill for in my white ruffled dress and my white Easter bonnet and carrying my white parasol. Well, Harry and Virginia Dooley came up and shoved me down into a huge mudhole.... [Later that day] ... Lizzie Pearl and I sneaked back over to their back yard and yanked the chirping heads off of every one of their colored Easter chicks—We murdered them *all* with our bare hands! (55)

It is difficult to reconcile this portrait of Katty with the other that prevails. In Wayne's absence, she paints herself "with glee" as fully capable of retaliating violently against indignities she has suffered. In Wayne's presence, however, she regresses to the role of a child, even using baby-talk to soothe him as he pretends to grieve the loss of his brother: "Why we're all gonna do every little bitty thing we can do to unburden poor, old Papa Sweet Potato" (9).

Katty's regression is intriguingly linked to her apparent inability to carry a fetus to term. Because Wayne reduces Katty to a "twat," he continuously snuffs out her adult interiority, where interiority signifies not simply an emotional and physical readiness to bear children but also a mature knowledge of the terrain of one's own imagination, memory, and will. This link between male sexuality and the death of female interiority is reiterated elsewhere in *The Wake* when Collard abruptly propositions Slade: "Brocker, honey ... you gonna leave me forever unravished?" (46–47). With his eye on Marshael instead, Brocker Slade refuses, and Collard, affronted, strikes back: "Oh, Marshael. Right, Marshael. Well, that's all right then. 'Course she's nothing like me. She doesn't caress death and danger with open legs" (47). Here Collard represents heterosexual intercourse as an act of heroic bravado, a potentially fatal sacrifice on the woman's part. (The metaphor also evokes the literal risk of death that women face during childbirth.) Later, her observation that sex with men threatens the death of the female subject is explicitly linked to Katty's instinctive regression. As Slade serenades Marshael from outside her window, Collard, protecting her sister as well as herself, throws a nest of bird's eggs at him, then assigns him responsibility: "Look! Now you've made me murder these baby eggs! I've done murder!" (62). Just as Collard sacrifices the embryonic lives of birds in a feeble attempt to ward off the dangers of Slade's predatory and at this time unwanted sexual advances toward Marshael, so Katty has killed Easter chicks to signify her resistance to the conventions of feminine obsequiousness, perhaps even to the expectation of motherhood. It is no accident of the text that Katty remains childless, her body expelling the embryonic fruits of her sexual relations with Wayne to preserve what little interiority is left her by their marriage. She controls her uterus if nothing else.

Although these narratives of "murder" intuitively link Katty and Collard, Collard is distinguished by openly resisting the imposition of patriarchal conventions. As we have seen, she furiously rejects sexual harassment from her brother-in-law Wayne, and in another memorable scene, as he insists that Marshael attend Jamey's wake, like it or not, Collard mocks him: "Look, just because you'll always have the taste of leather in your mouth, doesn't mean the rest of us have to" (67). Turning upon Wayne the equestrian metaphor previously applied to herself, Collard scorns him for having accepted the patriarchal bridle. Reversing the sign, she emphasizes the double standard by which men profit, and women suffer, from submitting to patriarchy—we know that Wayne has become a powerful small-town banker, Katty his slave. Yet it is also Collard who most articulates the toll of women's resistance against patriarchy. Ambivalent toward Slade, whom she once invited to "ravish" her, Collard is even more ambivalent toward her own reproductive freedom. In a magnetic scene, she recounts for the other women the aftermath of her abortion, which she imagines to be a violent act:

> I went out and ate fried chicken. Got a ten-piece bucket filled with mashed potatoes and gravy, coleslaw, and a roll. First it tasted good and greasy and gooey. Then I felt like I was eating my baby's skin and flesh and veins and all. I got so sick—(58)

In contrast to Ashbe's flippant scheme to parlay an abortion into a Tokyo vacation in *Am I Blue,* this painful memory illustrates the anguishing material consequences of Collard's resolve not to be bridled. It leaves her not simply "sick," but nightmarishly guilty. Again Henley records the cost of women's liberation in graphic images of animal dismemberment.[15] Associating the fetus and the fried chicken, which is the third appearance in *The Wake of Jamey Foster* of the trope of fowl destroyed (Easter chicks/bird eggs/fried chicken) as a sign of challenge to the conventions of gender, especially of the obligation to nurture, Collard imagines herself feeding off her own interior: "I felt like I was eating my baby's skin and flesh and veins." From another point of view, though, Collard is not a cannibal but a survivor. In this instance, to reject the fetus is to preserve her nascent claim to self-determination. Perhaps it is that claim that produces as much guilt as the abortion itself.

If Henley's plays collectively forecast the high price yet to be paid by virtually everyone for the manifold inequities long borne by women, the most expansive treatment of this idea is in *Crimes of the Heart*. Not the fairy tale of female bonding that Lorimar made it out to be in its 1986 production, *Crimes of the Heart* studies the origins and effects of domestic abuse, tracing the rise and fall of its principal heroine's rage, fingering the female conspirators of culturally sanctioned violence against women, exposing the link between sexism and racism, suggesting the often grave costs of women's coming to know themselves as wholly volitional beings.

Hovering over the MaGrath family in *Crimes of the Heart* is a curse as particular as any in Ibsen, Tennessee Williams, or Sam Shepard, and as general as post-classical Western culture itself: long ago, the matriarch of the MaGrath clan, in fury and despair, hanged herself and her cat in the fruit cellar of the family home. Her suicide affirmed for her daughters the ideological link between women's exercise of self-determination and death, a link dating at least from early Christian constructions of Eve's primal disobedience.[16] *Crimes of the Heart* dramatizes its continuing damage to the next generation, especially through the fallout from Babe and Zackery Botrelle's exploded marriage. Long physically abused by "the richest and most powerful man in all of Hazlehurst" (21), Babe has denied the significance of her own fractures and bruises, breaking free only after watching Zack maul Willie Jay, her fifteen-year-old African-American lover. Although Babe is enraged by Zack's racism and his consequent physical abuse of Willie Jay,[17] Babe's first response is to think of suicide, as her mother had done, then epiphanically to reject suicide as a viable response to explosive anger:

Why, I was gonna shoot off my own head! . . . I thought about
Mama . . . how she'd hung herself. Then I realized—that's right, I
realized how I didn't want to kill myself! And she—she probably
didn't want to kill herself. (49)

Instead, fittingly, she shoots Zack in the belly, inflicting *quid pro quo* an
ironic even if uncalculated revenge on a "bully" who had threatened to
cut out Willie's "gizzard" (42, 49). Though Babe is no avenger, her
shooting Zackery might seem to presage a heroine's decisive new commitment to self-determination. But near the end of *Crimes of the Heart*
Henley dashes that hope, having Babe comically regress toward suicide.
Without success she tries to hang, then to asphyxiate herself in a gas
oven. Babe suffers the by-now-familiar arc: once vented, her rage
boomerangs. In effect she mentally implodes, just as her compatriot
Marshael does in *The Wake*. Recall that Marshael, though liberated
by her husband's death from one cycle of emotional neglect, is still
furiously angry at him, confessing that she feels as if "a hole's been shot
through me, and all my insides have been blown out somewhere else"
(*Wake*, 43).

In earlier plays, heroines abort their rage or, what amounts to the
same thing, turn it inward, for obliquely palpable reasons that spectators
must infer. In *Crimes*, however, the playwright delivers a direct cause of
Babe's reversal, namely Zackery's intention to commit her to the Whit-
field psychiatric hospital (114). His plan disorients but also catalyzes
Babe, who "slams the phone down and stares wildly ahead: He's not.
He's not. . . . I'll do it. I will. And he won't" (114). The indicative verbs
here signify that Babe again turns to suicide as the only gesture of self-
determination available in a universe otherwise controlled by those such
as her estranged lawyer-husband, who is ominously confident that psychiatric clinics stand ready to isolate, punish, and perhaps reprogram
women who, in their rage, repudiate the hegemony of men. Zackery is
obviously a "total criminal" (43), as Babe's defense lawyer claims. Yet
Henley insists we not dismiss him as an aberrant loner, but see him as
an integral member of a community that permits, even expects, men to
abuse women, and that expects women to cope with it by clinging to the
theorem of female martyrdom. That theorem is best expressed in a
colloquial commonplace by Elain, the ex-beauty queen, who counsels
Carnell on her loss of the Miss Firecracker title: "Just try to remember

how Mama was enlightened by her affliction" (*Firecracker*, 80). Though none of the women in *Crimes of the Heart* has in so many words similarly advised Babe to tough out Zackery's abuse, Babe nevertheless has learned well not to expect others to validate her supposedly unfeminine rage, neither before nor after she shoots Zackery. Thus when her sister Lenny and cousin Chick question Babe as to motive, she is virtually mute, offering only that she "didn't like [Zackery's] looks" (27). Obviously ridiculous, this red herring intensifies her silence. Elizabeth Stanko observes that abused women's silence "is linked to an understanding of [their] powerlessness; it is a recognition of the contradictory expectations of femaleness and probable judgments others commonly render about any woman's involvement in male violence."[18] Henley sharpens her critique of women who collude with oppressive forces by depicting Babe's attorney Barnette Lloyd as steadfastly supportive of his accused client, suggesting how little one's gender necessarily dictates one's politics.

Indeed, in small ways and large, Lenny and especially Chick reproduce the inequities of gender that have been insinuated into every social discourse. Lenny, for example, anticipates Zack's psychiatric prescription, telling Meg, "I believe Babe is ill. I mean in-her-head ill" (17). Lenny fails to see how her diagnosis reinforces a double standard of provocation, in which men's "retaliatory behavior is acceptable," and women's is not.[19] But it is cousin Chick, who works the system well enough to have been accepted to membership in the Hazlehurst Ladies' Social League, who is Zackery's far more malignant if still unwitting conspirator. Deploying the concept of "shame" to police other women, Chick consistently attacks what she takes to be the MaGraths' lack of obedience to a code of womanhood that emphasizes decorum, not subjectivity; submission, not independence. She is not simply a watchdog, but a burlesque[20] obsessed by "the skeletons in the MaGraths' closet" (6) her anger rising as the sisters' violations mount. After spying Meg returning from a night with Doc, for example, Chick bashes Meg in order to recruit Lenny into conscious alliance with the model of suffocating female subjectivity endorsed by the Ladies' Social League.[21] Chick pities not Meg but Lenny:

You must be so ashamed! You must just want to die! Why, I always said that girl was nothing but cheap Christmas trash! . . . Meg's a low-class tramp and you need not have one more blessed thing to do with her and her disgusting behavior. (112)

When Lenny refuses to concede Meg's depravity, Chick explodes, inadvertently revealing the root of her anger:

> I've just about had my fill of you trashy MaGraths and your trashy ways: hanging yourselves in cellars; carrying on with married men; shooting your own husbands! . . . [*Turning toward Babe*] And don't you think she's not gonna end up at the state prison farm or in some — mental institution. Why, it's a clear-cut case of manslaughter with intent to kill! . . . That's what everyone's saying, deliberate intent to kill! And you'll pay for that! Do you hear me? You'll pay! (112–13)

"Manslaughter," from the lexicon of law, aptly describes Chick's judgment of the MaGraths' violations, their budding refusals to "pay" into a patriarchal discourse that brands women "cheap Christmas trash," that blames the victim for spouse abuse, that again insinuates death as the inevitable consequence of women's self-determination ("you must just want to die!"). In Chick's eyes, resistance is indeed man/slaughter.

Against Chick's slavish dependence upon pernicious communal values, Henley juxtaposes Meg's apparently fierce independence. Faced with the artifacts of her sister's medical history, for example, which records the consequences of Zack's spousal violence, Meg rants, "This is madness! Did he do this to her? I'll kill him; I will — I'll fry his blood!" (43); in the Senecan image Meg boldly claims the prerogative of revenge abdicated by most of Henley's other heroines. And later, she quells Babe's self-criminations by erasing the privileged line between sanity and madness, declaring, "Why, you're just as perfectly sane as anyone walking the streets of Hazlehurst, Mississippi" (119); in Meg's circuitous compliment we may hear an indictment of the citizenry for continuing to tolerate domestic violence.

In these moments of bravado Meg seems stronger than Babe for openly resisting the forces under which Babe has long suffered, but elsewhere Henley suggests that Meg likewise suffers from deep ambivalence about the scope and strength of her own freedom. Feigning heroic indifference toward the dangers of smoking, for example, she reiterates the link between women's self-determination and death that led her mother to hang herself in the fruit cellar: "That's what I like about [smoking], Chick—taking a drag off of death. . . . Mmm! Gives me a sense of controlling my own destiny. What power! What exhilaration! Want a drag?" (28). Unlike Lenny and Babe, who seemed glued to Hazlehurst, Meg has attempted to wrest her destiny away from the Ladies' Social League by exiling herself to Los Angeles, a move that demonstrates autonomy and mobility. In L.A., though, she has met failure. Once an aspiring singer, she has succumbed to clerking for a dog food company (23), and in her words has recently gone "insane," winding up in the psychiatric ward of L.A. County Hospital (85). The cause, as we gradually come to see, is the residual effects of her mother's suicide. Much like Carnelle in *Miss Firecracker,* who laments that "people've been dying practically all my life," and "I guess I should be used to it by now" (12), Meg has stoically attempted to block out the pain of having been the one to discover her mother's body.[22] Yet Babe recalls that during girlhood outings to the public library and the Dixieland Drugstore,

> Meg would spend all her time reading and looking through this old black book called *Disease of the Skin.* It was full of the most sickening pictures you've ever seen. Things like rotting-away noses and eyeballs drooping off down the sides of people's faces, and scabs and sores and eaten-away places [At Dixieland Drugs, examining a crippled-children poster, Meg would say] "See, I can stand it. I can stand it. Just look how I'm gonna be able to stand it." (66–67)

The memory illustrates Meg's resolve to steel herself against loss, an early decision that continues to sabotage her life as an adult. Reversing the usual pattern in Henley's plays, it has been Meg who abandoned her sometime lover Doc, rather than vice versa, during Hurricane Camille: returned from L.A., she confesses to him, "It was my fault to leave you. I was crazy. I thought I was choking. I felt choked!" (84). Meg's fear of "choking"[23] not only recalls her mother's suicide by hanging, but also illuminates what is for her virtually a synaptic link between romantic alliances with men and the potential snuffing out of her own life. But, she tells Doc, ""I was crazy." Apologizing, labelling her earlier perceptions of risk as signs of mental illness, Meg now repudiates her own intuition and thus repatriates herself into the Hazlehurst community. À la Elain in *Miss Firecracker,* she too "comes home."

Meg's maneuver is consonant with the pattern of surrender that is woven through Henley's scripts. We may conclude that these heroines engage in quasi-feminist rebellion, if they engage in it at all, for psychological rather than political motives. Babe makes the point best when she refutes what is to her the alarming possibility that she intended her interracial liaison with Willie Jay to be a political statement: "I'm not a liberal! I'm a democratic! I was just lonely! I was so lonely. And he was so good" (48). Babe's verbal slip—an adjective for a noun—reveals an inarticulate command of the political, at least disqualifying her from playing the conscious iconoclast. As in this instance, Henley's heroines seem not to recognize as such the feminist awakenings that bubble to the surfaces of their consciousnesses, as they seek to repair and preserve their lives within the system they have inherited. Yet they come to life inside Henley's crucible of populist tragicomedy, in which regressive comic fantasies and tragic aspirations collide; osmotically the heroines have absorbed some of the energies of the feminist movement, and in their own ways, they grope toward liberty.[24]

NOTES

1. On the implications of community for Henley's characters, other commentators have tended to read more optimistically. Hargrove, for example, finds "ultimately cheering and sustaining" the fact "That each plays ends with two or more characters joined together in a bond of human solidarity" (Nancy D. Hargrove, "The Tragicomic Vision of Beth Henley's Drama," *Southern Quarterly,* 22: 4 [1984] 69); Harbin emphasizes the "awakened sense of the restorative powers of familial trust and communion" in *Crimes of the Heart,* but concedes that the other plays leave characters suspended in "hopeless resignation" (Billy J. Harbin "Familial Bonds in the Plays of Beth Henley," *Southern Quarterly,* 25: 3 [1987), 88, 93); Laughlin, emphasizing *Crimes of the Heart,* too, claims it "proposes a vision of women bonding with each other and dramatizes a joyful celebration of this bond" (Karen L. Laughlin, "Criminality, Desire and Community: A Feminist Approach to Beth Henley's *Crimes of the Heart,*" *Women and Performance: A Journal of Feminist Theory,* 3: 1 [1986], 48). I argue that Henley dramatizes a far more ambiguous vision of community, of "female bonding" in particular.

2. For discussion of politically radical heroines in the tradition of Southern proletarian fiction, see Sylvia Jenkins Cook, "Poor Whites, Feminists, and Marxists," in *From "Tobacco Road" to Route 66* (Chapel Hill, 1976), 98–124.

3. Years in parentheses refer to the date of first production.

4. Beth Henley, *The Miss Firecracker Contest* (Garden City, NY, 1985), 38. Hereafter cited as *Firecracker*.

5. Beth Henley, *Crimes of the Heart* (New York, 1982), 19. Hereafter cited as *Crimes*.

6. Beth Henley, *The Wake of Janey Foster* (New York, 1983), 12. Hereafter cited as *Wake*.

7. Harbin mistakenly argues that Marshael's "grim suffering remains unrelieved throughout the play" (93).

8. Beth Henley, *Am I Blue* (New York, 1982), 23.

9. Mary Field Belenky *et al.*, *Women's Ways of Knowing: The Development of Self, Voice, and Mind* (New York, 1986), 82.

10. Belenky points out that many women start a transition to subjectivist autonomy and power only after experiencing a crisis in their trust of male authority (58).

11. Gordon Braden, *Renaissance Tragedy and the Senecan Tradition: Anger's Privilege* (New Haven, 1985), 2.

12. George Mariscal, "The Other Quixote," in Nancy Armstrong and Leonard Tennenhouse, eds., *The Violence of Representation* (New York, 1989), 113.

13. Belenky, 104. Belenky is citing N. Livson and H. Peskin, "Psychological Health at Age 40: Predictions from Adolescent Personality," in D. Eichorn *et al.*, eds., *Present and Past in Mid-Life* (New York, 1981), 191.

14. Edmund L. Epstein, *The Ordeal of Stephen Dedalus: The Conflict of the Generations in James Joyce's "A Portrait of the Artist as a Young Man"* (Carbondale, IL., 1971), 10.

15. Henley uses the technique to comic advantage when Marshael bites the ears off a chocolate Easter rabbit as the play opens.

16. Elaine Pagels cites Tertulian, a second-century Carthaginian theologian, excoriating women: "You are the devil's gateway ... You are she who persuaded him whom the devil did not dare attack ... *do you not know that every one of you is an Eve?*" See *Adam, Eve, and the Serpent* (New York, 1988), 63 (her emphasis).

17. Belenky *et al.* observe that abused women often respond by continuing to care for others, but not for themselves (166).

18. Elizabeth Stanko, *Intimate Intrusions: Women's Experience of Male Violence* (London, 1985), 72. Laughlin (43) says that "Elissa Gelfand and others have highlighted the tendency of (predominantly male) criminologists to explain

the female criminal's surprising departure from the expected patterns of inactivity and domesticity as 'monstrous'."

19. James Ptacek, "Why Do Men Batter Their Wives?" in Kersti Yllö and Michele Bogard, eds., *Feminist Perspectives on Wife Abuse* (Newbury Park, CA, 1988), 145.

20. Jacobs traces the literary evolution of caricatures of the southern poor white to William Byrd II's *History of the Dividing Line* (1728), not published until 1841, but circulating in manuscript much earlier. Robert D. Jacobs, "*Tobacco Road:* Lowlife and the Comic Tradition," in Louis D. Rubin, Jr., ed., *The American South: Portrait of a Culture* (Baton Rouge, 1980), 206–26. Hargrove notes that Chicks' name fits her: she "is nervous, nosy, and bossy, verbally 'pecking' at everyone" (63).

21. Laughlin observes that Chick's "attempts to divide or degrade the Magrath [sic] sisters play directly into the hands of the patriarchal order" (55).

22. Hargrove admires the characters' collective "strength or stoicism," declaring that "perhaps the dominant theme of her drama ultimately is the value of love" (55).

23. See Mac Sam's ironic observation, "I was almost choked to death by my mama's umbilical cord at birth" (*Firecracker,* 63).

24. Thanks to my colleagues Linda K. Hughes, Robert Donahoo, and Rob McDonald for reading earlier drafts of this essay, and especially to Steven Wozniak for his encouragement and counsel. An earlier version of this essay was presented on 14 February 1992 before a session of the Southern Humanities Conference, meeting at the University of North Carolina, Chapel Hill. Thanks to Professors Annette Cox for inviting me and Roberta Rosenberg for good conversation about *Crimes of the Heart.*

CHAPTER 11

My Words to Victor Frankenstein above the Village of Chamounix

Performing Transgender Rage

SUSAN STRYKER

INTRODUCTORY NOTES

The following work is a textual adaptation of a performance piece originally presented at "Rage! Across the Disciplines," an arts, humanities, and social sciences conference held June 10–12, 1993, at California State University, San Marcos. The interdisciplinary nature of the conference, its theme, and the organizers' call for both performances and academic papers inspired me to be creative in my mode of presenting a topic then much on my mind. As a member of Transgender Nation—a militantly queer, direct action transsexual advocacy group—I was at the time involved in organizing a disruption and protest at the American Psychiatric Association's 1993 annual meeting in San Francisco. A good deal of the discussion at our planning meetings concerned how to harness the intense emotions emanating from transsexual experience—especially rage—and mobilize them into effective political actions. I was intrigued by the prospect of critically examining this rage in a more academic setting through an idiosyncratic application of the concept of gender performativity. My idea was to perform self-consciously a queer gender rather than simply talk about it, thus embodying and enacting the concept simultaneously under discussion. I wanted the formal structure of the work to express a transgender aesthetic by replicating our abrupt, often jarring transitions between genders—challenging generic

Reprinted by kind permission of Gordon and Breach Science Publishers, Inc., from *GLQ* 1:3, 237–54. Copyright © 1994 by Gordon and Breach Science Publishers, Inc.

classification with the forms of my words just as my transsexuality challenges the conventions of legitimate gender and my performance in the conference room challenged the boundaries of acceptable academic discourse. During the performance, I stood at the podium wearing gen-derfuck drag—combat boots, threadbare Levi 501s over a black lace body suit, a shredded Transgender Nation T-shirt with the neck and sleeves cut out, a pink triangle quartz crystal pendant, grunge metal jewelry, and a six-inch long marlin hook dangling around my neck on a length of heavy stainless steel chain. I decorated the set by draping my black leather biker jacket over my chair at the panelists' table. The jacket had handcuffs on the left shoulder, rainbow freedom rings on the right side lacings, and Queer Nation-style stickers reading SEX CHANGE, DYKE, and FUCK YOUR TRANSPHOBIA plastered on the back.

MONOLOGUE

The transsexual body is an unnatural body. It is the product of medical science. It is a technological construction. It is flesh torn apart and sewn together again in a shape other than that in which it was born. In these circumstances, I find a deep affinity between myself as a transsexual woman and the monster in Mary Shelley's *Frankenstein*. Like the mon-ster, I am too often perceived as less than fully human due to the means of my embodiment; like the monster's as well, my exclusion from human community fuels a deep and abiding rage in me that I, like the monster, direct against the conditions in which I must struggle to exist.

I am not the first to link Frankenstein's monster and the transsexual body. Mary Daly makes the connection explicit by discussing transsexu-ality in "Boundary Violation and the Frankenstein Phenomenon," in which she characterizes transsexuals as the agents of a "necrophilic invasion" of female space (69–72). Janice Raymond, who acknowledges Daly as a formative influence, is less direct when she says that "the problem of transsexuality would best be served by morally mandating it out of existence," but in this statement she nevertheless echoes Victor Frankenstein's feelings toward the monster: "Begone, vile insect, or rather, stay, that I may trample you to dust. You reproach me with your creation" (Raymond, 178; Shelley, 95). It is a commonplace of literary criticism to note that Frankenstein's monster is his own dark, romantic double, the alien Other he constructs and upon which he projects all he cannot accept in himself; indeed, Frankenstein calls the monster "my own vampire, my own spirit set loose from the grave" (Shelley, 74). Might I suggest that Daly, Raymond and others of their ilk similarly construct the transsexual as their own particular golem?[1]

The attribution of monstrosity remains a palpable characteristic of most lesbian and gay representations of transsexuality, displaying in unnerving detail the anxious, fearful underside of the current cultural fascination with transgenderism.[2] Because transsexuality more than any other transgender practice or identity represents the prospect of destabilizing the foundational presupposition of fixed genders upon which a politics of personal identiy depends, people who have invested their aspirations for social justice in identitarian movements say things about us out of sheer panic that, if said of other minorities, would see print only in the most hate-riddled, white supremacist, Christian fascist rags. To quote extensively from one letter to the editor of a popular San Francisco gay/lesbian periodical:

> I consider transsexualism to be a fraud, and the participants in it . . . perverted. The transsexual [claims] he/she needs to change his/her body in order to be his/her "true self." Because this "true self" requires another physical form in which to manifest itself, it must therefore war with nature. One cannot change one's gender. What occurs is a cleverly manipulated exterior: what has been done is mutation. What exists beneath the deformed surface is the same person who was there prior to the deformity. People who break or deform their bodies [act] out the sick farce of a deluded, patriarchal approach to nature, alienated from true being.

Referring by name to one particular person, self-identified as a transsexual lesbian, whom she had heard speak in a public forum at the San Francisco Women's Building, the letter-writer went on to say:

> When an estrogenated man with breasts loves a woman, that is not lesbianism, that is mutilated perversion. [This individual] is not a threat to the lesbian community, he is an outrage to us. He is not a lesbian, he is a mutant man, a self-made freak, a deformity, an insult. He deserves a slap in the face. After that, he deserves to have his body and mind made well again.[3]

When such beings as these tell me I war with nature, I find no more reason to mourn my opposition to them—or to the order they claim to represent—than Frankenstein's monster felt in its enmity to the human race. I do not fall from the grace of their company—I roar gleefully away from it like a Harley-straddling, dildo-packing leatherdyke from hell.

The stigmatization fostered by this sort of pejorative labelling is not without consequence. Such words have the power to destroy transsexual lives. On January 5, 1993, a twenty-two-year-old pre-operative transsexual woman from Seattle, Filisa Vistima, wrote in her journal, "I wish I was anatomically 'normal' so I could go swimming. . . . But no, I'm a mutant, Frankenstein's monster." Two months later Filisa Vistima committed suicide. What drove her to such despair was the exclusion she experienced in Seattle's queer community, some members of which opposed Filisa's participation because of her transsexuality—even though she identified as and lived as a bisexual woman. The Lesbian Resource Center where she served as a volunteer conducted a survey of its constituency to determine whether it should stop offering services to male-to-female transsexuals. Filisa did the data entry for tabulating the survey results; she didn't have to imagine how people felt about her kind. The Seattle Bisexual Women's Network announced that if it admitted transsexuals the SBWN would no longer be a women's organization. "I'm sure," one member said in reference to the inclusion of bisexual transsexual women, "the boys can take care of themselves." Filisa Vistima was not a boy, and she found it impossible to take care of herself. Even in death she found no support from the community in which she claimed membership. "Why didn't Filisa commit herself for psychiatric care?" asked a columnist in the Seattle *Gay News*. "Why didn't Filisa demand her civil rights?" In this case, not only did the angry villagers hound their monster to the edge of town, they reproached her for being vulnerable to the torches. Did Filisa Vistima commit suicide, or did the queer community of Seattle kill her?[4]

I want to lay claim to the dark power of my monstrous identity without using it as a weapon against others or being wounded by it myself. I will say this as bluntly as I know how: I am a transsexual, and therefore I am a monster. Just as the words "dyke," "fag," "queer," "slut," and "whore" have been reclaimed, respectively, by lesbians and gay men, by anti-assimilationist sexual minorities, by women who pursue erotic pleasure, and by sex industry workers, words like "creature," "monster," and "unnatural" need to be reclaimed by the transgendered. By embracing and accepting them, even piling one on top of another, we may dispel their ability to harm us. A creature, after all, in the dominant tradition of Western European culture, is nothing other than a created being, a made thing. The affront you humans take at being called a "creature" results from the threat the term poses to your status as "lords of creation," beings elevated above mere material existence. As in the case of being called "it," being called a "creature" suggests the lack or loss of a superior personhood. I find no shame, however, in acknowledging my egalitarian relationship with non-human material Being; everything emerges from the same matrix of possibilities. "Monster" is derived from the Latin noun *monstrum*, "divine portent," itself formed on the root of the verb *monere*, "to warn." It came to refer to living things of anomalous shape or structure, or to fabulous creatures like the sphinx who were composed of strikingly incongruous parts, because the ancients considered the appearance of such beings to be a sign of some impending supernatural event. Monsters, like angels, functioned as messengers and heralds of the extraordinary. They served to announce impending revelation, saying, in effect, "Pay attention; something of profound importance is happening."

Hearken unto me, fellow creatures. I who have dwelt in a form unmatched with my desire, I whose flesh has become an assemblage of incongruous anatomical parts, I who achieve the similitude of a natural body only through an unnatural process, I offer you this warning: the Nature you bedevil me with is a lie. Do not trust it to protect you from what I represent, for it is a fabrication that cloaks the groundlessness of the privilege you seek to maintain for yourself at my expense. You are as constructed as me; the same anarchic womb has birthed us both. I call upon you to investigate your nature as I have been compelled to confront mine. I challenge you to risk abjection and flourish as well as have I. Heed my words, and you may well discover the seams and sutures in yourself.

CRITICISM

In answer to the question he poses in the title of his recent essay, "What is a Monster? (According to *Frankenstein*)," Peter Brooks suggests that, whatever else a monster might be, it "may also be that which eludes gender definition" (219). Brooks reads Mary Shelley's story of an over-reaching scientist and his troublesome creation as an early dissent from the nineteenth-century realist literary tradition, which had not yet at-tained dominance as a narrative form. He understands *Frankenstein* to unfold textually through a narrative strategy generated by tension be-tween a visually oriented epistemology, on the one hand, and another approach to knowing the truth of bodies that privileges verbal linguisti-cality, on the other (199–200). Knowing by seeing and knowing by speaking/hearing are gendered, respectively, as masculine and feminine in the critical framework within which Brooks operates. Considered in this context, Shelley's text is informed by—and critiques from a wom-an's point of view—the contemporary reordering of knowledge brought about by the increasingly compelling truth claims of Enlightenment science. The monster problematizes gender partly through its failure as a viable subject in the visual field; though referred to as "he," it thus offers a feminine, and potentially feminist, resistance to definition by a phallicized scopophilia. The monster accomplishes this resistance by mastering language in order to claim a position as a speaking subject and enact verbally the very subjectivity denied it in the specular realm.[5]

Transsexual monstrosity, however, along with its affect, transgender rage, can never claim quite so secure a means of resistance because of the inability of language to represent the transgendered subject's move-ment over time between stably gendered positions in a linguistic struc-ture. Our situation effectively reverses the one encountered by Franken-stein's monster. Unlike the monster, we often successfully cite the culture's visual norms of gendered embodiment. This citation becomes a subversive resistance when, through a provisional use of language, we verbally desire the unnaturalness of our claim to the subject positions we nevertheless occupy.[6]

The prospect of a monster with a life and will of its own is a principal source of horror for Frankenstein. The scientist has taken up his project with a specific goal in mind—nothing less than the intent to subject nature completely to his power. He finds a means to accomplish his desires through modern science, whose devotees, it seems to him, "have acquired new and almost unlimited powers; they can command the thunders of heaven, mimic the earthquake, and even mock the invisible world with its shadows. . . . More, far more, will I achieve," thought

Frankenstein. "I will pioneer a new way, explore unknown powers, and unfold to the world the deepest mysteries of creation" (Shelley, 47). The fruit of his efforts is not, however, what Frankenstein anticipated. The rapture he expected to experience at the awakening of his creature turned immediately to dread. "I saw the dull yellow eyes of the creature open.... His jaws opened, and he muttered some inarticulate sounds, while a grin wrinkled his cheeks. He might have spoken, but I did not hear; one hand was stretched out, seemingly to detain me, but I escaped" (Shelley, 56, 57). The monster escapes, too, and parts company with its maker for a number of years. In the interim, it learns something of its situation in the world, and rather than bless its creator, the monster curses him. The very success of Mary Shelley's scientist in his self-appointed task thus paradoxically proves its futility: rather than demonstrate Frankenstein's power over materiality, the newly enlivened body of the creature attests to its maker's failure to attain the mastery he sought. Frankenstein cannot control the mind and feelings of the monster he makes. It exceeds and refutes his purposes.

My own experience as a transsexual parallels the monster's in this regard. The consciousness shaped by the transsexual body is no more the creation of the science that refigures its flesh than the monster's mind is the creation of Frankenstein. The agenda that produced hormonal and surgical sex reassignment techniques is no less pretentious, and no more noble, than Frankenstein's. Heroic doctors still endeavor to triumph over nature. The scientific discourse that produced sex reassignment techniques is inseparable from the pursuit of immortality through the perfection of the body, the fantasy of total mastery through the transcendence of an absolute limit, and the hubristic desire to create life itself.[7] Its genealogy emerges from a metaphysical quest older than modern science, and its cultural politics are aligned with a deeply conservative attempt to stabilize gendered identity in service of the naturalized heterosexual order.

None of this, however, precludes medically constructed transsexual bodies from being viable sites of subjectivity. Nor does it guarantee the compliance of subjects thus embodied with the agenda that resulted in a transsexual means of embodiment. As we rise up from the operating tables of our rebirth, we transsexuals are something more, and something other, than the creatures our makers intended us to be. Though medical techniques for sex reassignment are capable of crafting bodies

that satisfy the visual and morphological criteria that generate naturalness as their effect, engaging with those very techniques produces a
subjective experience that belies the naturalistic effect biomedical technology can achieve. Transsexual embodiment, like the embodiment of
the monster, places its subject in an unassimilable, antagonistic, queer
relationship to a Nature in which it must nevertheless exist.

Frankenstein's monster articulates its unnatural situation within the
natural world with far more sophistication in Shelley's novel than might
be expected by those familiar only with the version played by Boris
Karloff in James Whale's classic films from the 1930s. Film critic Vito
Russo suggests that Whale's interpretation of the monster was influenced
by the fact that the director was a closeted gay man at the time he made
his Frankenstein films. The pathos he imparted to his monster derived
from the experience of his own hidden sexual identity.[8] Monstrous and
unnatural in the eyes of the world, but seeking only the love of his own
kind and the acceptance of human society, Whale's creature externalizes
and renders visible the nightmarish loneliness and alienation that the
closet can breed. But this is not the monster who speaks to me so
potently of my own situation as an openly transsexual being. I emulate
instead Mary Shelley's literary monster, who is quick-witted, agile,
strong, and eloquent.

In the novel, the creature flees Frankenstein's laboratory and hides in
the solitude of the Alps, where, by stealthy observation of the people it
happens to meet, it gradually acquires a knowledge of language, literature, and the conventions of European society. As first it knows little of
its own condition. "I had never yet seen a being resembling me, or who
claimed any intercourse with me," the monster notes. "What did this
mean? Who was I? What was I? Whence did I come? What was my
destination? These questions continually recurred, but I was unable to
solve them" (Shelley, 116, 130). Then, in the pocket of the jacket it took
as it fled the laboratory, the monster finds Victor Frankenstein's journal,
and learns the particulars of its creation. "I sickened as I read," the
monster says. "Increase of knowledge only discovered to me what a
wretched outcast I was" (Shelley, 124, 125).

Upon learning its history and experiencing the rejection of all to
whom it reached out for companionship, the creature's life takes a dark
turn. "My feelings were those of rage and revenge," the monster declares. "I, like the arch-fiend, bore a hell within me" (130). It would

have been happy to destroy all of Nature, but it settles, finally, on a more expedient plan to murder systematically all those whom Victor Frankenstein loves. Once Frankenstein realizes that his own abandoned creation is responsible for the deaths of those most dear to him, he retreats in remorse to a mountain village above his native Geneva to ponder his complicity in the crimes the monster has committed. While hiking on the glaciers in the shadow of Mont Blanc, above the village of Chamounix, Frankenstein spies a familiar figure approaching him across the ice. Of course, it is the monster, who demands an audience with its maker. Frankenstein agrees, and the two retire together to a mountaineer's cabin. There, in a monologue that occupies nearly a quarter of the novel, the monster tells Frankenstein the tale of its creation from its own point of view, explaining to him how it became so enraged.

These are my words to Victor Frankenstein, above the village of Chamounix. Like the monster, I could speak of my earliest memories, and how I became aware of my difference from everyone around me. I can describe how I acquired a monstrous identity by taking on the label "transsexual" to name parts of myself that I could not otherwise explain. I, too, have discovered the journals of the men who made my body, and who have made the bodies of creatures like me since the 1930s. I know in intimate detail the history of this recent medical intervention into the enactment of transgendered subjectivity; science seeks to contain and colonize the radical threat posed by a particular transgender strategy of resistance to the coerciveness of gender: physical alteration of the genitals.[9] I live daily with the consequences of medicine's definition of my identity as an emotional disorder. Through the filter of this official pathologization, the sounds that come out of my mouth can be summarily dismissed as the confused ranting of a diseased mind.

Like the monster, the longer I live in these conditions, the more rage I harbor. Rage colors me as it presses in through the pores of my skin, soaking in until it becomes the blood that courses through my beating heart. It is a rage bred by the necessity of existing in external circumstances that work against my survival. But there is yet another rage within.

JOURNAL (FEBRUARY 18, 1993)

Kim sat between my spread legs, her back to me, her tailbone on the edge of the table. Her left hand gripped my thigh so hard the bruises are

still there a week later. Sweating and bellowing, she pushed one last time
and the baby finally came. Through my lover's back, against the skin of
my own belly, I felt a child move out of another woman's body and into
the world. Strangers' hands snatched it away to suction the sticky green
meconium from its airways. "It's a girl," somebody said. Paul, I think.
Why, just then, did a jumble of dark, unsolicited feelings emerge word-
lessly from some quiet back corner of my mind? This moment of mira-
cles was not the time to deal with them. I pushed them back, knowing
they were too strong to avoid for long.

After three days we were all exhausted, slightly disappointed that
complications had forced us to go to Kaiser instead of having the birth
at home. I wonder what the hospital staff thought of our little tribe
swarming all over the delivery room: Stephanie, the midwife; Paul, the
baby's father; Kim's sister Gwen; my son Wilson and me; and two other
women who make up our family, Anne and Heather. And of course Kim
and the baby. She named her Denali, after the mountain in Alaska. I
don't think the medical folks had a clue as to how we all considered
ourselves to be related to each other. When the labor first began we all
took turns shifting between various supporting roles, but as the ordeal
progressed we settled into a more stable pattern. I found myself acting
as birth coach. Hour after hour, through dozens of sets of contractions,
I focused everything on Kim, helping her stay in control of her emotions
as she gave herself over to this inexorable process, holding on to her
eyes with mine to keep the pain from throwing her out of her body,
breathing every breath with her, being a companion. I participated, step
by increasingly intimate step, in the ritual transformation of consciousness surrounding her daughter's birth. Birth rituals work to prepare the
self for a profound opening, an opening as psychic as it is corporeal.
Kim's body brought this ritual process to a dramatic resolution for her,
culminating in a visceral, cathartic experience. But my body left me
hanging. I had gone on a journey to the point at which my companion
had to go on alone, and I needed to finish my trip for myself. To
conclude the birth ritual I had participated in, I needed to move something in me as profound as a whole human life.

I floated home from the hospital, filled with a vital energy that
wouldn't discharge. I puttered about until I was alone: my ex had come
over for Wilson; Kim and Denali were still at the hospital with Paul;
Stephanie had gone, and everyone else was out for a much-needed walk.

Finally, in the solitude of my home, I burst apart like a wet paper bag and spilled the emotional contents of my life through the hands I cupped like a sieve over my face. For days, as I had accompanied my partner on her journey, I had been progressively opening myself and preparing to let go of whatever was deepest within. Now everything in me flowed out, moving up from inside and out through my throat, my mouth because these things could never pass between the lips of my cunt. I knew the darkness I had glimpsed earlier would reemerge, but I had vast oceans of feeling to experience before that came up again.

Simple joy in the presence of new life came bubbling out first, wave after wave of it. I was so incredibly happy. I was so in love with Kim, had so much admiration for her strength and courage. I felt pride and excitement about the queer family we were building with Wilson, Anne, Heather, Denali, and whatever babies would follow. We've all tasted an exhilarating possibility in communal living and these nurturing, bonded kinships for which we have no adequate names. We joke about pioneering on a reverse frontier: venturing into the heart of civilization itself to reclaim biological reproduction from heterosexism and free it for our own uses. We're fierce; in a world of "traditional family values," we need to be.

Sometimes, though, I still mourn the passing of old, more familiar ways. It wasn't too long ago that my ex and I were married, woman and man. That love had been genuine, and the grief over its loss real. I had always wanted intimacy with women more than intimacy with men, and that wanting had always felt queer to me. She needed it to appear straight. The shape of my flesh was a barrier that estranged me from my desire. Like a body without a mouth, I was starving in the midst of plenty. I would not let myself starve, even if what it took to open myself for a deep connectedness cut off the deepest connections I actually had. So I abandoned one life and built this new one. The fact that she and I have begun getting along again, after so much strife between us, makes the bitterness of our separation somewhat sweet. On the day of the birth, this past loss was present even in its partial recovery; held up beside the newfound fullness of my life, it evoked a poignant, hopeful sadness that inundated me.

Frustration and anger soon welled up in abundance. In spite of all I'd accomplished, my identity still felt so tenuous. Every circumstance of life seemed to conspire against me in one vast, composite act of invalidation and erasure. In the body I was born with, I had been invisible as the person I considered myself to be; I had been invisible as a queer while the form of my body made my desires look straight. Now, as a dyke I am invisible among women; a transsexual, I am invisible among dykes. As the partner of a new mother, I am often invisible as a transsexual, a woman, and a lesbian—I've lost track of the friends and acquaintances these past nine months who've asked me if I was the father. It shows so dramatically how much they simply don't get what I'm doing with my body. The high price of whatever visible, intelligible, self-representation I have achieved makes the continuing experience of invisibility maddeningly difficult to bear.

The collective assumptions of the naturalized order soon overwhelmed me. Nature exerts such a hegemonic oppression. Suddenly I felt lost and scared, lonely and confused. How did that little Mormon boy from Oklahoma I used to be grow up to be a transsexual leatherdyke in San Francisco with a Berkeley Ph.D.? Keeping my bearings on such a long and strange trip seemed a ludicrous proposition. Home was so far gone behind me it was gone forever, and there was no place to rest. Battered by heavy emotions, a little dazed, I felt the inner walls that protect me dissolve to leave me vulnerable to all that could harm me. I cried, and abandoned myself to abject despair over what gender had done to me.

Everything's fucked up beyond all recognition. This hurts too much to go on. I came as close today as I'll ever come to giving birth— literally. My body can't do that; I can't even bleed without a wound, and yet I claim to be a woman. How? Why have I always felt that way? I'm such a goddamned freak. I can never be a woman like other women, but I could never be a man. Maybe there really is no place for me in all creation. I'm so tired of this ceaseless movement. I do war with nature. I am alienated from Being. I'm a self-mutilated deformity, a pervert, a mutant, trapped in monstrous flesh. God, I never wanted to be trapped again. I've destroyed myself. I'm falling into darkness. I am falling apart.

I enter the realm of my dreams. I am underwater, swimming upwards. It is dark. I see a shimmering light above me. I break through the plane of the water's surface with my lungs bursting. I suck for air—and find only more water. My lungs are full of water. Inside and out I am surrounded by it. Why am I not dead if there is no difference between me and what I am in? There is another surface above me and I swim frantically towards it. I see a shimmering light. I break the plane of the

water's surface over and over and over again. This water annihilates me.
I cannot be, and yet—an excruciating impossibility—I am. I will do
anything not to be here.

> I will swim forever.
> I will die for eternity.
> I will learn to breathe water.
> If I cannot change my situation I will change myself.

In this act of magical transformation
I recognize myself again.

I am groundless and boundless movement.
I am a furious flow.
I am one with the darkness and the wet.

And I am enraged.

Here at last is the chaos I held at bay.
Here at last is my strength.
I am not the water—
I am the wave,
and rage
is the force that moves me.

Rage
gives me back my body
as its own fluid medium.

Rage
punches a hole in water
around which I coalesce
to allow the flow to come through me.

Rage
constitutes me in my primal form.
It throws my head back
pulls my lips back over my teeth

opens my throat
and rears me up to howl:
: and no sound
dilutes
the pure quality of my rage.

No sound
exists
in this place without language
my rage is a silent raving.

Rage
throws me back at last
into this mundane reality
in this transfigured flesh
that aligns me with the power of my Being.

In birthing my rage,
my rage has rebirthed me.

THEORY

A formal disjunction seems particularly appropriate at this moment
because the affect I seek to examine critically, what I've termed
"transgender rage," emerges from the interstices of discursive practices
and at the collapse of generic categories. The rage itself is generated by
the subject's situation in a field governed by the unstable but indissoluble
relationship between language and materiality, a situation in which
language organizes and brings into signification matter that simultaneously eludes definitive representation and demands its own perpetual
rearticulation in symbolic terms. Within this dynamic field the subject
must constantly police the boundary constructed by its own founding in
order to maintain the fictions of "inside" and "outside against a regime
of signification/materialization whose intrinsic instability produces the
rupture of subjective boundaries as one of its regular features. The affect
of rage as I seek to define it is located at the margin of subjectivity and
the limit of signification. It originates in recognition of the fact that the
"outsideness" of a materiality that perpetually violates the foreclosure

of subjective space within a symbolic order is also necessarily "inside" the subject as grounds for the materialization of its body and the formation of its bodily ego.

This primary rage becomes specifically transgender rage when the inability to foreclose the subject occurs through a failure to satisfy norms of gendered embodiment. Transgender rage is the subjective experience of being compelled to transgress what Judith Butler has referred to as the highly gendered regulatory schemata that determine the viability of bodies, of being compelled to enter a "domain of abjected bodies, a field of deformation" that in its unlivability encompasses and constitutes the realm of legitimate subjectivity (16). Transgender rage is a queer fury, an emotional response to conditions in which it becomes imperative to take up, for the sake of one's own continued survival as a subject, a set of practices that precipitates one's exclusion from a naturalized order of existence that seeks to maintain itself as the only possible basis for being a subject. However, by mobilizing gendered identities and rendering them provisional, open to strategic development and occupation, this rage enables the establishment of subjects in new modes, regulated by different codes of intelligibility. Transgender rage furnishes a means for disidentification with compulsorily assigned subject positions. It makes the transition from one gendered subject position to another possible by using the impossibility of complete subjective foreclosure to organize an outside force as an inside drive, and vice versa. Through the operation of rage, the stigma itself becomes the source of transformative power.[10]

I want to stop and theorize at this particular moment in the text because in the lived moment of being thrown back from a state of abjection in the aftermath of my lover's daughter's birth, I immediately began telling myself a story to explain my experience. I started theorizing, using all the conceptual tools my education had put at my disposal. Other true stories of those events could undoubtedly be told, but upon my return I knew for a fact what lit the fuse to my rage in the hospital delivery room. It was the non-consensuality of the baby's gendering. You see, I told myself, wiping snot off my face with a shirt sleeve, bodies are rendered meaningful only through some culturally and historically specific mode of grasping their physicality that transforms the flesh into a useful artifact. Gendering is the initial step in this transformation, inseparable from the process of forming an identity by means of which we're fitted to a system of exchange in a heterosexual economy. Authority seizes upon specific material qualities of the flesh, particularly the genitals, as outward indication of future reproductive potential, constructs this flesh as a sign, and reads it to enculturate the body. Gender attribution is compulsory; it codes and deploys our bodies in ways that materially affect us, yet we choose neither our marks nor the meanings they carry.[11] This was the act accomplished between the beginning and the end of that short sentence in the delivery room: "It's a girl." This was the act that recalled all the anguish of my own struggles with gender. But this was also the act that enjoined my complicity in the nonconsensual gendering of another. A gendering violence is the founding condition of human subjectivity; having a gender is the tribal tattoo that makes one's personhood cognizable. I stood for a moment between the pains of two violations, the mark of gender and the unlivability of its absence. Could I say which one was worse? Or could I only say which one I felt could best be survived?

How can finding one's self prostrate and powerless in the presence of the Law of the Father not produce an unutterable rage? What difference does it make if the father in this instance was a pierced, tatooed, purple-haired punk fag anarchist who helped his dyke friend get pregnant? Phallogocentric language, not its particular speaker, is the scalpel that defines our flesh. I defy that Law in my refusal to abide by its original decree of my gender. Though I cannot escape its power, I can move through its medium. Perhaps if I move furiously enough, I can deform it in my passing to leave a trace of my rage. I can embrace it with a vengeance to rename myself, declare my transsexuality, and gain access to the means of my legible reinscription. Though I may not hold the stylus myself, I can move beneath it for my own deep self-sustaining pleasures.

To encounter the transsexual body, to apprehend a transgendered consciousness articulating itself, is to risk a revelation of the constructedness of the natural order. Confronting the implications of this constructedness can summon up all the violation, loss, and separation inflicted by the gendering process that sustains the illusion of naturalness. My transsexual body literalizes this abstract violence. As the bearers of this disquieting news, we transsexuals often suffer for the pain of others, but we do not willingly abide the rage of others directed against us. And we do have something else to say, if you will but listen to the monsters: the possibility of meaningful agency and action exists, even within fields of domination that bring about the universal cultural rape of all flesh. Be forewarned, however, that taking up this task will remake you in the process. By speaking as a monster in my personal voice, by using the dark, watery images of Romanticism and lapsing occasionally into its brooding cadences and grandiose postures, I employ the same literary techniques Mary Shelley used to elicit sympathy for her scientist's creation. Like the creature, I assert my worth as a monster in spite of the conditions my monstrosity requires me to face, and redefine a life worth living. I have asked the Miltonic questions Shelley poses in the epigraph of her novel: "did I request thee, Maker, from my clay to mould me man? Did I solicit thee from darkness to promote me?" With one voice, her monster and I answer "no" without debasing ourselves, for we have done the hard work of constituting ourselves on our own terms, against the natural order. Though we forego the privilege of naturalness, we are not deterred, for we ally ourselves instead with the chaos and blackness from which nature itself spills forth.[12]

If this is your path, as it is mine, let me offer whatever solace you may find in this monstrous benediction: May you discover the enlivening power of darkness within yourself. May it nourish your rage. May your rage inform your actions, and your actions transform you as you struggle to transform your world.

NOTES

1. While this comment is intended as a monster's disdainful dismissal, it nevertheless alludes to a substantial debate on the status of transgender practices and identities in lesbian feminism. H. S. Rubin, in a sociology dissertation in progress at Brandeis University, argues that the pronounced demographic upsurge in the female-to-male transsexual population during the 1970s and 1980s is directly related to the ascendancy within lesbianism of a "cultural feminism" that disparaged and marginalized practices smacking of an unliberated "gender inversion" model of homosexuality—especially the butch-femme roles associated with working-class lesbian bar culture. Cultural feminism thus consolidated a lesbian-feminist alliance with heterosexual feminism on a middle-class basis by capitulating to dominant ideologies of gender. The same suppression of transgender aspects of lesbian practice, I would add, simultaneously raised the spectre of male-to-female transsexual lesbians as a particular threat to the stability and purity of nontranssexual lesbian-feminist identity. See Echols for the broader context of this debate, and Raymond for the most vehement example of the anti-transgender position.

2. The current meaning of the term "transgender" is a matter of some debate. The word was originally coined as a noun in the 1970s by people who resisted categorization as either transvestites or transsexuals, and who used the term to describe their own identity. Unlike transsexuals but like transvestites, transgenders do not seek surgical alteration of their bodies but do habitually wear clothing that represents a gender other than the one to which they were assigned at birth. Unlike the transvestites but like the transsexuals, however, transgenders do not alter the vestimentary coding of their gender only episodically or primarily for sexual gratification; rather, they consistently and publicly express an ongoing commitment to their claimed gender identities through the same visual representational strategies used by others to signify that gender. The logic underlying this terminology reflects the widespread tendency to construe "gender" as the socio-cultural manifestation of a material "sex." Thus, while transsexuals express their identities through a physical change of embodiment, transgenders do so through a non-corporeal change in public gender expression that is nevertheless more complex than a simple change of clothes.

This essay uses "transgender" in a more recent sense, however, than its original one. That is, I use it here as an umbrella term that refers to all identities or practices that cross over, cut across, move between, or otherwise queer socially constructed sex/gender boundaries. The term includes, but is not limited to, transsexuality, heterosexual transvestism, gay drag, butch lesbianism, and such non-European identities as the Native American berdache or the Indian Hijra. Like "queer," "transgender" may also be used as a verb or an adjective. In this essay, transsexuality is considered to be a culturally and historically specific transgender practice/identity through which a transgendered subject enters into a relationship with medical, psychotherapeutic, and juridical institutions in order to gain access to certain hormonal and surgical technologies for enacting and embodying itself.

3. Mikuteit, 3–4, heavily edited for brevity and clarity.

4. The preceding paragraph draws extensively on, and sometimes paraphrases, O'Hartigan and Kahler.

5. See Laqueur, 1–7, for a brief discussion of the Enlightenment's effect on constructions of gender. Feminist interpretations of *Frankenstein* to which Brooks responds include Gilbert and Gubar, Jacobus, and Homans.

6. Openly transsexual speech similarly subverts the logic behind a remark by Bloom, 218, that "a beautiful 'monster,' or even a passable one, would not have been a monster."

7. Billings and Urban, 269, document especially well the medical attitude toward transsexual surgery as one of technical mastery of the body; Irvine, 259, suggests how transsexuality fits into the development of scientific sexology, though caution is advised in uncritically accepting the interpretation of transsex-

ual experience she presents in this chapter. Meyer, in spite of some extremely transphobic concluding comments, offers a good account of the medicalization of transgender identities; for a transsexual perspective on the scientific agenda behind sex reassignment techniques, see Stone, especially the section entitled "All of reality in late capitalist culture lusts to become an image for its own security" (280–304).

8. Russo, 49–50: "Homosexual parallels in *Frankenstein* (1931) and *Bride of Frankenstein* (1935) arose from a vision both films had of the monster as an antisocial figure in the same way that gay people were 'things' that should not have happened. In both films the homosexuality of director James Whale may have been a force in the vision."

9. In the absence of a reliable critical history of transsexuality, it is best to turn to the standard medical accounts themselves: see especially Benjamin, Green and Money, and Stoller. For overviews of cross-cultural variation in the institutionalization of sex/gender, see Williams, "Social Constructions/Essential Characters: A Cross-Cultural Viewpoint," 252–76; Shapiro, 262–68. For accounts of particular institutionalizations of transgender practices that employ surgical alteration of the genitals, see Nanda; Roscoe. Adventurous readers curious about contemporary nontranssexual genital alteration practices may contact E.N.I.G.M.A. (Erotic Neoprimitive International Genital Modification Association), SASE to LaFarge-werks, 2329 N. Leavitt, Chicago, IL 60647.

10. See Butler, "Introduction," 4 and *passim*.

11. A substantial body of scholarship informs these observations: Gayle Rubin provides a productive starting point for developing not only a political economy of sex, but of gendered subjectivity; on gender recruitment and attribution, see Kessler and McKenna; on gender as a system of marks that naturalizes sociological groups based on supposedly shared material similarities, I have been influenced by some ideas on race in Guillaumin and by Wittig.

12. Although I mean "chaos" here in its general sense, it is interesting to speculate about the potential application of scientific chaos theory to model the emergence of stable structures of gendered identities out of the unstable matrix of material attributes, and on the production of proliferating gender identities from a relatively simple set of gendering procedures.

WORKS CITED

Benjamin, Harry. *The Transsexual Phenomenon.* New York: Julian, 1966.

Billings, Dwight B., and Thomas Urban. "The Socio-Medical Construction of Transsexualism: An Interpretation and Critique." *Social Problems* 29 (1981): 266–82.

Bloom, Harold. "Afterword." *Frankenstein, or The Modern Prometheus.* New

York: Signet/NAL, 1965, 212–23. Orig. pub. "*Frankenstein,* or The New Prometheus." *Partisan Review* 32 (1965): 611–18.

Butler, Judith. *Bodies That Matter: On the Discursive Limits of "Sex."* New York: Routledge, 1993.

Daly, Mary. *Gyn/Ecology: The Metaethics of Radical Feminism.* Boston: Beacon, 1978.

Echols, Alice. *Daring to Be Bad: Radical Feminism in America, 1967–1975.* Minneapolis: U of Minnesota P, 1989.

Gilbert, Sandra, and Susan Gubar. "Horror's Twin: Mary Shelley's Monstrous Eve." *The Madwoman in the Attic.* New Haven: Yale UP, 1979. 213–47.

Green, Richard, and John Money, eds. *Transsexualism and Sex Reassignment.* Baltimore: Johns Hopkins UP, 1969.

Guillaumin, Colette. "Race and Nature: The System of Marks." *Feminist Studies* 8 (1988): 25–44.

Homans, Margaret. "Bearing Demons: Frankenstein's Circumvention of the Maternal." *Bearing the Word.* Chicago: Chicago UP, 1986. 100–19.

Irvine, Janice. *Disorders of Desire: Sex and Gender in Modern American Sexology.* Philadelphia: Temple UP, 1990.

Jacobus, Mary. "Is There a Woman in this Text?" *Reading Woman: Essays in Feminist Criticism.* New York: Columbia UP, 1986. 83–109.

Kahler, Frederic. "Does Filisa Blame Seattle?" Editorial, *Bay Times* [San Francisco], 3 June 1993, 23.

Kessler, Suzanne J., and Wendy McKenna. *Gender: An Ethnomethodological Approach.* Chicago: U of Chicago P, 1985.

Laqueur, Thomas. *Making Sex: Body and Gender from the Greeks to Freud.* Cambridge, MA: Harvard UP, 1990.

Meyer, Morris. "I Dream of Jeannie: Transsexual Striptease as Scientific Display." *Drama Review* 35, 1 (1991): 25–42.

Mikuteit, Debbie. Letter. *Coming UP!* Feb. 1986, 3–4.

Nanda, Serena. *Neither Man Nor Woman: The Hijras of India.* Belmont, CA: Wadsworth, 1990.

O'Hartigan, Margaret D. "I Accuse." *Bay Times* [San Francisco], 20 May 1993, 11.

Raymond, Janice G. *The Transsexual Empire: The Making of the She-Male.* Boston: Beacon, 1979.

Roscoe, Will. "Priests of the Goddess: Gender Transgression in the Ancient World." American Historical Association Meeting, 9 January 1994, San Francisco.

Rubin, Gayle. "The Traffic in Women: Notes on the 'Political Economy' of Sex." *Toward an Anthropology of Women.* Ed. Rayna R. Reiter. New York: Monthly Review P, 1975. 157–210.

Russo, Vito. *The Celluloid Closet: Homosexuality in the Movies*. New York: Harper and Row, 1981.

Shapiro, Judith. "Transsexualism: Reflections on the Persistence of Gender and the Mutability of Sex," *Body Guards: The Cultural Politics of Gender Ambiguity*. Ed. Julia Epstein and Kristina Straub. New York: Routledge, 1991. 248–79.

Shelley, Mary. *Frankenstein, or The Modern Prometheus*. Orig. pub. 1817. New York: Signet/NAL, 1965.

Stoller, Robert. *Sex and Gender*, Vol. 1. New York: Science House, 1968. *The Transsexual Experiment*. Vol. 2 of *Sex and Gender*. London: Hogarth, 1975.

Stone, Sandy. "The Empire Strikes Back: A Posttranssexual Manifesto." *Body Guards: The Cultural Politics of Gender Ambiguity*. Ed. Julia Epstein and Kristina Straub. New York: Routledge, 1991. 280–304.

Williams, Walter. *The Spirit and the Flesh: Sexual Diversity in American Indian Culture*. Boston: Beacon, 1986.

Wittig, Monique. "The Mark of Gender." *The Straight Mind and Other Essays*. Boston: Beacon, 1992. 76–89.

PART III

Rage in the Academy

CHAPTER 12

Class Matters

Symbolic Boundaries and Cultural Exclusion

SHARON O'DAIR

"I believe this community is a hard-hat community and very few hard hats take in Shakespeare. They're more *Oklahoma* types. I'd like to see [the company do] more things that the citizens of Garden Grove would come out to." So reasoned City Councilman Raymond T. Littrell, as he and other members of the council in my hometown of Garden Grove, California, decided in June 1988 to withdraw an $83,000 subsidy from the Grove Shakespeare Festival (Herman, 9). City councils sometimes debate the value of subsidizing arts organizations, and often the debate is conducted over cultural taste, the relative merits of *Oklahoma* and *Othello*, but seldom, I think, do naysayers suggest, as did Councilman Littrell, that the subsidy might be justified if the Grove Shakespeare Festival produced dinner as well as theater.

As of this writing, the Grove Shakespeare Festival still limps along, each year securing funding from various sources to make up the shortfall and to contribute to Orange County's cultural life. Shakespeare is hard to shake, even in a city almost adjacent to Disneyland, whose principal claim to fame is, locally, its part in a burgeoning Little Saigon and, nationally, its status as the corporate headquarters for a successful television preacher. In 1994, as I read and think and write about Shakespeare or the canon or literary theory, the fuss over the Grove Shakespeare Festival often comes to mind. When it does, I know that what bothers me about the councilman's remarks is not that they almost deny the very possibility of me, the daughter of a hard hat who grew up in Garden

Reprinted by kind permission of Temple University Press from *This Fine Place So Far from Home: Voices of Academics from the Working Class* (forthcoming).

Grove and became a Shakespearean, nor even that they homogenize and stereotype the working-class constituents the councilman is elected to represent. The problem is that basically the councilman is correct, and that as an academic I am implicated—seriously, strongly, probably permanently—in reasons why "very few hard hats take in Shakespeare."

I wish to discuss several of these reasons, reasons that, because I left the working class to claim a career in the academy, strike me as undeniable realities, obvious truths. These (shall we say) deeply experiential truths, however, are ones that colleagues in English departments, who usually lack the weight of my experience, tend to resist or to qualify— when they consider them at all. Yet I am convinced that until progressive academics in English confront rather than dismiss these kinds of experiences and arguments, we will be unable to extend to the working class the kinds of opportunities successfully extended in recent years to women and racial minorities. John Guillory, I believe, is correct: the category of class is incommensurable with that of race or gender, and the marginality of the working class "cannot be redressed by the same strategy of representation" that has worked, more or less, for women and racial minorities (11). Unless, therefore, we rethink our critique of the canon and of the university, "the category of class in the invocation of race/class/gender is likely to remain merely empty" (14).

To make that invocation less empty requires an understanding of why few hard hats take in Shakespeare, which in turn requires one to confront what are perhaps some hard truths about academic work and its functions in society. My first point, therefore, is that academics must acknowledge what one might call the liminal importance for the working class of reading books or, later on perhaps, wishing to write them. In a working class milieu, a child's desire to read books or to succeed in school signifies difference—not just emotional or intellectual difference but material difference as well. Consider this, for instance: the child must leave the home and even the neighborhood to find novels or stories to read, cajoling her skeptical, even fearful, parents to drive her to and from the public library, because in her own house, if she is lucky, the library consists of *Reader's Digest, Guideposts,* and her neighbor's fingered *National Enquirer.* The desires of this working-class child, if acted upon successfully, eventually separate a working-class child from her peers and family, and from her culture, as Annie Ernaux points out in her autobiographical novel *Cleaned Out:*

Books . . . books. . . . [My mother] believed in them, she would have given me books to eat if she could have, she carried them as if they were the Holy Sacrament, with two hands. . . . She told me to look after them, not to get them dirty. What she didn't realize was that these same books were shutting me off from her, taking me away from them and their cafe, showing me how awful it was. (77)

What the books offer is, partly, a window onto the attractions of a life of the mind. They also offer a glimpse of a life in which the culture of the school—taste, manners, a standard language, in short, the culture of the middle- and upper-classes—is not jarringly discordant with the culture of one's own everyday life. That culture, that life, is where you look for space, look for privacy, look for books—and find none. Instead, you do your homework under bad light at the kitchen table, ignoring as best you can the noise and noise and noise that surrounds you.

For good reasons, desire to read books or to succeed in school is often seen as a betrayal of the values and the integrity of the community. Working-class kids play sports or work on cars or take care of younger siblings; they don't read and study. Thus, " 'smart' boys are often labelled 'fags' [or] 'ass-kissers' . . . when they do well in class . . . [and] working-class girls suffer similar ostracism," report Stanley Aronowitz and Henry A. Giroux (12). Novelist Paul Monette describes a more physical response to such desires: "Dad . . . used to hit me for reading," seethes an adult and dying Tom in *Halfway Home* (19). In a memory that might be a refrain in this novel of violence and reconciliation, he sees himself "as a little kid, black crewcut and shoulders slumped, reading in secret so my father wouldn't beat me" (97; see also 167).

Cleaned Out records a French working-class university student's burden of shame and alienation, especially with respect to her parents, whose way of life she learns to disdain, whose way of life she must disdain if she is to learn. Indeed, this is the usual destiny of a child who accepts that goal: to abandon, seemingly with few regrets, the language and culture of her birth. As Lillian B. Rubin observes, upward mobility implies a value judgment: "those who climb up have a different sense of themselves and of their relationship to the world around them. . . . And whether they bear the lash of resentment of those they left behind, or the smile of approval of their newfound peers, the messages they get reinforce their self-image as not just different but better" (9). Nevertheless, a working-class student's shame and alienation can be aimed in the opposite direction, too, with respect to the knowledge and culture one is trying to acquire, the knowledge and culture that allows one a better life.

My parents knew early on that I was especially bright: on a trip home from college, I once found a letter my mother had written my father, who in 1960 had taken a long-term construction job in northern California because there was none at home. In the letter, amid details of siblings, the house, and the neighborhood, she briefly notes her joy and wonder at the doings of their four-year-old. By the time I was seven or eight, tests confirmed what they already knew, and I became unlike the working-class kids in my immediate neighborhood, separated from them during school hours and placed instead in a classroom of other bright children drawn from several elementary schools. They were, by and large, children who did not live the way I lived, whose families did not live the way my family lived. (The reasoning seemed to be that if I weren't tracked out, I might get on the wrong track.) To be sure, I took readily to the challenges of the advanced schoolwork—regular elementary school classes had bored me—and eventually I found it advantageous that the children of professionals liked me: I could watch their color television sets, listen to their Beatles records on big console stereos, and feel the freedom their large houses afforded. But even as a child I knew all this was not simply advantageous, and for many years I bore a double burden of guilt: among my middle-class friends I was embarrassed by my parents and my home, and among my working-class friends I was embarrassed by my intellectual privilege. Such separation, such opportunity, is a blessing and a curse.

I remember being chastised in fourth grade by the daughter of an aerospace engineer for saying ain't all the time; "ain't ain't in the dictionary," she sneered in a voice the entire class could hear. In 1964, ain't wasn't; but it was in the vocabulary of my neighborhood in Garden Grove, and stung though I was, I vowed at that moment never finally to cross to the other side, the side I was already tracked onto. And I like to think I haven't. Years and years of professional training—graduate school at Berkeley under the tutelage of Greenblatt, Fineman, Barish, et al., and six years teaching Shakespeare as an assistant professor at the University of Alabama—have not smoothed my rough edges. My colleagues have not liked my position, or the politics implicit in an essay like this one; and some of them fought bitterly and unsuccessfully to deny me tenure. Even my parents, who understand little of what I do for a living—"you teach how many hours a week?"—tease me about the occasional ungrammaticalness of my spoken English, me their English professor. I have refused to memorize and then recite lines of literature in conversation with colleagues, finding it too smooth, too genteel, a part of the role to resist. Often, in fact, I keep my professor's role firmly at arm's length; parts of the role, some of the behavior associated with the role, I avoid—or reinterpret—to suit myself. Clothes, haircut, the car I drive, the jokes I make in class: I am making this Hamlet my own, out of respect for my alienation and shame, alienation from and shame at what I've become, not only what I left.

No doubt all professors sprung from the working class know of what I speak, shame and alienation of various sorts, moving in one direction and then another, humiliations that should not count but do. Never knowing where to place a fork or spoon. Being told there's a proper way to skin a carrot. Laughing off awkwardness until it hurts. As Pierre Bourdieu explains,

> The manner which designates the infallible taste of the "taste-maker" and exposes the uncertain tastes of the possessors of an "ill-gotten" culture is so important, in all markets and especially in the market which decides the value of literary and artistic works, only because choices always owe part of their value to the value of the chooser, and because, to a large extent, this value makes itself known and recognized through the manner of choosing. What is learnt through immersion in a world in which legitimate culture is as natural as the air one breathes is a sense of the legitimate innate choice so sure of itself that it convinces by the sheer manner of the performance, like a successful bluff (9 1–9 2).

In Bourdieu's view, professors from the working class by definition possess "ill-gotten" culture; our performances always reveal us. But some of us, it seems, take some pleasure in revealing ourselves, in refusing a performance that we know will only betray us.

One might thus wish to claim that a working-class professor's refusal or appropriation of her role is revolutionary practice, and perhaps not in such a small way as it might seem. For when her performance differs from that of an upper-class white male, she challenges the norms of her society, since how a person performs a role influences the role itself, either by reinforcing others' (and one's own) expectations for the role or by opening up a possibility for change in them. Surely, for example, movements to democratize the canon result partly from decisions by individual scholars to interpret part of the professor's role differently from expectation, to take as objects of study texts that had not seemed to be appropriate to serious scholarship.

Undoubtedly, such an argument carries much truth: in the long run performance counts, our choices affect the structure of everyday life, the personal is political. Yet such truth does not, I think, obviate Bourdieu's functionalist model of reproduction through education. Like much sociology, Bourdieu's model does not suggest the impossibility of change but rather the difficulty of change within institutions, since, as Guillory notes (55–63), once established, institutions tend to persist. Institutions, Peter L. Berger and Thomas Luckmann observe, "confront the individual as undeniable facts" (60), facts that, despite one's potential for radical agency, will outlast the individual even as they antedate him or her.

This, then, is my second point: I am, and doubtless the reader is, part of an institution whose principal function in society is to distinguish, to separate, to launch the meritorious, however defined. The privileging of intellectual work, the judging of merit, is itself a principal way in which society reproduces itself. As Evan Watkins observes, in the United States "the boundary lines of class are drawn through a series of contact points staffed by intellectual workers . . . [who] 'earn their right' to be intellectual workers by having demonstrated their merit for the work in school" ("Intellectual," 204, 205). All of which suggests, as Richard Terdiman explains, that "there is always class in our classes" because "the act of classing itself presupposes power in the form of a superior instance authorized to decide the membership of the categories specified. A system of classes (of whatever kind) always implies evaluation, and hence its inevitable if guilty accompanist, subordination" (228).

I am writing this essay—rather than waitressing or driving a bus or cleaning up at Disneyland, like the kids I grew up with—in large part because the institution did that job on me. In class, the institution found me willing and appropriate, that is, meritorious, material on which to work. It then classed me accordingly. Thus, though I know that engaging the institution through my sometimes bizarre performance in the professor's role is progressive or at least disruptive, I also know that the institution still works to distinguish and separate and that I work to distinguish and separate. I know what every ex-working-class academic or professional knows: "school knowledge is loaded in class terms" (Aronowitz and Giroux, 12). The upwardly mobile working-class student is wrenched from the culture of her birth and reconstituted according to the norms of middle- and upper-class culture—standard English, taste, manners, and today, perhaps, political correctness. No more ethnic slurs, no more homophobia, no more hating everyone not of the clan. In class, we learn to class, as Terdiman suggests (227). And we learn that we belong no longer to the working class.

A continuing source of frustration for me as a writer and professor of English, and this is the third point I wish to address here, is the apparent controversy of this assertion: "Professors of English are not working-class." Again and again, in print, at conferences, in casual conversation, I encounter colleagues who gain a comfortable and secure living in institutions that sit atop a hierarchy of institutions geared toward the sorting and sifting of human lives and who at the same time claim solidarity with or deny their difference from those who have failed in or been failed by those very institutions. Among colleagues and friends, that is, resistance to recognizing the class positions of intellectuals is strong, and to me almost perverse, a series of refusals and excuses, such that almost any discussion of this issue becomes heated and, worse, convoluted and imprecise. Distinctions dissolve in a chorus of "but . . . but . . . buts": a professor's salary is but thirty or forty thousand dollars a year, hardly more than a plumber's or mechanic's; and the angst of a family like that in "Ordinary People" proves that life is miserable, too, for those in the upper-middle class; and the fact that ethnic working-class America has abandoned liberal politics, finding some comfort if not real help among the Republicans, shows that they are not worth our trouble or concern anyway.

I know and can understand, and indeed have explored in print, some of the reasons why some academics in English refuse to acknowledge their positions among the elites, and why others identify with the working class or claim working-class status: guilt, ideology, politics, ignorance, sheer human kindness all play their part (see O'Dair, "Vestments"). What concerns me, however, from the vantage of both theory and practice, is the possibility that attempts to dissolve class in sets of common experience actually constitute an abandonment of working-class people. Recently, for example, in light of its weakened position in the West, the left has determined that the working class "failed in its historical mission of emancipation" and thus no longer "represents the privileged agent in which the fundamental impulse of social change resides," as Ernesto Laclau and Chantal Mouffe observe (169, 177). But such a theoretical determination, with its attendant emphasis on new agents of change such as women, homosexuals, or people of color, does not and cannot eliminate the disadvantage of the working class. (Perhaps it can only make it worse, as once again, the working class is judged wanting, this time failing not just a course in history, but history itself.) Nor, I think, can such theoretical twisting and turning dodge the fact that class distinctions exist in the United States—it is, says Rubin, "a structured reality that there's no room at the top and little room in the middle" (211); and that educational institutions, including the academy, are vitally, perhaps essentially, involved in maintaining them—"schools appear the motor force where a system of class boundaries reproduces itself," as Watkins insists in *Work Time* (245).

A few years ago, I presented a paper at a conference dedicated to exploring class-bias in higher education. Tension developed from familiar debates about definitions of social class and the role of education in constructing class distinctions. Discussion became highly charged as the conferees gradually confronted the proposition that class bias is different from and thus cannot be equated with racial bias or sexual bias in the academy. But as bickering and fighting and posturing continued, slowly there emerged a sense that a lot of us indeed shared a certain kind of background, upbringing, and experience of education and the academy. Slowly people came to demand of speakers and of each other that they reveal themselves, to demand that someone who claimed to speak for us in fact be one of us. Suddenly, you had to have credentials of a different sort—not where you took your Ph.D. or where you taught now or whether you were something other than a white male—but what your father or your mother did for a living. Colleagues who answered "professor" or "physician" rather than "truck driver" or "bank teller" found themselves relegated to the margins, silent and awkward.

What I experienced there was, I imagine, something quite like what blacks or women felt a generation ago when they were organizing themselves and laying claim to a particular experience of America and the academy—a great and all-encompassing relief that others understand you and you understand them. Who cares what instrument to use on creme brule, or even how to spell it? What I experienced there was the matter, the weight and significance of class: class matters in ways that are painfully obvious to us and almost invisible to our colleagues who are not from the working class.

Let me sum up what Councilman Littrell from my hometown seems to intuit. For the working class, books take you away, and distinguish you from your peers; and they give you the power to judge others, or perhaps more accurately, books give others the power to judge you. The professor, situated in the academy and perhaps the supreme warder of books, institutionalizes subordination and thus class through her ability to evaluate, to pass on or to fail. The power of her authority, as Watkins points out, "visibly and immediately seems to control the outcome of the situation and visits its humiliations on you" ("Intellectual," 209).

Shakespeare, who succeeded in letters despite his small Latin and less Greek, expresses these points well, in Caliban's instructions to Stephano and Trinculo about how to overthrow Prospero:

> 'tis a custom with him
> I' th' afternoon to sleep: there thou mayst brain him,
> Having first seiz'd his books; or with a log
> Batter his skull, or paunch him with a stake,
> Or cut his wezand with thy knife. Remember
> First to possess his books; for without them
> He's but a sot, as I am, nor hath not
> One spirit to command: they all do hate him
> As rootedly as I. Burn but his books.
> (*The Tempest*, 3.2.85–93)

"Burn but his books," for surely it is Prospero's books that enable him to "control the situation and [visit] its humiliations" on Caliban, to inflict physical punishment on the recalcitrant slave: "tonight thou shalt . . . be pinch'd/As thick as honeycomb, each pinch more stinging/Than bees that made 'em" (1.2.327–32). And, of course, Prospero's books prove impossible to burn or to possess, and relations of power and privilege in *The Tempest* remain structurally unchanged. Still, it pleases me to think that Shakespeare reveled in the irony of including in this play celebrating the power of books an "abhorred slave" who succinctly anatomizes the uses of education for most workers: "You taught me language; and my profit on't/Is, I know how to curse" (1.2.365–66). With respect to power and privilege in late-twentieth-century America, class matters, and books, like Shakespeare's, map class. So it is that "the school functions as a system of credentialization by which it produces a specific relation to culture. That relation is different for different people, which is to say that it reproduces social relations" (56). That relation is different for different people, which is why the Councilman is correct: "very few hard hats take in Shakespeare." The hard hats who do find themselves in a position as conflicted and uneasy as that of the professor who grew up working class.

WORKS CITED

Aronowitz, Stanley, and Henry A. Giroux. *Postmodern Education: Politics, Culture, and Social Criticism.* Minneapolis: University of Minnesota Press, 1991.

Berger, Peter L., and Thomas Luckmann. *The Social Construction of Reality: A Treatise in the Sociology of Knowledge.* Garden City: Doubleday and Company, 1967.

Bourdieu, Pierre. *Distinction: A Social Critique of the Judgement of Taste.* Trans. Richard Nice. Cambridge: Harvard University Press, 1984.

Ernaux, Annie. *Cleaned Out.* Trans. Carol Sanders. Elmwood Park, IL: Dalkey Archive Press, 1990.

Guillory, John. *Cultural Capital: The Problem of Literary Canon Formation.* Chicago: University of Chicago Press, 1993.

Herman, Jan. "Grove Theatre's Supporting Cast: Enter the Philistines." *Los Angeles Times.* May 1988, Orange County ed., VI 9.

Laclau, Ernesto, and Chantal Mouffe. *Hegemony and Socialist Strategy: To-wards a Radical Democratic Politics.* Trans. Winston Moore and Paul Cammack. London: Verso, 1985.

Monette, Paul. *Halfway Home.* New York: Crown Publishers, 1991.

O'Dair, Sharon. "Vestments and Vested Interests: Academia's Suspicion of the Working Class." In *Working Class Women in the Academy: Laborers in the Knowledge Factory.* Ed. Michelle M. Tokarczyk and Elizabeth A. Fay. Amherst: University of Massachusetts Press, 1993.

Rubin, Lillian B. *Worlds of Pain: Life in the Working-Class Family.* 1976. New York: Basic Books.

Shakespeare, William. *The Tempest.* Ed. Frank Kermode. New York: Methuen, 1986.

Terdiman, Richard. "Is There Class in This Class?" In *The New Historicism.* Ed. H. Aram Veeser. New York: Routledge, 1989.

Watkins, Evan. "Intellectual Work and Pedagogical Circulation in English." In *Theory/Pedagogy/Politics.* Ed. Donald Morton and Mas'ud Zavarzadeh. Urbana: University of Illinois Press, 1991.

———. *Work Time: English Departments and the Circulation of Cultural Value.* Stanford: Stanford University Press, 1989.

CHAPTER 13

Second-Rate or Second-Rank

The Human Pyramid of Academe

SHENG-MEI MA

The academe, in the United States and elsewhere, is a human pyramid bound together by capitalist hypocrisy. A limited number of elite institutions perch on the precipitous tip of this pyramid like captains of industry, dominating the preponderance of resources, while the bulk of, in James Sosnoski's term, "Token Professionals" labor and sweat at the swampy bottom of this triangle to hold up the weight of the structure, subconsciously resigned to the fate of slaves carrying on their shoulders what Sosnoski calls the "Master Critics." A preference for this status quo is understandable amongst the ruling class if they were all apolitical academicians with a vested interest in remaining blind. But quite vexingly, a large number of leading intellectuals today are from the left (of Marxist, feminist, postcolonial, minority, queer, or other radical vintage), hence *theoretically* concerned with the ideology and fact of exploitation. They, ironically, preach their gospel of justice and equality from a privileged position in academe modeled after none other than capitalism—the concentration of resources, the hierarchy based on wealth and power. Even these leftists seem to partake comfortably in what Louis Althusser coins as the "Ideological State Apparatuses" since

> the reproduction of labor power requires not only a reproduction of its skills, but also, at the same time, a reproduction of its submission to the rules of the established order, i.e. a reproduction of submission to the ruling ideology for the workers, and a reproduction of the ability to manipulate the ruling ideology correctly for the agents of exploitation and repression, so that they, too, will provide

for the domination of the ruling class "in words." (Althusser, 132–33)

Regardless of political persuasions, the upper-class and the masses of "intellectual laborers" share a secret alliance in maintaining the illusion that this profession is not what it really is—a human pyramid—and the fact of standing on people's heads or being stomped into the mud is justified through the ability or the lack thereof of, among other things, "manipulat[ing] the ruling ideology . . . 'in words' "—i.e., one's facility with Theory.

By Theory, I mean philosophy in disguise, which has been in vogue for quite some time, despite an increasing backlash. Although every piece of critical scholarship has theory at its core, this kind of *high* Theory detaches itself from literary texts or any cultural artifacts. Pure thought in a vacuum, it addresses a select audience—other theorists, while average (less gifted?) professors stand in awe of the immense incomprehensibility of such intellection. It eventually evolves into a game of names, as Terry Caesar notes in "Theory in the Boondocks": "The same names, from the same universities, continue to speak to each other about the same questions" (226). This game of exclusion relies heavily on one's deployment of big names and their Theories, of performing mental gymnastics with ever-escalating levels of difficulty in order to compete in the ever-shrinking job market. Theory, innocent in and of itself, thus becomes the floor plan as well as the superstructure of this network of power/knowledge. It differentiates among contenders for positions, publications, grants, and conferences, meting out their fate and academic career. Theory makes the elite.

An insightful analysis of the use of theory comes from Paul Lauter's *Canons and Contexts* (1991). Lauter astutely distinguishes the aforementioned "formalist criticism" from his "canonical criticism" in terms of the former's heavy debt to "Continental philosophy" and its deep concern with "questions of epistemology" (134). Lauter is certainly not referring to New Criticism alone but includes criticism of a more recent kind which substitutes "theorists" for "poets" as unacknowledged legislators and which "separate[s] literary texts . . . as well as critical acts from history, . . . ignore[s] the particular role their work is playing in educational institutions and in society, . . . [and] turn[s] the domain of literature . . . into a 'vast, enclosed, textual and semantic preserve' "

(138). The privileging of theory, in Lauter's words, "deepen[s] the abyss
. . . between those who dwell in the towers of academe and those who
inhabit the trenches," exercising "practical criticism . . . in the classroom" (141).

Various proposals have been put forward to revamp the discipline and
to yoke together theory and practice. One of the arguments is Sosnoski's
Token Professionals and Master Critics (1994), which advocates that
theory or criticism be moved from a text-oriented to a person-oriented
practice and from its indefensibly objective pretension to a candidly
subjective position. Such innovative ideas, nevertheless, continue to
dwell around the borderland of academic discourse, overshadowed by a
select group of towering figures and their incessant, incestuous self-
reproduction in writing. The obstacle Sosnoski's subjective criticism (to
borrow from David Bleich's book with that title) confronts is evident
when Sosnoski acknowledges that he has recast in the voice of "the
implicating 'we' " (xxix) many personal anecdotes not unlike Terry
Caesar's in "On Teaching at a Second-Rate University." This calculated
move provides an aura of generality and objectivity to eschew the ava-
lanche of criticism suffered by Caesar, such as the report and letters in
The Chronicle of Higher Education, immediately after his courageous
(to those letter writers, outrageous) confessions (Sosnoski, xxiv–xxvii).

My strategy of forgoing any pretension to high Theory in Lauter's
definition derives from two reasons, both related to the praxis in the
classroom. First of all, to describe my experience at a teaching college
does not require the assistance of Theory, which I do not have the time
to take up fully anyway and which is never needed in grading student
papers from my four courses per semester. Theory is the luxurious
plaything of the upper-class in the academy, like playing golf at exclusive
country clubs for the rich. Caddies like me write whatever and whenever
we can, often without the leisure (or sheer agony and boredom) of
reviewing theorists first (the more abstruse the better). Secondly, to
resort almost entirely to my personal experience serves to subvert the
supremacy of Theory, the rule of the game set up by elite critics. My
lived experience then becomes the foundation of my oppositional discourse. I only lament that my language and thought have already been
contaminated by the academic trend toward high Theory. I too have
tried in vain to climb up from the huddled masses to the tip of the
pyramid through—what else?—theorizing for theorists. And I, alas,

continue to do so in my more formal scholarly writings, sustained by what Sosnoski describes as "the myth of advancement by merit," i.e., writing one's "way out of 'bad' jobs" (xvii).

At any rate, the whole issue of "second-rate" exploded in my face when I naively characterized myself as teaching at a "second-rate" university in two national conferences in the summer of 1993. I was immediately assaulted from both sides, by colleagues from first-rate and second-rate institutions.

Let me recall one incident which prompted me to say that first-rate institutions would reject such a label as vehemently as the lesser schools. I attended the annual meeting of the Association of Asian-American Studies (AAAS) at Cornell University, June 2–6, 1993. This was the first time I had participated in AAAS activities and there were many surprises. I was struck, for instance, by how many presenters were graduate students from the University of California system and from the Ivy League. This showed that AAAS was an organization for the future, a part of the surging tide of Asian-American power. The fact that most of the graduate students came from prestigious institutions only strengthened my conviction. But by the same token, the conference lacked real substance, as I listened to, in one paper after the other, graduate students theorizing theories.

One of the last sessions in the conference was on "Problems in the Teaching of Asian-American Studies." I attended that "practical" session with great interest, both because I had confronted many difficulties in trying to teach about the Asian-American experience "east of California" and expected some advice from the session and because the panelists were all distinguished professors from renowned institutions: University of California, Irvine; University of California, Berkeley; University of Colorado, Boulder; and State University of New York, Albany. The last panelist, an eminent sociologist, however, had recently moved from Albany to Duke. All the chairs of the sessions featuring the sociologist loved to mention this beneficial career move in their introductions of her. One was a bit too dramatic in stopping himself mid-way and whispering to her (just loudly enough for the microphone to pick up): "Am I allowed to reveal this?" Hypocrisy at its height, decorated by playacting.

As it turned out, four out of the five panelists and the discussant kept scribbling on their notepads throughout the Chair's introduction as well as the ensuing presentations. There was no doubt in anybody's mind that they were preparing their scripts while the session was actually in session. I sat in the front row and saw that the notepads were blank when they first sat down and that what they had written (and nothing else) became the basis for their subsequent presentations, which were all clearly extemporaneous—but not in a way that suggested brilliance in improvization. Some panelists appeared almost tripping over their own talks, whereas one professed that he did not have much to say. My suspicion was confirmed months later when only one presenter responded to the Chair's call for the panelists' papers—to be edited for a special issue of UCLA's *Amerasia Journal*. This off-handed treatment of a well-attended session betrays the low priority the experts give to teaching and pedagogy as well as their sheer arrogance. In contrast, when the panelists delivered their "scholarly" papers at this conference, they read, measuredly, from prepared scripts. Nevertheless, I was awed by the sight of eminent scholars making scrawls of their talks five minutes before their turn. I assumed that this was how distinguished scholars operated. (Since my trip to Cornell, I was inspired to postpone my own work until just before the deadline. But I invariably made a mess of it in the end. I guess I am not meant for greatness.) There was only one exception to this casual attitude. The professor from Colorado had to struggle to condense his twenty-five-page paper into ten minutes. His work ethic may reveal, ironically, an origin as "humble" as mine— he had been teaching at San Francisco State University for over ten years.

My anger began to build up. During the question session, I let them have it—in my feeble and second-rate way. I stated that their presentations were all California-based (thus having little to do with the area "east of California," which is much of the country) and were all concerned with first-rate institutions. The dynamics of teaching Asian-American materials at second-rate or teaching colleges (and there are apparently more of these schools than theirs) was utterly ignored. I might not have been as lucid as the above statements, since my remarks were marred by a trembling voice, which sprung from my suppressed rage over their hastily assembled and poorly thought-out presentations. The arms of all the panelists shot up after my question. In fact, the professor from Irvine could not even wait until I had finished and immediately began to refute my distinction between first- and second-rate. This argument over ratings continued for quite some time, totally brushing aside my point about teaching Asian-American texts, so to speak, in the real world. Had I been able to respond to the panelists' face-saving evasions, I would have said that I could understand and sympathize with their defensiveness, for no conscientious intellectual wished to admit one's privileges coexisted perennially with, if not themselves posited upon, someone else's being deprived of them. But such is the inescapable fact of competition in capitalism. In the educational system as it stands now, there has to be a broad base to buttress the elite institutions, or who is going to teach the populace and to grapple with the statistics of literacy, one of the cornerstones of democracy? To say otherwise would be disingenuous. After the session, I in fact walked to the professor who had been lauding teaching colleges over his own, Irvine, and asked him to exchange schools with me. (He asserted earlier that he would send his child to a teaching college, but that remains to be seen.) He could come to my school, I suggested, and carry my teaching load and I could enjoy Irvine for a few months. He dodged. Even if he had accepted my offer, I doubt that Irvine (not so much my school) would comply.

This hierarchy of institutions, faculty, and students was reflected in the conference structure itself. I, with my rich experience of teaching Asian-American texts, had to sit in the audience and listen to some talk scribbled minutes before. I was not alone. There was at least one other man in the room using similar texts at a community college in California, who was invited by one of the panelists to give his view, *after* the issue of first- and second-rate (and the nagging suspicion of exclusion) was brought up. If nothing else, I think I had succeeded in disquieting the calm waters of Asian-American Studies, though just for one afternoon. The panelists and the audience, I trust, will simply return to their respective circle and remember this episode as an aberration caused by a disgruntled—whoever he is—from a college—whose name escapes them.

Reflecting now, I am most concerned with the false hope this session as well as the entire conference created for the bulk of the audience, who were graduate students. These young men and women would take away from Cornell the sense that Asian-American Studies or Ethnic Studies in general is associated with first-rate institutions. Resources for Asian-American Studies or any other discipline are indeed concentrated in schools like the ones they are attending, but certainly the dissemination of their expertise will involve a much broader view of America and academe. An extremely high percentage of them are going to wind up teaching, if they get jobs at all, at colleges like or less ideal than mine (I suspect that the community college professor was once the panelist's student at Berkeley!), having to contend with limited resources and research time, in addition to perhaps a widespread provincialism and uneasiness over the contentious, potentially political Ethnic Studies.

On the other hand, second-rate schools are not about to swallow that label, either. Still reeling from the clash at Cornell, I flew to California to attend the conference on "Rage! Across the Disciplines" at California State University, San Marcos (June 10–12, 1993), and presented an early draft of "The Politics of Teaching Asian-American Literature Amidst Middle-class, Caucasian Students 'East of California.' " This conference, due to its "newsworthiness" (as opposed to most conferences with a heavy scholarly bent), was covered by, among others, two major news agencies: Connie Chung's *Eye To Eye* on CBS and *U.S. News and World Report.*

In Chung's program, a three-day conference was condensed into thirty seconds, with the most inflammatory remarks taken out of context to satiate the audience's appetite for sensationalism. For instance, one militant feminist's paper and subsequent interview became: "White males have power because they are white and have penises." I only thank God that I was not the Chosen One to be put on the air.

I was not so lucky in *U.S. News and World Report.* The reporter, John Leo, caricatured the conference as "a marathon of pique," the title of his article. My presentation was bashed; quotes were taken from my paper and rearranged to support the writer's own bias. Among other distortions, Leo charged that I complained because "East Coast white students" refused to "see themselves as *guilty oppressors* of Asian-Americans" (emphasis mine). Consistent with his long-standing anti-academic and reactionary career, Leo portrayed me as name-calling whites, hence provoking the majority's pent-up anger over "political correctness." While such attacks against academe in news magazines are banal, Leo's acquired an added dimension of viciousness when he alleged that I had said "[I] was forced to teach at a second-rate college" because I was Asian. Throughout my twenty-page, thirty-minute paper, I used the term "second-rate" but once, but nowhere had I asserted that because of my ethnic background, I was condemned to a second-rate university. The reporter, indeed, had already implied that I was privileged rather than disadvantaged due to my ethnicity. His interpretation was based as much on twisted logic as on what he wished to read into my paper. In the end, he had completely mangled my argument, even though he added: "During the question period he [Ma] said this was, of course, an ironic statement, not to be taken literally." But no reader would remember this belated disclaimer; only one word stuck in their mind, evidenced by the reaction from the colleagues at my home institution, from students, and from students' parents.

After a long, at times heated, debate with a few colleagues at my home university over the great gap in implication between "second-rate" and "second-rank," I conceded that this linguistic subtlety escaped me when I wrote my paper, as it had eluded me when I had been at Cornell. I would have avoided a great deal of controversy had I switched to "second-rank." (Better still, I might have adopted Sosnoski's more polished phrases: "token professionals from mainstream [non-elite] American universities.") Having said that, it would be misleading to attribute the misunderstanding solely to the fact that English remains my second language. I take it also as an act of linguistic transgressiveness by a nonnative speaker, who has not yet mastered the entire range of euphemisms and the related decorum. Euphemisms and decorum tend to sugarcoat the unpleasant truth; and I unintentionally offended people's sense of propriety by vocalizing what was unspoken but understood. Yet by elucidating the cultural differences surrounding the word "second-rate," I intend once again to bring academic hypocrisy into sharp focus.

In my native tongue and in the minds of most Pacific Rim residents/ emigrants of Chinese descent, the hairsplitting distinction between "second-rate" and "second-rank" (What about "second-class"?) with reference to schools is nonsense. The educational systems in Taiwan, Hong Kong, Singapore, and China are so hideously competitive that schools, students, and faculty are stratified accordingly. "Erh-liu" or "second-rate," defined as "of inferior or mediocre quality" in Webster, is in fact used in the Chinese context to describe the status of certain institutions. The sense of inadequacy in this expression is not unfamiliar to, though not particularly welcome by, most Chinese associated with those institutions, who take the "offensive" word as spurring them on in their academic pursuit.

Americans—and I count myself as a hybridized Asian-American—

tend to find "second-rate" distasteful because it undermines their self-esteem and threatens to cancel their effort, as the cliché goes, "to be the best they can be." While the hierarchy in the Chinese language and society is inexcusably stifling, the drastically diverging connotations attributed to two almost identical words of four letters each (rate vs. rank) belie the unique way Americans view this world. Shaped by the myth of democracy and equality, Americans have refined their language to such an extent as to obliterate or at least downplay such issues as hierarchy and class, which, of course, exist all around us. This tendency to gloss over actual differences is compounded, in the U.S. academe, by the illusion of egalitarianism embraced by most intellectuals. Academicians here have traditionally felt that if there were any arena where people were treated equitably, it would be in their circle.

With his rich cross-cultural experiences of teaching abroad, Caesar makes the same point (and China is cited as his first example) by likening athletic rivalries between American universities and colleges to academic ones. Observing that it is impossible in any foreign country for a Robert Morris College to compete athletically with a University of Kansas, as is indeed the case in the first round of NCAA Division I basketball playoffs in 1990, Caesar concludes that such indeterminacies within the system "are distinctively American . . . [and] crucial to our mythologies about class or our beliefs about how education equalizes because they express an antagonistic energy or fluid evaluative possibility that no other country has in higher education" (*Conspiring*, 155). While critiquing this myth of "differences under erasure," even Caesar appears heartened by the fact that Robert Morris College "came close. It could have [beaten Kansas, ranked No. 2]" (154). But how rarely do such teams meet, how predictable the outcome is, and, ironically, how intensely Americans relish the prospect of cheering for the underdog, as I did for my school against Florida State with Sam Cassell in the 1994 NCAA basketball playoffs. At that moment, none of us wishes to remember the odds stacked against the underdog. Precisely to combat this national amnesia, my deployment of "second-rate" seeks to expose this facade and farce of impartiality ascribed to higher education—athletic, academic, or otherwise; I see far too many inequities in the system, such as between research universities and teaching colleges, not to point out the mirage we strain to keep up.

Caught between these two perceptions, however, are Chinese Americans. This is perhaps why Chinese Americans seem to harbor this drive to excel, for going down ever so slightly would only mean becoming "second-xxxx." This impulse for excellence often leads to brilliant performances from Chinese Americans, but it also creates generational conflicts between immigrant parents and their American-born children. For instance, what appears to the parents to be a second-rate school their Americanized child chooses to attend may be seen by the child as a first-rate school among second-rank institutions, which is, parenthetically, how my home university would like to characterize itself.

I was also led to use "second-rate" because—and this demonstrated my naivete as well as provincialism more than anything else—I picked up the term from Terry Caesar's essay "On Teaching at a Second-Rate University" in the *South Atlantic Quarterly,* a journal published by Duke. I was under the impression that since *SAQ* had published this piece, it must have become an accepted practice to distinguish between first and second rate in academic discourse. Disastrously unaware was I of the barrage of attack against Caesar in the *Chronicle of Higher Education,* nor did I heed Caesar's repeated musings on the utter silence of public discourse on the issue of second-rate. This placid ignorance was perhaps endemic to any second-rate condition, assisted in no small measure by the material circumstances—in my case, a library in dire need of expansion, an intellectual community deprived and demoralized, and other insufficiencies. Yet exactly because of this condition, I was instantly electrified by Caesar's brutally honest exegesis:

> Second-rateness is not solely a matter of variety of programs or size [of university], although each of these helps. . . . Arguably, it's not strictly a matter of provinciality or mediocrity, although each of these helps even more. . . . Second-rateness is ultimately a matter, more than anything else, of *perception.* I believe it was an Israeli poet who once said that "the difference between me and Auden is that I have to be aware of him, whereas he doesn't have to be aware of me." The second-rate always has to be aware of some greater measure of anything distinguished, from which its own lesser measure is derived. (*Conspiring,* 149; emphasis mine)

I was struck by how relative and volatile the hierarchy might be. Auden, indeed, was perceived by the Israeli to be a major poet, an assessment subject to some debate. On the other hand, the Israeli, though remaining anonymous, was after all cited, whereas hundreds of thousands of modern writers never even graced a footnote in scholarship. More significantly, I began to toy with the idea of the potential of subversiveness within the academic discourse in the vein of Caesar and, more dynamically, the postcolonial rewriting of Prospero and Caliban. If Aimé Césaire in *A Tempest* reversed Shakespearean roles and called into question the legitimizing Western hegemony, couldn't we grotesque "mimic men" deconstruct the system which reduced us to, slightly recasting Homi Bhabha's term, "not quite/not theoretical" ("Of Mimicry and Man," 132). Yet the paradox was that even as I sought to empower myself and others, I did so in the name of greater men—Césaire, Bhabha, and, ironically, Caesar, just as they had done in the name of Shakespeare and other canonical writers. Nonetheless, I began to feel that my oppositional discourse against the hypocritical academe might be echoed and appreciated.

I was sorely mistaken, more sober now after the backlash at Cornell and at my own school. My colleagues who are friendly enough to joke about my "Californian betrayal" are only the tip of the iceberg. Those who do not bring up the incident truly worry me, as I had received anonymous phone calls inquiring not too politely about my alleged remark and I had been informed (deliberately?) that parents of incoming freshmen had called the school for clarification of my alleged statement. Some students stormed into my office to demand an explanation and, in a culminating moment, a xeroxed copy of the *U.S. News* report was sent to me through the regular chain of command from the President's Office of my university. A person who called himself "a concerned taxpayer" in Virginia photocopied this report and mailed it to the President, with scribblings on the margins branding me "this ass" and "a disgrace to" my school. The document may have originated from some miffed individual but it gained in stature in terms of the great distance within the bureaucracy it had traveled—through the entire administration under which I continued to be employed as a tenure-track assistant professor.

The term "second-rate" is so insulting to both "Token Professionals" and "Master Critics" because, as I have argued, it exposes the institutionalized elitism and hypocrisy we as academics and society at large live by. After all, for any collection of human beings to maintain harmony and to function, certain taboos are required to define propriety, a transgression against which would be met with immediate condemnation and even punishment. The silence about "second-rate" institutions in academic discourse is one of these taboos. Without pondering one's inferior position, one could theoretically go about the business more efficiently. But by retrieving into scholarly debates such terms as second-rate, as harsh as they may sound, we impart to our profession some degree of honesty. This term does not have to be worn like a badge of victimhood and result in what Edward Said calls "the politics of blame"; instead, it enables us to map institutional reality. With the diagram of the pyramid in mind, the broad base of the structure could perceive the framework which weighs on the bottom and valorizes the top. This realization makes possible the revolution of turning the communication channel upside down. This "unnatural" process of the bottom speaking to the top invariably yields unique insights, as Carey McWilliams puts it in a different context:

> One of the best ways to view and understand a society is to see it from the bottom looking up. To be sure, the underview is incomplete. Bottom dogs see, know, and learn a lot but their perspective is limited. But they see more, I have come to believe, than those who occupy the middle and upper reaches; their view is less inhibited, less circumscribed. The view from down under exposes the deceits, self-deceptions, distortions, apostasies. . . . It offers a good, if limited, guide to what the society is really like, not what it professes to be. (xx)

Such a class-based, Marxist critique is well intentioned. But for it to truly function, the practitioner of this critique must be keenly aware of his or her own positionality, of the inherent paradox of a privileged person speaking for the subaltern. Arguably, the whole issue of second-rate closely resembles the contestation over subalternity. While considering myself somewhat privileged as an academician within this capitalist economy, I remain submerged in the subaltern class of this profession and my argument will close with some reflection on a personal story where facets of the subaltern intersect.

I did have a chance to catapult myself from the "bondage" of scholarly subaltern class at the Modern Language Association conference in Toronto in December 1993. I interviewed with, among other institutions, University of California, Riverside with its paradisal teaching load and abundant opportunities for leaves and internal grants. During the thirty-minute conversation (a generous allotment compared with some other interviews), I was pointedly asked what I thought of Gayatri Chakravorty Spivak's "Can the Subaltern Speak?" Due to "temporary insanity" about which I can not elaborate at this point, I blurted out that the critic was a hypocrite pretending to speak for the downtrodden from an enviable academic position. I went on to lecture the interviewers with respect to professional taboos such as "theory is the plaything of the upper class." My "deranged" mental state compelled me to assume a far more contentious persona than any level-headed interviewee would ever have, no matter how malcontent. Toward the end of the interview, the chair asked, with more civility than some schools that treated me like a wretched of the earth, how I would feel to be in a department where all felt that theory was central to what they were doing. I answered with a silly grin: "I thrive on debates."

Personal and immediate reasons aside, my explosive behavior derives, academically, from the elitism and hypocrisy that I witness in employment, publication, conferences—indeed the entire profession. While standing by this general observation, I concede now that my timing for eruption is off. One has to wait until being granted membership at any of the exclusive clubs before articulating unpleasant thoughts, which then miraculously acquire the status of a "debate," the lifestyle of the rich and famous among intellectual laborers. So here is a belated explanation for my outburst: while making statements like McWilliams' "bottom dogs" or Spivak's subalternity, it is incumbent upon us to examine how and why we are authorized to make such statements in the first place. The widespread lack of self-reflexivity in this matter is where academic hypocrisy lies. A case in point is Spivak. I admire Spivak's work for the Indian subaltern and, in particular, women, but I find her assessment regarding her own position rather disingenuous. In response to an interviewer's final question about her "prestigious position in a very prestigious university in the United States," Spivak states:

> Well, my position is not altogether prestigious. I have been now twice in print described as someone who only got in clandestinely

because of political correctness. . . . I don't think I am in a position
yet to utter a last word on this positioning. (Pheng 159)

The right-wing attack against her resembles John Leo's charge against
me, but if that exempts me or Spivak from scrutinizing institutionalized
elitism, we become our detractors' accomplices, guilty in acquiescing to
and profiting from the capitalist system. Spivak's strategy of invoking
right-wing criticism to circumvent any discussion of her shining stardom
versus masses of blurred extras in the show-biz of academe is deeply
troubling. But this self-defense stems from her self-appointed role as a
spokesperson for the subaltern. She has consistently maintained, as Arif
Dirlik derides in a footnote to his essay, "that she did not belong to the
'top level of the United States academy' because she taught in the South
and the Southwest whereas the 'cultural elite in the United States inhabit
the Northeastern seaboard or the West Coast' " (330; the single quotation marks refer to Dirlik citing from Spivak's *The Post-Colonial Critic*,
114). Dirlik concludes his footnote rather satirically: "Since then Spivak
has moved to Columbia University." Yet Dirlik inadvertently taunts
himself as well: his quibble is published in the renowned *Critical Inquiry*
and written at the renowed site of Duke University, a first-rate institution
despite its location in the South. As such, these leading intellectuals carry
on debates not unlike family squabbles and contend over who truly
represent the subaltern in some of the most prestigious scholarly spaces.

I do not mean to be a carping critic, drawing evidence either from the
closing gesture of dismissal in Spivak's highly intellectual interview or
from one mocking footnote among the other thirty-five well-documented
ones in Dirlik's essay. Yet it is Spivak who comments disparagingly,
again in a footnote to "Can the Subaltern Speak?", that the European
thinkers' influence over U.S. academia comes primarily from their translated interviews rather than book-length works. Consequently, I am
merely subjecting Spivak to a reading of the "peripherals," for I am just
as shallow as the next American academician. (Incidentally, "Can the
Subaltern Speak?" analyzes a conversation between Michel Foucault and
Deleuze from Foucault's *Language, Counter-Memory, Practice: Selected
Essays and Interviews*.) I know people may accuse me of venting personal gripes or, at best, performing dubious critical moves by focusing
on the margins of academic discourse, but where else in their seamless
arguments can one discover ruptures of personal voices of these distin-

guished scholars, Marxist or not? After all, it is in their interest not to interrogate the human pyramid of academe which you and I live off— or under.

WORKS CITED

Althusser, Louis. "Ideology and the Ideological State Apparatuses (Notes Towards an Investigation)." In *Lenin and Philosophy and Other Essays.* Trans. Ben Brewster. New York: Monthly Review Press, 1971. 127–86.
Bhabha, Homi. "Of Mimicry and Man: The Ambivalence of Colonial Discourse." *October* 28 (1984): 125–33.
Caesar, Terry. *Conspiring with Forms: Life in Academic Texts.* Athens: University of Georgia Press, 1992.
———. "On Teaching at a Second-Rate University." *The South Atlantic Quarterly* 90.3 (Summer 1991): 449–67.
———. "Theory in the Boondocks." *Yale Journal of Criticism* 6.2 (1993): 221–35.
Dirlik, Arif. "The Postcolonial Aura: Third World Criticism in the Age of Global Capitalism." *Critical Inquiry* 20.2 (Winter 1994): 328–56.
Eye To Eye. Hosted by Connie Chung. CBS. 23 June 1993.
Foucault, Michel. *Language, Counter-Memory, Practice: Selected Essays and Interviews.* Trans. Donald F. Bouchard and Sherry Simon. Ithaca: Cornell University Press, 1977.
Lauter, Paul. *Canons and Contexts.* New York: Oxford University Press, 1991.
Leo, John. "A Marathon of Pique." *U.S. News and World Report* 12 July 1993, 22.
McWilliams, Carey. Introduction. In Carlos Bulosan. *America Is in the Heart.* Seattle: University of Washington Press, 1973. vii-xxiv.
Pheng, Cheah. "Situations of Value: Gayatri Chakravorty Spivak on Feminism and Cultural Work in a Postcolonial Neocolonial Conjuncture." *Australian Feminist Studies* 17 (Fall 1993): 141–61.
Sosnoski, James. *Token Professionals and Master Critics: A Critique of Orthodoxy in Literary Studies.* Albany: State University of New York Press, 1994.
Spivak, Gayatri Chakravorty. *The Post-Colonial Critic: Interviews, Strategies, Dialogues.* Ed. Sarah Harasym. New York: Routledge, 1990.

CHAPTER 14

The Rage of Innocents

On Casting the First Stone in a Sea of Cultural Pain

DON KEEFER

Within the walls of academia, most all of us feel ourselves to have become casualties in the war over political correctness. Some PC proponents have lost their jobs for their fight for cultural parity. A few PC-opponents may have lost their jobs for their resistance or lack of compliance with the new trends within the academy. Many have been wounded on both sides. Robert Hughes, in *The Culture of Complaint,* describes our society as a growing population of cry-babies. We have become thin-skinned and preoccupied, he says, with the negative, and many bask in the self-righteous bath of victimhood.[1] Advocates for the victims wrap themselves in the mantle of self-proclaimed goodness. Many live in a state of fear that they will be the next victims, that their ideas will be dismissed because of their political-color or because of the color of the person speaking. Courses will be derailed by a student or students who feel entitled by their cultural identity to disrupt the flow. It is just as likely or unlikely that a professor in a nontraditional course, for example, women's studies, be treated with disrespect as a professor of a traditional, more canonical course. White males complain they cannot get hired. Females of all colors and males of color complain they cannot get promotions. We all rage inwardly or outwardly about our innocence.

To be honest, however, these incidents are like the acts of real violence in our society. They are sparse in the grand scheme of things. But it only takes one incident in the community to set in motion the well-oiled gears of fear and suspicion. With fear, the mind clamps shut. With suspicion, a seed of resentment grows into a stone. Just as in urban settings, we now live behind protective bars, and we are often armed with alarms and weapons, likewise in academia each side confronts the other in the debates over political correctness, with a monumental stoniness that only partially covers the protective bars, alarms, and weapons from sight. We are in a cold civil war.

The campaign for political correctness is essentially a war on the prejudice against peoples deemed by larger society to be different in a way that makes them somehow lesser people. Cornel West describes this as an intellectual paradigm shift:

I would go so far as saying that a new kind of cultural worker is in the making, associated with a new politics of difference. These new forms of intellectual consciousness advance reconceptions of the vocation of critic and artist, attempting to undermine the prevailing disciplinary divisions of labor in the academy, museum, mass media and gallery networks, while preserving modes of critique within the ubiquitous commodification of culture in the global village. Distinctive features of the new cultural politics of difference are to trash the monolithic and homogeneous in the name of diversity, multiplicity and heterogeneity; to reject the abstract, general and universal in light of the concrete, specific and particular; and to historicize, contextualize and pluralize by highlighting the contingent, provisional, variable, tentative, shifting and changing.[2]

Some subset of this movement of new cultural workers is, therefore, more militantly and insistently challenging the mechanisms of past and present social cruelty that have been used to demean, demote, and demoralize groups that do not fit the advertised and institutionalized ideals of mainstream society. West cleverly calls this *malestream* society![3] It is the radical fringe of the new workers that seem to be more about policing the thought and speech of others than increasing the grounds of affirmation in the groups that they advocate.

The term, PC, captured for the traditional liberal and conservative alike what was problematic about the new cultural practices associated with the war on prejudice and xenophobia. It coalesced into an orthodoxy which was rendered all too predictable in its dogmatism and repertoire of subjects for condemnation. Group think replaced individualism. The individual was being written out of history.[4] The greatest sin of PC, however, was its evangelical zeal. Despite their obvious limitations, the horror stories are emblematic and legendary.

Case in point: A University of Michigan student was disciplined under a newly enacted Hate Speech policy for expressing the idea in one of his classes that homosexuality is a disease, treatable by therapy.[5] The Supreme Court struck down the policy as violating the First Amendment right of free speech. Where this case is discussed, discussion does not go into depth about how the student expressed his idea nor about what type of punishment the University of Michigan issued. Our opinions about these minimal details will serve as an index of our political correctness. That is, there is a preferred attitude to have about this issue. The politically correct approach is that "words harm" and that an enlightened society must act to prevent such injury which may impede a student's educational potential. What seems so lamentable is that there seems to be no middle ground. We are not allowed to ask about context or tone. In the abstract, it would appear that an entire classroom of students was deprived of an opportunity to learn. An opportunity to discuss what constitutes normalcy, nature, disease, who decides, and so on was derailed to protect anyone in the class who might happen to be homosexual.

For example, certain sections of Plato's *Symposium* will provoke a discussion of homosexuality. Sometimes students will argue that homosexuality is immoral because it is unnatural. Why, I ask? Because there can be no issue from the sexual union of two members of the same sex. Why pray tell then is 99 percent of heterosexual sex considered natural, when were we convinced of natural issue we wouldn't risk sexual union? Invariably, this leads to an interesting discussion of many important topics that would have been missed had the student been bullied by political correctionism into silence.

Nonetheless, to ask more questions, to question political correction is politically incorrect.

There is a core value in the PC movement which I imagine few of us rejecting. Every human deserves to be treated with dignity. Nothing expresses that more deeply than the educational mission of the university. In the new world of participatory, interactive pedagogies, blind grading may not be enough to insure full access to educational offerings. More and more we find ourselves called to work with students' cultural funds and background to maximize their potential. The core value of PC, civility, aims at a professional ethic of openness in academia which protects all involved, students and faculty alike, from the sorts of intolerance that may have derailed the educational mission in the past. Hence much to admire exists in the heart of what inspires PC: a great concern for civility and its link to improving the mission of our universities. These noble goals are underwritten by a sense of historical human tragedy: Western history, far from being a pure progression of human moral and technological achievement, is one of missed opportunities, of oppression, torture, cultural eradication, genocide. It is a sorrowful narrative that forms the potential plotlines for the narratives of individual women, blacks, and gays in our culture and members of the Third World who are victims of colonialism. Such cultural sensitivity is itself admirable.

All this comes at a time when there is much in the larger world to worry about. Hate is on the rise. Anti-Semitism is apparent from the recent Nation of Islam flap, where Louis Farrakhan and a disciple claimed that a high percentage of Jews were responsible for the colonial slave trade.[6] Homophobic violence. Violence against women. Religious intolerance here and abroad in central circle of hell, Bosnia, could shake one's confidence in humanity. It would appear that the world could use a bit of political correcting!

The question is what went wrong here? How did the almost saintly values of the PC movement come to incite a civil war, a rage, in the university?

To answer this question, I will look not to key events. All of us have our stories. Some of us have personal incidents of such clashes. What is apparent is that the host of anecdotes that we currently traffic in do nothing more than confirm our convictions. In other words, as interesting as the incidents may be, as provocative or definitive of the problems that traditional or nontraditional faculty face in this regard, they will only serve to reveal symptoms of some deeper academic dis-ease.

While the values of PC fit well a progressive and enlightened university environment, it is in their execution that the problems begin. Their academic style of criticism and debate is quite often confrontational, dismissive, and mean-spirited. This combative interactive style is facilitated by a "hermeneutic of suspicion," that is, a foregrounding of the imputed selfish motives of any speaker, that is a constant in the interpretation, analysis, and criticism of their "texts." The results of this genetic, psychoanalytic snooping are then systematically ranked in a for-us/against-us category. For example, in coming out against PC, some would say, I am expressing my anger and hurt at their decade long attack on white males. It is my hurt that fuels this attempt to reclaim the turf lost to non-white, non-males. As such, I am an enemy.

This style and methodology lead to two inconsistencies that are not tolerable in any setting dedicated to the fair exchange of ideas. First, even when the hermeneutic of basic motivation is applied consistently, the psychoanalysis is inconsistent and biased in its moral coloring. One group is viewed as having fundamentally base, selfish, self-serving, pow-ermongering motives (whichever group is in power), the other has fully acceptable or even superior motivation. But all too often one method is employed to benignly interpret the protected group and another method is to hunt for the ill-will in the words of the oppressing group. Thus, the political correctionists are psychologically lax in their readings of their own. According to Cornel West, this desire to protect the endangered peoples made it virtually impossible to fight against the Clarence Thomas nomination for the Supreme Court.[7] Secondly, it appears that in drawing a protective circle around endangered peoples, the PC seek to protect themselves from their own methods of suspicion. That is, they remain above suspicion. It is this fundamental inconsistency regarding who is suspect that makes for the sense that the intellectual and social space for free and fair exchange of ideas is being sundered.

I hear a voice that wonders about the myth of academic free and fair exchange of ideas. Who among us has not been measured by length of our vita? Who among us has not felt snubbed by someone convinced they were more naturally or prestigiously endowed in their field? And it wasn't that long ago when the question of what philosophers had to say about women would have been taken as relevant to the central issues of philosophy as the siblings of Lady MacBeth to interpretation of Shakespeare. There never was a level playing field, the voice intones. Lamentably so, but is it progress towards greater cultural justice, that new wounds and new hierarchies based merely on group-identifications are formed?

A consequence of the politically correct depth-psychological search and destroy mission to eradicate prejudice is a style of intolerance not tolerable within the academic community. This style resorts to name-calling and moral shaming. In her recent review of Kate Roiphe's new work on the problem of date rape on college campuses, *The Morning After*, bell hooks chastised Roiphe's work for failing to take into account the experience of African-American women.[8] Because hooks had little if any analysis and criticism of other aspects of Roiphe's book, it was not clear that she had done anything more than consult the index and count citations to black authors and references to women of color.

The political zeal of those mobilized towards the politics of difference actually flows from a sense of moral outrage. Sexism, like ethnocentrism, and racism are not merely politically problematic postures in a democratic society. They are forms of moral failing. At an institutional level, they form the basis of social injustice or unfair discrimination. A society has morally failed to the extent that it permits such practices. Likewise, individuals, deemed, for example, as racist or sexist, are judged to be disposed to discriminate against others on the basis of complexion, hair length, biology and so on. They are judged rightly as morally corrupt. The charge of sexism or racism is no small moral charge—not to be taken lightly.

It is certain that being raised in a polarized, fragmented, unequal society will engender prejudicial attitudes and stereotypes that would predispose one towards forms of sexual and racial cruelty and discrimination. The survey of our nation's public schools by Jonathan Kozol reveals tragic inequities between urban educational settings, which serve principally poor black families and the educational resources in the affluent suburban settings.[9] If education is the key to an individual's future, then we are providing defective keys to many of our most deprived citizens. Certainly, this is the measure of continued racism in America on an institutional level. While we are making great strides in higher education and business, with greater democratization, we still live in a society that can be said to betray bias against women. A survey of women living in large U.S. cities reports that women feel unsafe in their neighborhoods at night.[10] A large number of them take self-imprisoning precautions to be secure. Thus in our "free society," women are not equally free to be outside at night.[11] Women are so endangered by domestic violence that virtually every state has a task force devoted to the issue. Fully a third of public hospital emergency visits by women are due to domestic violence. These are just the most blatant signs of our living in a racist and sexist society. Being raised in these conditions is likely to create anger on one side and a morally numbing sense of privilege on the other. But, just as survivors of child abuse are capable of recognizing and overcoming their disposition to continue the cycle of abuse, so too can the good people of our unequal society break the cycle of social and cultural cruelty. Too often, the charges of sexism or racism are leveled at individuals who become the scapegoats for punishing the society's institutional inequities. In these cases, such moral condemnations are often ill-conceived at best, baseless and sometimes injurious in real life terms, at worst.

Consider: In a debate over the work of Robert Mapplethorpe between a Catholic conservative professor of philosophy and one of his young black female students, words became hot. This professor found the infamous photos obscene. The student defended them as Art. She may have questioned the professor's motivation for his condemnation. He reacted by telling her she had "bad breeding." The conservative professor immediately apologized for having lost his temper. He was contrite for having behaved "unprofessionally." She was, however, not to be placated. She took the matter to the administration by lodging a formal complaint of racism against the professor. Though no formal action was taken, the administration apparently sided with the student in its sympathies. The professor, so disappointed by the lack of moral support he received from his institution, took it as a vote of no confidence in him and opted for an early retirement. The reality is, the administration had lost all confidence in its own moral intelligence and moral courage to adjudicate charges of discrimination. If a member of a protected peoples feels hurt, their perspective and judgment appears to be the final court of decision. It may be true that this retired professor held homophobic, sexist, and racial prejudices as part of his cultural inheritance, but the real issues here are actual racial discrimination and whether or not the harm done in his insulting reaction is irreparable. Suppose we agree that he meant to question this student's upbringing. He was speculating offensively that had this student been brought up properly she would not entertain such ideas which he took to be reprehensible. It is still possible that this black student looks back on the whole lamentable history of blacks in America. The choice of the term, *breeding,* calls to mind, slavery and chattel. Hard not to take offense. I don't doubt the offensive nature of this episode. But why do we resort to discipline prior to a clarification and atonement which would dignify all involved?

These reflections point out the moral fundamentalism that political correctionists embrace. Thus far I have shown that PC proponents display intolerance for difference of opinion that makes the movement suspect in academic quarters. I have questioned the consistency of the values. I have shown administrations aligning themselves with the movement in sometimes cowardly ways. I would not be surprised to find a greater number of times when administrations cower in the opposite direction, when they ought to be acting to protect students or fellow faculty threatened by discriminatory practices. All of this goes some distance to explaining the growing frustration and anger directed against those coming to be called the "thought police." Despite the sharing of a professional ethic of civility and equal access to education, we form a divided camp. Now I have pointed my finger at them—calling them moral fundamentalists. In the next section, I want to sketch what such moral fundamentalism is, and why we should be committed to avoiding it.

I take my cue from the American philosopher, William James, in his construction of a moral philosophy cognizant of a pluralistic universe— that is a human world composed of more than one person, where there is complexity of goods and claims.[12] James concludes that morality and its claims rest not on divine command, logic, or some transcendental realm, but that "[t]the only possible reason why any phenomenon ought to exist is that such a phenomenon is actually desired."[13] In a universe populated by diverse claimants then, James writes, "[T]here is some obligation wherever there is a claim."[14] The moral of James's view, the aim the philosopher of morals should have, is "to satisfy at all times *as many demands as we can*. That act must be the best act, accordingly, which makes for the *best whole,* in the sense of awakening the least sum of dissatisfactions. . . . [T]hose ideals must be written highest which *prevail at the least cost.*"[15] James further distinguishes profound distinction in the purview of this already complicated moral stance:

The deepest difference, practically, in the moral life of man is the difference between the easy-going and the strenuous mood. When in the easy-going mood the shrinking from present ill is our ruling consideration. The strenuous mood, on the contrary, makes us quite indifferent to present ill, if only the greater ideal be attained.[16]

James's view is not unproblematic. He is ultimately too deferential to tradition.[17] Some may find it hard to distinguish James here from Bentham and his hedonic calculus. Nonetheless, in James we see an attempt to work out a complex, democratic, and potentially muscular sense of what it can take to make the world less evil. Witness the shift from the easy-going mode of living to the strenuous moral nature depicted in Oscar Schindler. James rejects the possibility of a final transcendental picture of an ethical world. In Richard Rorty's terms, there is no final vocabulary in which the values of the world will ultimately be best described.[18] This is a view that leaves open the possibility of dissension, conflict, and shifts of value. For all its flaws, it gives us a complex view against which to describe moral fundamentalism.

Moral fundamentalism is the absolute privileging of any single value or claim or subset of claims from the total universe of demands. Such privileging winds up setting the demands of one group, or certain demands in the population, at the expense or loss of others and the justification for the priority will be in some sense axiomatic. James's target here is theistic ethics. James acknowledges that if God is among the universe of claimants, then God would win hands down. Nevertheless, he notes, given the vagaries of divine commandment and such, conflicts of interpretation of what God really wants, human ethics and divine ethics are on at least equal footing.[19] The equal footing recalls Rawls's calculation of justice behind the veil of Ignorance. What is challenging about James's view is that it shifts the philosophical ethics search for principles and a calculus for ranking to the more complex question of what sort of life does one want to live? The equal footedness of answers to this question, in James's pluralistic universe or Rawls's Original Position negate morally simple or merely ego-centric approaches to the question. Moral fundamentalists are not moved by their reasoning. Eschewing egoism, and apparently self-interest, they would say they have a higher mission.

In fact, one may be more likely to find that the politically correct are guilty whites in search of salvation. At a major college, a professor of literature introducing a noted black poet, publicly declared her unworthiness to introduce such an illustrious ambassador from the oppressed peoples of the world, saying, "I don't know what a fish-belly white is doing introducing this eminent black poet!" The badge of proof of admission to the recent Whitney Biennial exhibition in New York City was a badge of admission to the politically correct self-loathing brigade. It was a button that was embossed with the message: "I would never dream of being a white person." What underlies this self-loathing and public self-flagellation is the axiom of evaluation basic to the moral fundamentalism of the PC: nothing short of radical affirmative action in every aspect of human, personal, and social life is sufficient to apologize and make restitution to the groups that have been mistreated by Western civilization. Thus the original sin of being white can only be atoned for by constant intonements of *mea culpae* and encouragement of others to recognize the extant mangled heritage of groups oppressed by whips and chains of the white man and to lament what could have been but wasn't. The horrible politically correctionist stigma of being male can only be shed by ceasing to speak, judge, or even look upon another with desire. Finally, moral salvation can only be attained by the humanist through admission of his own cultural fraudulence. The simple and noble sympathies for the victims of our lamentable histories has been turned into a dance of moral exhibitionists who strut their righteousness as a badge of their saintly, simultaneously self-denying and self-promoting natures.

Ironically, we find the perpetuation of racial stereotypes—some of them capable of perpetuating continued feelings of insecurity. Brent Staples, a writer on cultural affairs for the *New York Times,* writes about his graduate school experience at the University of Chicago, School of Psychology.[20] He was greeted by a German professor, who said that it may be hard for him, but white people have been very bad by black people and that she would be sure to get him through. It led him to question his adequacy for graduate school, despite a sterling academic performance as an undergraduate. African-American students are capable of rather strong reproach for the patronizing attitudes of white professors. In such cases, they assert their desire to have their own space to be who they are, not to be burdened with being a spokesperson or exemplar of their race. Just as the more common type of moral fundamentalist puts general and abstract principles ahead of particular and concrete situations and people, so the PC fundamentalist often puts genera above the individual members of the group.

The social cost of the dwelling on the negative is increasingly recognized by women and blacks as they attempt to shift the spotlight onto positive aspects of their histories and present successes. Rhode Island is establishing an African-American Heritage Museum which will provide a repository of images of pride and honor as well as the record of slave trade and other injustices. Its sponsors are quite adamant about the one-sidedness of the historical picture that young blacks receive. Naomi Wolfe's recent book, *Fire with Fire,* challenges the victimography that she charges is written into much of modern feminism that she finds ultimately disempowering.[21]

What is at stake for these groups is their *group autonomy. A* people have group autonomy when they are "regarded by others as the foremost interpreters of their historical-cultural traditions, it being understood that the aim of others is not to show that those traditions should be jettisoned by the group of adherents."[22] The great enduring cruelty of multigenerational enslavement during the age of American slavery was the eradication of their cultural and historical memories, what Orlando Paterson calls, *natal alienation.*[23] Laurence Thomas notes:

> One would not expect a natally alienated people to have group autonomy, as one would not expect such a people to have socially unencumbered affirmation. . . . Racism against blacks is the view that blacks are incapable of full moral and intellectual maturity. It is next to impossible to hold that view about people while simultaneously regarding them as the foremost interpreters of their own historical-cultural traditions.[24]

I take it as fairly straightforward that the consequences of low expectations of performance and capability to one's self-image are low self-esteem, a sense of hopelessness, and high potential for failure. How much more multiplied and disabling when such low expectations and social stigma are reflected by the world around you about your race or gender. On this score, proponents of diversity, multicultural education, and the politically correct have been allies in the search for affirmations of cultural worth. But Thomas finds the approach wrong headed. As he implies, it ghettoizes the culture, in this case of black Americans:

> It would seem that one of the best ways to get others to respect one is to get them to respect the observations that one makes about them. For, psychologically, this makes it very difficult not to take one seriously when one speaks about oneself. Thus, it may be that one way for a people to achieve group autonomy in a hostile society

is by becoming an authority on things that the members of that society value. It may be necessary for blacks to take this course in the United States. It may be a mistake to think that focusing simply upon the black experience, by way of rap music or film or dance, will ensure the moral and political standing of blacks in oppressive societies. For these accomplishments, important as they are, do not suffice to command the respect of nonblacks.[25]

I am here reminded of Oprah Winfrey's wise counsel, "The greatest argument against prejudice is excellence." While excellence is for the moment based upon the standards and practices of the culture that hasn't accepted blacks on their own terms, Thomas and Winfrey are both pragmatic moralists in reckoning their projects in terms of the real world. It is not the only viable strategy, but it does give pause to the endless affirmations of the PC movement which appear on Thomas's logic to be unhelpful.

There are two further problems with the moral fundamentalism of the political correctionist. They share with some of their brethren on the religious right an almost Herculean indifference to the suffering of others and virulent intolerance for any other viewpoint. I do not want to paint all Christians with this brush, but historically, Christians since Roman times have relished the suffering of sinners, who refused the word. Tertullian wrote about how the damned would be treated during the second coming and how this would be part of the faithful's reward.[26] Aquinas constructed a heaven which overlooked the punishment of the sinful in hell, so that good folks in heaven could better appreciate their lofty reward![27] Likewise, the political correctionists sniff out discourse like hermeneutic bloodhounds hunting for an indictable clue. When an idea is deemed offensive, they rush to the scene ready for disciplinary action. Sometimes it is a patronizing reprimand. Sometimes, it is a public shaming. Sometimes one must lose one's head. (I imagine an Aquinian politically correct academic heaven where the labor-force of new cultural workers look down from their ivy paradises onto the hell of retirement communities where the damned have been sent to stew in their irrelevance and self-importance!)

None of this should be taken to indicate that we shouldn't correct one another, share our misgivings about one another to one another, that we would do best to keep quiet. But both fundamentalists insist that there is only one conversation to have. Certain subjects can be viewed only one way. On this, the PC fundamentalists have another striking analogy with some extreme Christian fundamentalists: it is a kind of hermeneutic monism. Many religions have special codes for interpreting God's message through the world. In some religions this is a secret code. Hermeneutic monism would hold that all symbolism finds its meaning in but one final translation. It might be possible to construct hermeneutic monisms for pop psychology for example. Like the religious fundamentalism search for signs of Satan's work in our world, the politically correct police are hard at work detecting signs of oppression from the ruling party in every cultural product that they encounter.

Analogous to playing rock and roll records backwards to search for the words of the devil, such films as *Fatal Attraction* are interpreted to become warnings from patriarchal culture of social costs of women in the workplace. It is interesting how the two can blend into one another, Eve's taste of the corporate apple leads to the temptation of the family man, Adam, and her subsequent transformation into a death-dealing, castrating Medusa. In another example, some members of the speech protection police demand that the word Man can never be used to refer to both men and women inclusively. Every assumption of inclusion of women under the use of the word man is suspect, now as well as in the past. In a bit of twisted logic, the use of the word, man, to refer to both men and women, as in the Bill of Rights, is seen as ultimately demeaning to women.

What is ironic about this power spin strategy is its departure, or convenient ignorance of the prevalence in today's humanist community of hermeneutic indeterminacy. Many have taken the hermeneutic circle to be a basic condition of perception. In other words, theory and background assumptions, feelings, influence what we see. *There is no innocent eye.* Moreover, most of the political correctionists are dedicated deconstructionists. They have fixed upon those infinitesimal details in the parade of words to enunciate the hidden biases, to invert hierarchies, to call into question the ruling assumptions. I see much of this as continuous with the Socratic mission of the humanist agenda. But the hobgoblin of this small mind wants greater consistency. Just as James thinks that moral pluralism ought to humble us into a more cautious, humane, democratic moral philosophy, so should our hermeneutic insights about filters and meaning humble us to accepting a much more complicated universe of textual readers. In this sense, the readers of the PC squad deploy as imperialistic a reading of texts as any of the most strenuous New Critics and the Positivists of the late 1940s.

I have little doubt that so much of the bashing that goes on in these academic circles is a measure of continuing frustrations and a sense of impotence over the problems that plague the larger society. Traditional scholarship is an easy and durable target. Writing in the margins has become centralized, yet the authority of the new work in cultural studies is often tenuous and despite the growing numbers of new scholars, their power is quite localized to their camps. Students approach school as consumers today. They bring consumer-like demands to the table filtered through their ethnicity and gender that they have been told is their essential identity marker. No doubt the backlash, the bashing of PC comes from the sense of erosion of the student pool to more 'sexy' courses, the brazen interrogation by students and fellow faculty of traditional approaches, and the sense of that administrations are being held hostage to these new values. On this last issue, Richard Bernstein reported a lamentable incident in the *New York Review of Books*.[28] The University of New Hampshire has fired one of its professors for sexual harassment. According to the article, the culpable act here was that some of the professor's lecture was deemed by some of the female students as offensive. The professor is seeking a higher court ruling on the matter. As always in these anecdotes, we have the bare bones event rendered for maximum moral outrage. But the climate these stories produce are very much like how we hear when we learn a friend has been mugged on an avenue that we frequent. We begin to feel vulnerable to these sorts of attacks.

One of the criteria of sexual harassment is that certain actions, words, or images are capable of creating a chilly climate which inevitably interferes with the victim's ability to do her or his job properly. This reasoning has been properly extended to the academic setting to adjudicate cases where one person has acted in such a way as to interfere with another's learning. It seems to me that we are on the verge of academic harassment, where we have the creation of a chilly climate where it is becoming increasingly hard to do our job for fear of offending someone who may turn out to have a politically correct ax to grind. I suspect that this is the fundamental issue here. Academic freedom has been abused in the past—perhaps by the UNH professor. The inquisitorial approach can only lead to silence and blandness. It is the conversation that is threatened—a conversation upon which education in our day is based.

I was given a lesson in the worth of this conversation recently. In a seminar on aesthetics and the practices of art, one of my students did a presentation on the marginalization of women in art history as well as the current art scene. She was armed to the teeth with statistics. How many women were models, how many women were displayed in galleries and so on. It was clear from this catalog of inequities that the art world was far from kind to women. I should add that all of my students are fine arts or design majors; they all have an obvious future stake in these issues. After documenting the sexism apparent from these stats, the student felt compelled to speculate how she would deal with it. She said that she would not get involved. She would look for a different market place than this New York cosmopolitan, international cutting edge, avant garde, high rollers venue. Her fellow students were appalled. One student noted that statistics are just that. Easy to interpret however you like. Another complained that there were stories behind those statistics. But the most appalling thing to the students was that she had surrendered, allowed herself to be undone by the negativism. I suspect that what happened that night taught these students valuable insights about how the picture of the world they carried around might effect their sense of how they see themselves and their prospects. These were lessons that never would have been learned had the logic of female victomography reigned chillingly supreme that night. My suspicion runs high about this, because it was a night of learning for me.

I want to conclude by considering how much the political correction movement is born out of the basic academic ethos itself. It is not the bastard Edmund striking back on his father to blind him with a knife. It is more likely the daughters Lear whose tongues have been sharpened more piercing than a serpent's tooth at their father's table. What I mean by this is that academia has been since its founding a place of discriminating judgment. One only needs to think of Abelard, whose use of logic circumvented the dictates of the Church, to realize that Occam's Razor was often used for non-metaphysical reasons. But more recent moments of intolerance can be found in the cultural writings of Theodor Adorno, Walter Lippman, Alan Bloom, and Camille Paglia. What lies at the heart of academic intolerance is most often an elitism that puts academics beyond judgment. Consider the familiar sort of culturally critical charge. Almost everyone agrees that watching television is harmful to the viewer. All will agree that it stupefies. All hold that its fare numbs the viewer to real world problems. However, almost everyone who adheres to this indictment of television viewing exempts themselves from the deleterious effects of television. Likewise, ideology studies depict the common man as a puppet of the ruling class, while the critical social scientist is safe beyond the reach of ideology. What this indicates is that in relation to its enveloping culture, the university has taken an elitist and self-serving view of that culture. The point is that for quite some time the essence of the humanist was critical judgment. That is the ability to justifiably rank objects in the world on some scale of value. The cataclysmic events of this century probably make critical social judgment all the more urgent than the discrimination of taste. So I take the line between Theodor Adorno's dismissive indictment of jazz as a cultural narcotic for the poor and Catherine MacKinnon's claim that magazines, such as *Playboy*, are a cultural stimulant to rape to be a rather short one.[29] What may throw one off the scent is that so much of PC is anti-elitist, supposedly. It is not clear that PC succeeds in its underprivileged populism. Many a literary theorist who beats the drums for diversity has harshly punished the substandard linguistic abilities of the very students who are underprivileged in this society. Interestingly, some of the greatest sticklers for grammar turn out to be the most vociferous editors of social attitudes of our time.[30] Occasional articles in *The Chronicle of Higher Education* have noted the apparent hypocrisy.

In speculating about the judgmental nature of academia, I can suggest only the barest alternative. Whether it is for the sake of certainty or the appearance of expert authority, we have too often stayed defiantly on a train that we suspect or others are telling us will not take us where we want to go. Critical perception is not something we can or should give up. However, we could become better listeners whose challenges are not to silence, but to provoke richer and deeper understanding of the world. When in doubt, we could use our creative imaginations to construct more rationalizing contexts for the propositions of others we would so quickly otherwise dissect and reject. To paraphrase Wordsworth, we murder to reject.

Thus words can harm. Words matter. We have been reckless in the past. But they are more likely to do irreparable damage if the conversation is stifled and arrested. Making sure this is the broadest conversation which includes as many voices as possible is as daunting a charge as James's moral philosophical suggestion that *we seek to create a world where as many desires are satisfied as possible,* but it has the advantage of being fully human. The history of words and actions of our complex society has created a sea of cultural pain and mistrust. It is into those gray and turgid waters I cast these words in the hope that we may come to converse more humanely.

NOTES

Many thanks go to Pembroke State University, its Philosophy and Religion Department, and the Matchette Foundation for its sponsorship of this lecture delivered at PSU on February 10, 1994. Particular thanks go to Jeffrey Geller for his invitation. His comments on an earlier version of this paper were crucial to the shaping of this one.

1. Robert Hughes, *The Culture of Complaint: The Fraying of America,* (New York: Oxford University Press, 1993). See also Wendy Kaminer, *I'm Dysfunctional, You're Dysfunctional* (New York: Vintage Press, 1993).

2. Cornel West, *Keeping Faith: Philosophy and Race in America,* (New York: Routledge, 1993), 3.

3. Ibid., 4.

4. This comment begs for much deeper investigation. The rejection of methodological individualism by structuralist social science as an explanatory model has given way to what might be called "methodological socialism," where a social group's experience and ideology becomes the locus of explanation. This coupled with any acknowledgment of a fractured society or cultural relativism quickly yields a rich pluralistic hermeneutic. We soon relaize that not all group perspectives are created equal. This gives rise to the politics of culture that underwrites much of the political correctionist's motivation and theorizing. Methodological socialism is neutral on the competing visions of the world. What it offers every group, every individual who has determined to see the world through his group, is instant legitimation. This in itself might not be problematic even in practice if the bits of the world interpreted by each group were not the other groups. But the real situation is that each group has its own view of the other groups. Historically, this has denied group autonomy (discussed below) to blacks, for example. Now, the leveling process of methodological socialism gives way to a contest of interpretations of group identities. Within the scheme of the politics of difference, this means that the contest will be won only by constant agitation and political and cultural action—Cornel West's new cultural workers?

Jeffrey Geller, in his reaction to this paper, likened the new politicians of difference to Socrates' combatants, Glaucon and Thrasymachus in Plato's *Republic*. This would mean that ultimately the PC movement is no more than the cultural and political opportunism (egoism at a group level) underwritten by postmodernism and nihilism. I am persuaded by this reading for some portion of the movement. However, I wish to resist this view for a number of reasons. It is quite possible that many of the noisiest agitants on PC patrol are simply genuinely concerned for their charges. Far from being nihilistic, opportunistic sophists, they see themselves as continuing in behest of the humanist tradition.

5. Jon Wiener, "Free Speech for Campus Bigots?" *Nation*, February 20, 1990, reprinted in *Bigotry, Prejudice and Hatred: Definitions, Causes and Solutions*, edited by Robert M. Baird and Stuart E. Rosenbaum, (Buffalo: Prometheus, 1992), 87.

6. It is interesting to note that Islamic trading of African slaves continued till quite recently in such countries as Saudi Arabia. Slavery under Islam is not as racially annihilating as it was in the American experience. Nonetheless, slavery is slavery, and the nations of Islam did play a formidable role in slave trade during colonial times. See Hughes, ibid., 140–47.

7. Cornel West, "The Pitfalls of Racial Reasoning," in *Race Matters*, (Boston: Beacon Press, 1993), 23–32.

8. bell hooks, "Review," *New Republic*, January, 1994.

9. Jonathan Kozol, *Savage Inequalities* (New York: Crown Books, 1991).

10. Stephanie Riger and Margaret Gordon, *The Female Fear: The Social Cost of Rape* (Urbana, IL: University of Illinois Press, 1991), 8–22.

11. Ibid., 118.

12. William James, "The Moral Philosopher and the Moral Life," reprinted in J. McDermott, *The Writings of William James*, (Chicago: University of Chicago Press, 1977), 615–16.

13. Ibid., 617.

14. Ibid, 617.

15. Ibid., 623.

16. Ibid., 627.

17. Ibid., 624. James writes, "The presumption in cases of conflict must always be in favor of the conventionally recognized good. The philosopher must be a conservative, and in the construction of his casuistic scale must put the things most in accordance with the customs of the community on top." Either we are past this sense of community today, or there really do seem to be times when the community's own scale seems in need of a critique and challenge.

18. As developed in Richard Rorty's *Contingency, Solidarity, and Irony* (Cambridge: Cambridge University Press, 1989), ch. 1.

19. James, op. cit., 618–19.

20. Brent Staples, *Parallel Time, Growing up Black and White* (New York: Pantheon Books, 1994), 196–97.

21. Naomi Wolf, *Fire with Fire* (New York: Random House, 1994).

22. Laurence Thomas, *Vessels of Evil* (Philadelphia: Temple University Press, 1993), 182.

23. Ibid., 160–65. Paterson's term is developed in his *Slavery and Social Death* (Cambridge, MA: Harvard University Press, 1982).

24. Thomas, ibid., 185.

25. Ibid., 188.

26. Tertullian, *De Spectaculius,* ch. 29, following. I owe this reference to Friedrich Nietzsche's *Genealogy of Morals,* First Essay, section 15, in Walter Kaufmann, ed., *Basic Writings of Nietzsche* (New York: Modern Library, 1968), 485. Likewise the quote from Aquinas.

27. Saint Thomas Aquinas, *Summa Theologiae, III, Supplementum,* Q. 34, Art. 1: "In order that the bliss of the saints may be more delightful for them and that they may render more copious thanks to God for it, it is given to them to see perfectly the punishment of the damned."

28. Richard Bernstein, "Guilty IF Charged," *New York Review of Books,* January 13, 1994, 11–14.

29. See Catharine MacKinnon, *Feminism Unmodified: Discourses in Life and Law* (Cambridge: Harvard University Press, 1987), 138.

30. Steven Pinker, "Grammar Puss: The Fallacies of the Language Mavens," *New Republic,* vol. 210, no. 5, issue 4124 (January 15, 1994): 19–26.

INDEX